Legacy

What would a sustainable economy look like? What would it take to live within our environmental means? *Legacy* answers these questions, setting out the key features of the sustainable economy. It explains what it would take to properly maintain different types of capital, why polluters would have to pay, why the current generation would have to fund the necessary maintenance of our natural assets and why we would have to save to invest. The message is a tough one: we are way off course in terms of meeting these conditions and we cannot escape the consequences. This book explains what we would have to do to mend our ways. In doing so, it highlights the feebleness of current approaches to net zero and biodiversity loss as well as our great neglect of the core infrastructures, and why we are not meeting our duties to the next generation. This title is Open Access.

Sir Dieter Helm is Professor of Economic Policy at the University of Oxford and Fellow in Economics at New College, Oxford. From 2012 to 2020, he was Independent Chair of the UK Natural Capital Committee, providing advice to the government on the sustainable use of natural capital. He provides extensive expert advice to governments, regulators and companies across three key areas: Energy & Climate; Regulation, Utilities & Infrastructure; and Natural Capital & the Environment. Dieter is a Vice President of the Exmoor Society, a Vice President of Berkshire, Buckinghamshire and Oxfordshire Wildlife Trust and an Honorary Fellow, Brasenose College, Oxford.

Legacy

How to Build the Sustainable Economy

Dieter Helm

University of Oxford

CAMBRIDGE
UNIVERSITY PRESS

Shaftesbury Road, Cambridge CB2 8EA, United Kingdom

One Liberty Plaza, 20th Floor, New York, NY 10006, USA

477 Williamstown Road, Port Melbourne, VIC 3207, Australia

314–321, 3rd Floor, Plot 3, Splendor Forum, Jasola District Centre,
New Delhi – 110025, India

103 Penang Road, #05–06/07, Visioncrest Commercial, Singapore 238467

Cambridge University Press is part of Cambridge University Press & Assessment,
a department of the University of Cambridge.

We share the University's mission to contribute to society through the pursuit of education,
learning and research at the highest international levels of excellence.

www.cambridge.org
Information on this title: www.cambridge.org/9781009449229

DOI: 10.1017/9781009449212

First published 2024

A catalogue record for this publication is available from the British Library

Library of Congress Cataloging-in-Publication Data
NAMES: Helm, Dieter, author.
TITLE: Legacy : how to build the sustainable economy / Dieter Helm, University of Oxford.
DESCRIPTION: Cambridge, United Kingdom ; New York, NY : Cambridge
University Press, 2024. | Includes bibliographical references and index.
IDENTIFIERS: LCCN 2023028322 | ISBN 9781009449229 (hardback) |
ISBN 9781009449212 (ebook)
SUBJECTS: LCSH: Sustainable development. | Economic development – Environmental aspects.
CLASSIFICATION: LCC HC79.E5 H4554 2024 | DDC 338.9/27–dc23/eng/20230720
LC record available at https://lccn.loc.gov/2023028322

ISBN 978-1-009-44922-9 Hardback
ISBN 978-1-009-44918-2 Paperback

To Amelia, Jake and Ralph

'Be realistic, demand the impossible.'

Student slogan in Paris 1968, quoted in Odd Arne Westad,
The Cold War: A World History, London: Allen Lane, p. 379.

'Two roads diverged in a wood, and I—
I took the one less travelled by,
And that has made all the difference.'

'The Road Not Taken' by Robert Lee Frost, 1915

CONTENTS

PREFACE

In my lifetime, the world's population has more than doubled, the climate has warmed and many of the species that were common when I grew up are now scarce or gone. I have spent much of my career watching these dark clouds gathering. My previous books – *Natural Capital, Green and Prosperous Land* and *Net Zero*[1] – have set out how to think about these problems through the lens of natural capital.

The future is what we make it. It is open-ended and what I have tried to do in this book is to set out what that future could look like if it is to be sustainable, what it would be like if we actually lived within our environmental means and hence if we chose an optimistic path and faced up to climate change and biodiversity loss head on.

It would be a brave green world and radically different from the way we live now. It requires the greatest economic transformation to our overwhelmingly carbon-based economy in less than three decades, to get away from the current 80 per cent global reliance on fossil fuels. We would have to stop burning the rainforests and plundering the oceans, while decarbonising agriculture, transport, heating and cooling, and do all this as the population goes on upwards for several decades to come and people in developing countries aspire to Western standards of living. Otherwise, our legacy will condemn the next generation to a poverty of nature, against which their lives will be constrained.

[1] D. Helm (2015), *Natural Capital: Valuing the Planet*, New Haven: Yale University Press; (2020), *Green and Prosperous Land: A Blueprint for Rescuing the British Countryside*, revised edn, London: William Collins; and (2021), *Net Zero: How We Stop Causing Climate Change*, revised edn, London: William Collins.

The more I thought about the scale of the challenges and our feeble responses, the more I became disillusioned with conventional economic answers. The economics toolbox is still remarkably reliant on the theories developed almost 100 years ago, in the years of high theory of the 1920s and 1930s, an intellectual world view created by names still familiar today and who continue to dominate our economic debates, like John Maynard Keynes and Friedrich von Hayek and others perhaps less familiar like John Hicks. Today's economists and the textbooks that set out their ideas are heirs to this older tradition. Their great theories have dominated economic policy debates ever since: in privatisation, liberalisation and competition; in the debate between monetarists and Keynesians; and most recently in the responses to the great financial crash and the shock of Covid.

It is the ghosts of Keynes, Hayek and Hicks that lurk behind today's economists' prescriptions. None had a primary concern with the environment. Many of their tools break in the hands of the sustainable economy: it is not about marginal changes to discrete bits of the economy and cost–benefit analysis; it is not primarily about utility, utilitarianism and making people happy; and it is not about maximising aggregate demand and printing money and creating ever larger piles of debt. To put my cards on the table, I am not a utilitarian and I am not a Keynesian. I don't think maximising utility is all there is to life. The citizens of my sustainable economy have entitlements and rights, as well as duties and obligations to others now and to the next generation. The purely consumerist lens will not suffice, not as currently promoted by governments, companies and the media.

Whilst I have borrowed the bits that help, like the pricing of pollution and the provision of public goods, my sustainable economy is a long way away from the conventional economics, and further still from the Keynesian macroeconomics which places short-term consumption at the heart of economic policy. Its focus is on the longer term, on assets, systems, balance sheets and capital maintenance, on radical uncertainty and citizens and the obligations to the next generation. My academic colleagues may not like the result, but then the conventional economic models are helping to send us towards the environmental cliff edge. The way out is not to boost retail sales, borrow to pay for what we cannot otherwise afford, and hope that the spending will lead to lots of economic growth, just assuming the longer term will take care of itself.

I struggled with the temptation to make this a very academic book, to lock horns directly with mainstream economics and its guiding theories. You may feel I have given in too much to the temptation, but throughout my aim is to take the general reader with me, and to provide a comprehensive overview of the sustainable economy, rather than give detailed supporting references for each and every component part. I plan to turn to the more academic exposition later on.

In writing this, the thought often struck me that maybe I have been just wasting my time describing what to many must seem a utopian dream. But then the reality struck in a simple one-liner: what is not sustainable will not be sustained. We are either going to have to change the fundamentals of our economies and sort out the pollution we cause and the erosion of the fundamental natural capital, or we will face the disaster of much more warming and the consequences of losing a lot more of earth's rich biodiversity. There is simply no escape. Utopia or dystopia: we can choose which path we want to be on.

It is a good idea to know where you want to get to before setting off. This is my best shot at trying to define this end point, what the sustainable economy would look like, one where we humans live in greater harmony with nature, and the battle against nature has ended. I don't shy away from how radical this would be. I don't assume we will choose to do what is necessary, but if we don't we should not delude ourselves about how it will otherwise end.

ACKNOWLEDGEMENTS

All ideas are ultimately borrowed from someone else. I have the great good fortune to spend my career amongst many people much cleverer than me, and who have shaped and critiqued my arguments.

I started out under Amartya Sen's supervision, and he got me to help John Hicks compile his collected papers whilst I was simultaneously working on my thesis. For me, Sen's deep pluralistic and tolerant version of liberalism based upon justice, in turn grounded in capabilities, is the best way to think about what we owe to other people, and I have used some of his ideas to shape how I think about the legacy we should pass on to the next generation and its citizens. Understandably, despite lots of attempts to persuade him otherwise, he never really worked out the implications for the design of welfare states and the broader economy, and although the environment was important to him, he never wrote much directly on the issues, to the best of my knowledge.

John Hicks made the great years of high theory in the 1930s come alive and he helped me to see through much of what became the Keynesian enthusiasms. He once remarked to me that Keynes was so busy doing so many things that he never really had time to work out his ideas properly.

These are the two biggest influences on me from academic economics and I have borrowed the capabilities approach for my sustainable economy from Sen, and the Labour Standard to develop my Consumption Standard from Hicks.

Amongst my contemporaries, the two biggest influences on me have been Colin Mayer, who taught me to take accounts seriously,

and Cameron Hepburn, whose constant comments and criticisms have been an inspiration to me.

During my time as chair of the Natural Capital Committee, Georgina Mace and Kathy Willis helped me appreciate the science of biodiversity. Ian Bateman is the stand-out environmental economist, and discussions with him helped shape my views on cost–benefit analysis. In rejecting much of the sort of economics Ian excels at, I learnt so much from him.

I am grateful for comments on and conversations about earlier drafts from Joe Grice, Tony Ballance, Chris Bolt, Stephen Glaister, Edward Barbier, David Vines, Laurence Lustgarten, Iain Smedley, Alex Teytelboym and Anthony O'Hear.

Academics shape debates, but our environmental problems will not be solved uniquely in ivory towers like Oxford. I have spent much time with civil servants across Whitehall and in Brussels, and with politicians. The latter include outstanding MPs, and a string of ministers and prime ministers. Though it is fashionable to criticise them, and indeed criticism is essential to democracy, I have learnt from them, not least because they have the art of appealing to voters – us. They, too, are the ones who will need to step up to the plate to avoid us going over the environmental cliff. Michael Gove was the reforming Secretary of State for the Environment, Food and Rural Affairs, challenging vested interests, and the architect of both the UK's Agriculture and Environment Acts. Rory Stewart's short time as Secretary of State for International Development offered a glimpse of what could have been done. I learnt a lot from both.

I am grateful to Chris Stark, the outstanding Chief Executive of the Climate Change Committee for his patient responses to my comments and challenges, Julia King, Mike Thompson, Glenys Stacey and James Bevan. Thanks, too, to Nick Barter, Julian Harlow and Rebecca McIlhiney.

Amongst the think-tanks and non-government organisations (NGOs), I am grateful for continuous engagements with Shaun Spiers and Richard Benwell.

None of course is responsible for any errors or omissions and none can be assumed to agree with all or any of my arguments, especially as this book is so much against the conventional intellectual and policy currents.

Cate Dominian has yet again beavered away at my scribbles and copyedited it all. Without her skills, support and good humour the book would never have seen the light of day. Jenny Vaughan has, as ever, been wonderfully helpful on the administrative side.

Thanks to Philip Good and Chris Harrison at Cambridge University Press for their enthusiastic and professional support.

Thanks finally to New College. The Warden and Fellows of New College, Oxford have continued to provide the best of all academic environments within which to write this book. It is the students and their contemporaries who will determine whether we – and New College – take the sustainable path.

ABBREVIATIONS

AGR	advanced gas-cooled reactor
AI	artificial intelligence
CCC	Climate Change Committee
CCS	carbon capture and storage
CEGB	Central Electricity Generating Board
COP	Conference of the Parties
Covid	severe acute respiratory syndrome coronavirus 2 (SARS-CoV-2)
DDT	Dichlorodiphenyltrichloroethane
Defra	Department for Environment, Food and Rural Affairs
ECB	European Central Bank
ESG	environmental, social and governance
EU	European Union
EU ETS	European Union emissions trading scheme
GDP	gross domestic product
GMO	genetically modified organism
HS2	a planned high-speed rail project for England
IAM	integrated assessment model
IEA	International Energy Agency
MMT	Modern Monetary Theory
mRNA	messenger ribonucleic acid
NGO	non-governmental organisation
NHS	National Health Service (UK)
OPEC	Organization of the Petroleum Exporting Countries
ppm	parts per million

QE	quantitative easing
R&D	research and development
RAB	regulatory asset base
UN	United Nations
UNFCC	United Nations Framework Convention on Climate Change
USO	universal service obligation
VAT	value-added tax

1 INTRODUCTION

It can't go on like this. The concentration of carbon in the atmosphere is marching on relentlessly, adding two parts per million (ppm) every year since 1990, remarkably even during the lockdowns in the pandemic years. Coal, oil and gas still make up 80 per cent of the world's energy, the same as they did back in 1970. Global temperatures are already up over 1°C; 1.5°C will probably be crossed at some stage in this decade, and the pathway points towards at least 3°C. No serious progress on climate change has been made despite thirty years of trying.

The story on biodiversity is more complex, but every bit as bad. The rainforests are diminishing and, in some cases, burning. Parts of the Amazon are now net emitters of carbon. The oceans are more acidic, the great rivers polluted and there has already been an insect Armageddon. On current trends, one of the great extinction events of geological history is well under way.

These are the facts, neither optimistic nor pessimistic. They are the result of the great economic expansion mainly since 1900. Fossil fuels made it possible to feed a global population that increased from 2 billion to now 8 billion. This expansion made us all consumers, and we all bought into and became dependent upon a continuous increase in gross domestic product (GDP). The diesel and petrol engines replaced horses, sail and even steam engines. Tractors, and fertilisers, produced by the Haber Bosch process, transformed agriculture. Plastics have become ubiquitous. Cars became a part of everyday life and flying around the globe reached the masses in developed countries. Electricity, generated mainly by coal, transformed both industry and domestic life, and gas heated homes. At the end of the twentieth century, the energy-intensive internet, smartphones and laptops began to usher in a whole new way of working, aided by robots, and genetics have already yielded the ability to manipulate the very stuff of life.

Most of human economic consumption (and most pollution) has happened since 1900, and most people have lived since then too. For thousands of years, the human population was small and vulnerable to famines and plagues, and economic growth barely existed until the eighteenth and nineteenth centuries. Life was short, nasty and brutish for too many people who lived before 1900. Nature kept populations in check.

All of this great fossil-fuel-driven economic growth has yielded great benefits: longer healthy lives, better food, better housing and, in the developed countries, a standard of living unimaginable for all but the very rich in previous centuries.

Not everyone of course has benefited: the two world wars left millions dead, and murderous regimes like Mao's China and Pol Pot's Cambodia killed lots of their own people. Poorer countries suffered from the legacy of colonialism, and there were terrible famines, like that in Darfur in the mid-1980s, yet by the end of the twentieth century poverty was in general retreat. A global Malthusian nightmare of mass starvation was avoided, as food production kept pace with population growth. Eight billion are better fed in 2020 than the two billion were in 1900.

This extraordinary transformation in both population and economic prosperity is now largely taken for granted. There is a lot to like about this. Extending further the great twentieth-century benefits to the fast-rising populations in Africa, India and to those caught in the middle incomes of China, the Middle East and much of Latin America is an obvious and understandable aspiration. By 2050, Nigeria's population alone will have doubled and probably be larger than that of either Europe or the US. Why shouldn't Nigeria's prospective half a billion people live like those in the developed countries do now?

The promise of the endless progress often seemed too good to be true, and scratch below the surface of the consumer nirvana it has created, and which we continue to vote for, and doubts emerge. Are we all really so much better off? The inconvenient truth, the first of many, is that all of this has come at a terrible price to the environment. Those green facts will not go away. The twentieth century was one that pushed nature back hard. Chemicals killed the pests and diseases, and in the process destroyed much of the insect life. Rivers and lakes have been grossly polluted. Rainforests retreated. Biodiversity declined. Extinctions mounted. The twentieth century was a great boom for us as consumers, but it also created the prospect of an unfolding environmental disaster. It had costs, and we are now beginning to face its environmental price.

It is now pretty clear to everyone that the current pathway is not sustainable. What follows, if this is true, is that it will not be sustained. It can't go on and it won't go on. There will be an environmental reckoning, and it has already begun to materialise, whether or not there are dramatic tipping points to come. The twenty-first century might have inherited all the technology and wealth built in the twentieth century, but it has also inherited all the environmental consequences too, neatly summarised in the facts of climate change and biodiversity loss.

We face a stark choice. We can either act now and head off further damage, or we can live with the consequences as and when our economic way of life is no longer sustained. The former opens up the possibility of transforming our economy into the sustainable one now, by tackling our problems head on. It is an exciting prospect for humanity. The latter takes us over the cliff like the lemmings, with all the suffering and damage that might bring. Billionaires might fantasise about moving to another planet, or at least retreating to a special bubble for the very rich to enjoy whilst the rest of humanity struggles to cope. For the rest of us (and for them too), there is no Planet B.

This book sets out the main building blocks of the sustainable economy – what the economy would look like if we lived within our environmental means. It answers the question: how could we get onto the sustainable path when the general population is more concerned with getting from today to tomorrow, affording what are now seen as necessities and doing as much consuming as possible? Unwilling to face up to the costs of Covid and its lockdowns and furlough schemes; unwilling to pay the higher costs of energy? Most of the world aspires to live like Americans and Europeans (or at least the better-off ones). People in developing countries want to eat more meat, drive their own cars and have broadband, clean water and air conditioning. The Americans and the Europeans do not want to sacrifice their consumption to help the developing world. On the contrary, they want more. Transfers of money are pathetically small, and even these are widely resented.

Turning around climate change, getting out of that 80 per cent dependency on fossil fuels, is a very big ask. Doing it in just over twenty-five years, by 2050, is a transformation without precedent in economic history. Halting the destruction of biodiversity is, if anything, an even bigger challenge, especially given where the biodiversity that is left actually is – in Brazil, the Democratic Republic of Congo, the countries along the Mekong and the great free-for-all vastness of the oceans. It is not hard to look at the lives of ourselves and those around us and realise that we can't go on like this, even with lots of new technologies, consuming ever more of the one planet we have.

Reorientating our economic approach to life does not mean that consumption is unimportant, that it does not matter whether we can meet our needs and that we cannot have more economic growth. That is the mistake many environmentalists make. They say that economic growth caused our problems, and we *therefore* should move to a no-growth economy to make things better. It can easily lead to a kind of arcadian nostalgia, a desire for the simpler life, forgetting many of the hardships that went with it, and especially for the poor.

There is something to be said in favour of this kind of low-impact, off-grid lifestyle, but what it neglects is the great human capacity for ideas and the creation of new technologies. It is these that enable each generation to build on the shoulders of the knowledge created by the previous generations. It allows us to decode the genetics of the coronavirus and develop a vaccine in a matter of days, and head off a repeat of the tragedy that the Spanish Flu caused towards the end of the First World War. It allows the internet to deliver to us huge access to knowledge, information and social contacts that could feature only in science fiction just a few decades ago. It gives us the science to be able to understand the causes of climate change and how ecosystems work. Human progress is not an evil to be stopped in its tracks. Sustainable economic growth will enable future people to be better off, in the sense of having better assets, more knowledge and in the process a better understanding of how to manage and sustain our world. But it must be sustainable, a genuine enlightenment.

To this must be added an element of humility. Instead of forecasting the future and tweaking the economic interventions to keep the economy on its maximum growth pathway, it would be better to admit, despite the great scientific advances, just how ignorant about the future we (and especially economists) still are. Instead of trying to make people, especially future people, happy, we should try to achieve a humbler objective: to ensure that we pass on to them a set of assets at least as good as we inherited, so they can choose how to live their lives armed with the wherewithal to do so.

The fundamental building block of the sustainable economy is us, as *citizens*, as members of a society with rights and obligations to each other, and who must cooperate together for the economy to work and for our lives to be fulfilled. We are entitled to inherit from the last generation a habitable world, and we are obliged not to make it worse for those who follow us. That is the overarching principle of the sustainable economy, to which other secondary principles (the 'polluter-pays' and the 'precautionary' principles) are added.

For us as citizens to participate in society and the economy, we need a stable climate, a thriving biodiversity and infrastructure networks. We need the knowledge embedded in ideas, science and technologies. We need to have access to health services, education, and we increasingly need a broadband connection, as well as affordable access to clean water, sewerage and rubbish disposal, reliable electricity available on demand, and roads and railways and airports. Take away any one of these and the citizens are vulnerable to being excluded from society and the economy.

All of the above come in *systems* – the natural, physical, human and social capitals. All comprise assets. They are the more important primary assets. Of these, the natural assets, what nature gives us for free and what makes life on this planet the wonderful cornucopia of opportunities that these provide, are the most important. Without natural capital, nothing else is possible. These natural assets come in two sorts: non-renewable and renewable natural capital. Our modern economy is based upon the non-renewables – things like oil, coal, gas and iron ore – and increasingly on nickel, lithium, cobalt and copper (used for wind and solar generators and in batteries for electric vehicles). These are all extracted from the earth's crust. Once burnt or refined or purified, they provide energy and materials that literally build our world. There is a good reason why the last 200 years have seen the world population go from less than 2 billion to 8 billion. It is called coal and oil and iron ore and the other core minerals.

We overwhelmingly depend on these non-renewable natural capital assets. We always will. Our generation is extracting and, in the case of fossil fuels, burning them without much regard to what will be left for future generations, and without any serious regard for the pollution that is a by-product of their use. Few realise that the new low-carbon technologies will take mining onto a whole new and vast industrial scale.

In the sustainable economy, we can go on using up these non-renewable natural capitals, provided we compensate the next generation for the fact that we have had the benefits that they cannot have (because these capitals have been used up) and we deal with the pollution their extraction, refining and use cause. The fact that we are a very long way from meeting these conditions does not mean they cannot be met. We could have national sovereign wealth funds to provide compensation to the next generation, and we could deal with the pollution. But mostly we do not, and that means that we need to change our unsustainable ways quickly. Turning from oil, gas and coal to cobalt, lithium, nickel and copper is not an escape from these responsibilities, but so far there is no evidence that we are compensating future generations for their depletion or dealing with the major pollution caused by mining for these 'low-carbon' minerals.

Renewable natural capital is even more important. It is alive, the stuff that nature will keep on giving us for free as long as we do not deplete it so that it can no longer reproduce itself. Think of the cod and herring swimming around in the North Sea, the Atlantic and beyond. We have been eating them for millennia. In the sustainable economy, the catch is capped so that the fish stocks remain at a healthy margin above the thresholds that would tip them over into the non-renewable category, even to extinction.

Behave selfishly, campaign for bigger and bigger fish quotas, and deplete the stocks too far, and then it is not just that there will soon not be any fish and chips, and kippers, but all future people also will not have these. The value of renewable natural capital is open-ended. People in 100,000 years' time could enjoy cod and herring, provided we treat these fish as assets-in-perpetuity and refrain from the sorts of reckless and destructive practices that are prevalent in modern fishing. Mega industrial trawlers now extend the destruction to deeper waters, stripping out fish stock wherever they still remain.

This open-ended value adds one further dimension to the sustainable economy. Nature does not come in discrete bits and discrete species. Everything in nature depends upon everything else. Unlike the claims of conventional economic theories, based upon discrete and atomistic consumers ('agents' in the economic literature), and discrete bits of capital which can be substituted at the margin for each other, the great renewable natural capital systems of the rainforests, the soils (with much more carbon than the atmosphere), the river catchments and the oceans are integrated ecosystems. They cannot be substituted for anything else.

The sustainable economy is starkly different from that of conventional economics, whose views we are exposed to every day, from the politicians and industrialists who are what Keynes called the 'slaves of defunct economists'. The primary assets, with the exception of the non-renewable natural capital, are all assets-in-perpetuity. They need to be maintained and, in many cases, not only be restored but also enhanced for us and the next generation to thrive. They are the essential building blocks of the sustainable economy and the state they are in is what politicians and the public should all be talking about, and what we should be worrying about.

With these assets in good shape, citizens are able to choose how to live their lives because the systems give them the capabilities to do so. Future citizens are enabled to be free to choose. To make these choices, citizens need these assets-in-perpetuity. They cannot do without them.

Basing the sustainable economy on citizens opens up a very different vista. Instead of GDP and the cash-based national accounts which tell us very little about the underlying state of the primary assets, the sustainable economy needs very different accounts. Accounts should answer the question as to whether the economy is on a sustainable path, and whether current consumption is consistent with leaving the next generation with a set of assets at least as good as those we inherited. GDP won't tell you this. Conventional economists look at the flows of goods and services, the flows of expenditures and the flows of incomes. The sustainable economy starts with the balance sheet of the assets and asks how well the stocks of these assets are being stewarded. In the example above, it is about the *stocks* of fish, not just how many we are catching. The former can be declining while the catches are going up, increasing GDP.

These accounts are anything but boring. Accounts shine a torch on what is going on. There should be a continuous updating on the state of the primary building blocks of the economy, an exercise that is more like William the Conqueror's Domesday Book than estimating GDP. Accounts should tell us every year how well we are doing in sustaining the primary assets. The balance sheet should be net of maintaining the assets, of any spending necessary to fix damage to the climate, to biodiversity, to the energy systems and to other core utility system networks *in perpetuity*. These costs of maintenance should be a charge to the nation's current account, analogous to a business's profit and loss account.

What might look like an arcane accounting detail has really radical implications in the sustainable economy. What is left for us to spend now is *net* of having first made good any damage we have done. If you own a house and have neglected to fix a hole in the roof, you will not pretend that you are better off and can spend more because the money has not been spent on fixing the roof. On the contrary, your house would be worth less; you would in effect be eating up your capital, mortgaging the future for the benefit of your spending today. Try constructing your own household balance sheet and see how few assets you have to fall back on. That is what we have been doing at the national and global scale in not paying for the capital maintenance. We have not been maintaining our personal or our national capital.

Proper accounts for the sustainable economy result in a very different set of national budgets. Imagine if finance ministers presented sustainable accounts. These would show the state of the primary assets, and would include an item on the current account subtracting the monies needed to properly maintain the value of the assets on the balance sheet. The amount of capital maintenance required for the hospitals, schools, railways, energy systems, water and broadband to prevent any deterioration would be subtracted, as would the more general cost of the environmental damage to natural capital. What is left would be a lot less for governments and us to spend. It would be a sobering collision with reality.

The sustainable economy treats debt very differently. Across most developed countries, finance ministers are borrowing to pay for both current spending and for capital maintenance (where it is being done at all). In the sustainable economy, the purpose of debt is to finance new enhancements *after* the existing assets have been properly maintained. The next generation gets the debts and the new *additional* assets to match, so they are at least as well off. At present, they get both debts and the degraded assets. All of the above is also true for you and me. Borrowing to spend, armed with credit, is a dangerous path to follow.

The next generation is properly respected in the sustainable economy, and the accounts tell us whether we are making sure that they will have the assets that provide the capabilities for them to choose how to live their lives. They keep us honest. The enhancements they get, which will include a significant amount of new knowledge, ideas and technologies, increase their opportunities, and they incentivise us to look to increase these because they pay for these if they are genuine enhancements. We borrow from them, and they get to repay the debt. This is why economic growth in the sustainable economy is possible. The accounts tell us if we are over-consuming and messing up their inheritance.

The investments in enhancements need savings to back the debts. Savings must equal investment. Saving is forgone consumption. The sustainable macroeconomic economy sets up the framework within which this is facilitated. A glance at where we are now tells us we are a very long way from this pathway. Interest rates have stayed well below inflation for the last quarter of a century, incentivising spending and borrowing and disincentivising savings and investment. It is no accident that productivity growth rates are widely exceptionally low and, in the absence of the incentives to save, the debt has had to be partly monetarised through quantitative easing (QE). It is not accidental that printing money has led to inflation and it is no accident that it has resulted in greater inequality. None of this is consistent with the sustainable economy.

It would be painful to get onto the sustainable macroeconomic path. We would have to pay for the capital maintenance, and we would have to save for the investment. Together, these are two big whammies to our current consumption, and together illustrate how far we are living beyond our sustainable means.

There is one more hit our consumption has to take to get onto the sustainable path. An obvious requirement is that pollution is internalised in the economy by making polluters pay. Following the polluter-pays principle would be another very radical departure from the status quo. Today's pollution is typically paid for by the polluted, who get the costs in terms of dirty air, poor-quality rivers and pesticides in their food. They are often the poor. In almost all major economies, farmers are subsidised to pollute, and expect to get subsidised fuel, and even subsidies to own land. The 'ask' of government by farming lobbyists is that farmers should be paid to provide public goods, paid to husband the carbon in the soil, paid to reduce nitrate run-offs and even paid to store water for irrigation. In effect, farmers claim the right to pollute, and if they are to take the environment into account, they want to be paid to do so. The fishing industry looks to be compensated for any loss of fishing grounds. At the global scale, Brazil expects to be paid not to cut down more of the Amazon rainforest.

This is all the wrong way around. If polluters pay, the relative prices of polluting goods and services go up, and those of the less-polluting ones go down. The price of fossil fuels goes up, as does the price of beef raised on cleared Amazonian forests and the price of palm oil from the cleared South East Asian rainforests. The price of local food becomes relatively cheaper than the price of food flown around the world, as the transport costs to the environment are added in.

Why then don't we make polluters pay and internalise these costs, and thereby make the economy more efficient? The answer reveals yet another inconvenient truth: the ultimate polluters are you and me. Companies do not produce stuff for the fun of it: they do it for profit, and profits come from selling stuff we demand. Whilst it is convenient to pretend that it is all the fault of dirty businesses and for activists to glue themselves to the doors of big (Western) companies and the banks that finance them, it is best to bear in mind that these businesses are selling petrol and diesel to us, and the petrochemicals industry is making the plastics and synthetic materials for the clothes and shoes we buy. The act of buying this stuff is the act of causing the pollution that its production entails. All that 80 per cent fossil fuels is for you and me.

With this further inconvenient truth in mind, it is hardly surprising that voters resist carbon taxes and increases in fuel and aviation taxes, wanting to have all this stuff but not wanting to pay its full costs. Yet by sidestepping our responsibilities as citizens, the pollution costs do not go away. Worse, whilst demanding that companies clean up their acts, we do nothing much to curtail our own polluting habits.

This is where it gets personal. To see how this would work for you, try drawing up a diary of your daily spending and divide it up according to your best guess of its environmental impacts. To get to the sustainable economy, now try rewriting it excluding the polluting stuff: the petrol, diesel, heating gas and oil, the palm oil, the plastics and the cardboard, and the non-renewable energy used for all the IT gadgets. If you use cryptocurrencies, try to work out how incredibly harmful they can be.

What the polluter-pays principle does is to go behind that spending and helps to change it. It puts us as citizens at the heart of the economy and at the heart of addressing climate change and biodiversity loss. That beef from Brazil, that palm oil from Malaysia, all that polluting stuff would now cost us more, and in some cases a lot more. We might not completely stop buying the polluting stuff, but we would use a lot less of it.

The inconvenience of us being the polluters goes deeper. It means that, because we are not paying the full costs of the stuff we consume, we are all living beyond our sustainable means. It means sustainable consumption will have to be lower, even if it can rise over time as sustainable economic growth builds on the basis of new ideas and technologies. We can get better off, but only from a lower sustainable level, one that internalises all those pollution costs in your diary.

This gives us the three big adjustments to our consumption: deducting the costs of capital maintenance so we are not consuming our primary capital assets; setting aside savings to fund investment; and paying for the pollution we cause.

Together, these require a very significant adjustment, and the burden would be most acutely felt by the less well-off. That means that social justice has to play a big part in the transition to the sustainable economy. Making sure that future generations have general access to the core systems, to health and education, to the body of knowledge and ideas, and to the natural environmental systems will not be enough to ensure that everyone has sufficient capability to choose how to live their lives. They will need enough income to spend on private goods and services, a problem that the switch from an unsustainable to a sustainable consumption path will exacerbate, given the scale of the claims already on current consumption, and the fact that pollution will be priced into the shopping basket. The sustainable economy embeds social justice within it, and social justice will be essential to the transition from here to there.

The way this is usually dealt with is through social security systems, funded by taxation. There are means-tested benefits for the poor and progressive taxes on the rich. But there are several obvious and well-known problems with these conventional approaches to social justice. They can undermine the incentives to work, inhibit contributions to the sustainable economy and lead to unemployment, and, despite the costs, still leave a lot of people in poverty.

The alternative is to break the link between wages and benefits. Flexible wages give people the incentive to work at whatever wage rates clear the market. Universal basic income is an idea that seeks to make this break. It does this by giving all citizens a sufficient income and therefore eliminates poverty. In the sustainable economy, this would be on top of the access to the core system assets, and together these would deliver social justice, so that all citizens have the capabilities to participate in society.

The obvious problem is that it would be (very) expensive. Eliminating poverty is never going to be cheap. Yet this, too, can be addressed pragmatically. It can have a high cut-off point, to exclude the better-off to whom the basic income will not make any difference to their choices. It becomes a universal safety net for the least well-off. A second constraint can be created by tying the level of basic income to the performance of the economy as a whole. The basic income could be a dividend on the national balance sheet, and so add a second advantage. Citizens would now have a direct stake in the economy, and the basic income has to carry only the costs that the economy can bear as a result of its productivity performance over time. A national fund, backed by the national balance sheet, provides a means to the end of the relief of poverty, and it does so in a way that leaves the economy on a sustainable path. Most or all get a pay-out from the fund, and the pay-out is only what can be afforded without jeopardising the prospects of the next generation.

The sustainable economy now has its core assets and these are properly maintained. It has enhancements that are paid for by borrowing, and savings equal investment. Polluters pay, so that the economy is efficient because all the costs are internalised. Social justice is achieved by providing both the assets and a modified form of universal basic income based on a national dividend.

That leaves regulatory structures and the constitution. The institutions of the sustainable economy will need to be underpinned by a systems regulatory framework and by a constitution that embeds the principle to leave the assets in at least as good condition for the next generation and embeds the rights and duties of current and future citizens. The tyranny of the current majority needs to be limited by giving the interests of the next generation constitutional protection.

You might by now be thinking that whilst it may be interesting to know what the sustainable economy would look like, and how big a departure from the status quo it might be, its uncomfortable implications are going to deter anyone from seriously following its design. That may well be the sad fact about our politics and our generational selfishness. It might even be a true representation of human nature. But, in thinking this, the conclusion that follows cannot be escaped, and cannot be repeated too often. If you recognise that the current way of doing things is unsustainable, then you also have to accept the conclusion that follows: *it will not be sustained.*

The consequences of global warming do not go away because we refuse to address its fundamental causes. Our current path leads to nasty carbon and biodiversity crunches. The difference between now and earlier generations is that these crunches are getting closer, and we know it. It is within this century that quite a lot of the consequences will be felt, within the lives of our children and grandchildren. It is getting ominously close. This might not be 'our last century' as some alarmists have predicted, but there is nothing inevitable about the human species escaping the extinction that has already hit 98 per cent of the species that have ever lived. The rules of the sustainable economy tell us what we need to do. We can do it now and head off the worst of what is coming because of the actions of our selfish generation; or we can be forced onto the sustainable economy path later. A key difference is that the latter is almost certainly going to be a lot more painful than the former. Nature, of course, doesn't care one way or the other. Unsustainability has to end. How it ends remains to be seen.

Which brings us to the upside of the sustainable economy. It is not all doom and gloom, and reduced standards of living. In the sustainable economy, we probably will ultimately end up better off because the things that are valuable get valued. Better-quality air, better-quality water, better-quality seas, less global warming and more biodiversity are all really quite nice. Much of what we buy is not necessarily what we might really want if we thought about what it is doing to us. Do we really want to be obese, have less healthy lives and a painful old age? Do we really need to go to packed beaches strewn with litter through ever-more-crowded airports? And do we really need all the stuff the advertisers get ever better at targeting to us? Being sustainable can be quite liberating.

The point about our environmental crises is that we are all in this together. Just tackling climate change will require an economic transformation on a scale never seen in economic history, from an overwhelmingly fossil-fuel-based economy to one that is very different, within the space of a couple of decades or so. Rising to this challenge will be bracing, but it will also be exciting and packed with new ideas and technologies, and could bring with it the sort of social cohesions that past threats such as wars have brought. Keynes, writing in 1940 about *How to Pay for War*, proposed a switch from consumption to investment for the war effort. We need a switch from consumption to investing for our natural environment on a similar scale now. It was done then, and it can be done now.

2 THE NEXT GENERATION

Sustainability is all about the future, and the sustainable economy is one that has a future. It is about stewardship, about making sure we do not make such a mess of our planet that the next generation's possibilities are curtailed. How we think about the future, and in particular the next generation, is the first building block of the sustainable economy.

I recently gave a lecture to a large international group of students finishing their school education, in which I set out some of the environmental challenges they will face. Aged 15–18, these students are the next generation who are coming of age. A few of them will make it to 2100. It occurred to me that it was like presenting to people born in the years immediately after the First World War and wondering what their world in 2020 would be like.

By 2050, this next generation will be in their mid-30s, many with children of their own and already connected to the generation after themselves. By 2075, they will be contemplating retirement. They are the people we need to look in the eye and account for our stewardship – or lack of it – as we pass the baton on to them. And throughout this chapter, it is this audience who are what the arguments are all about.

If we are going to honour the current generation's obligations to them, we need to ask what their world will look like at these milestone dates – how hot the climate is likely to be; how much biodiversity might remain; what science they may have; and what technologies might be available to them – from the baseline we are leaving behind.

The next generation will have its own legacy to pass on to the generation that comes afterwards. What matters is that we leave an inhabitable planet, and a robust legacy of assets. We should leave them our houses, our infrastructures, our knowledge and ideas, our institutions and an environment in a fit state, and only so much debt as to be covered by new assets that we have created for them.

What matters is not about making sure they are happy and have lots and lots of utility, and a higher GDP as environmental economists would have us concentrate on. It is about equipping them for their open-ended future, and not mucking up the planet so badly that they lack the basics of an equitable and stable climate and lots of biodiversity, and the core infrastructures and knowledge. We need to treat them as new citizens and not just as the economists' future utility-maximising machines. Whether, armed with these assets, they are happy or sad is not our business, unless that sadness comes from the depleted set of opportunities they confront.

Saints and Sinners

This is what we owe them, and is as far as we can reasonably be expected to go. It is also what we are failing to achieve. The next generation, those people already with us, is as far as our altruism should stretch. To see why this is the realistic limit of our concerns, rather than all future peoples, ask yourself: how much do you really care about the future compared with getting through today? Take a look at what you're going to spend on today. How far have you really thought through whether your choices seriously take much account of the imprint they will make on the next and future generations? You might try to do some recycling, buy less plastic-wrapped stuff and eat less meat, but few really think through the carbon embedded in their daily routines. The finger points to all those foreign holidays, fast fashions and fast foods.

Even if we do care a bit, carrying on as 'normal' remains the default mode of our consumption. Amongst those who claim to be environmentalists, the majority fly just as much as the rest of us, sometimes more so. When I was recently asked to fly to Bali to speak at a conference on climate change, the organisers did not see the irony.

(I did not go.) Ask the many children who joined in the Extinction Rebellion demonstrations what their holiday plans are and what clothes and fashions they follow, and the answers are 'normal' too. This is not meant as a personal criticism (though it is good to keep a record of one's own carbon footprint), but rather to provide an insight into what constitutes the context for designing policies to better meet our obligations. Assuming a world of environmental saints is not going to get us sinners to take the practical and realist steps necessary to provide a decent legacy to the next generation.

This dose of realism stands in stark and remarkable contrast to what some economists and philosophers claim – that there is no obvious reason to discriminate against people on the basis of when they live – and the conclusions they then draw. Since nobody decides when their lives are to be lived, it is argued that there is no good reason to discriminate against those who will live in the future. The policy they recommend is that we should be purely impartial, and forever.

Rather than look at human nature as it is and stretch out our concerns to just the next generation, leading thinkers like Nick Stern (on climate change) and Partha Dasgupta (on biodiversity) would have us follow this impartiality principle.[1] We should not focus more on the needs of those living now and less on those in the future. All are counted as one – now, tomorrow, in 2100 and in 10,000 years' time. We should be altruistic impartial saints. But we obviously do. We violate this time-invariant impartiality principle all the time. It is basic to our existence. Your spending probably illustrates this, and your carbon and environmental diaries would spell this out. A possible reward in the future is worth less than money in your pocket now. All of us do this discounting of the future, ranking current consumption as more important than postponed consumption, preferring instant gratification to the possibility of our own future happiness, let alone that of other people. This is not a sin, but rather a fact of our human nature.

Short-termism myopia is not without merit on an individual basis. It is quite rational. Taking that holiday now rather than when you are older and possibly dead makes a lot of sense. Better spend it now than regret it later, or no longer have the opportunity to do so at all. Many of our major personal decisions are complicated by not

[1] See N. Stern (2007), *The Economics of Climate Change: The Stern Review*, HM Treasury, Cambridge: Cambridge University Press; and P. Dasgupta (2021), 'Final Report – The Economics of Biodiversity: The Dasgupta Review', 2 February.

knowing when we will die and not knowing how long our health will hold up. Savings for pensions and putting aside something for a rainy day postpone consumption. Take a look at your bank statements, and the trade-offs you have made. How precautionary are you when it comes to pensions, health risks and possible future rainy days?

For most of human history this myopia has been a pretty successful strategy. The battle against nature, the battle for resources and consumption now, has confronted a forgiving natural world, rich in the cornucopia of the natural capital we have inherited. The battle against nature has been pretty successful so far, but no longer. The problem with building the sustainable economy on our own myopia, our discounting the future to prioritise the present, is that it might (and probably will) lead to environmental disaster. The interests of society are not the same as the sum of the interests of the individuals who make it up. It is not at all clear why society as a whole should follow our individual myopic paths. Instead, rules are needed to keep us on the straight and narrow.

Climate Change and Nuclear Power

To see why myopia is no longer going to work, take a very practical question: is tackling future climate change a good economic investment to make now from the perspective of our own personal interests? For many people the answer is 'yes' if it does not cost them much (demonstrating a bit of altruism), and 'no' if it does require them to pay a bit more now for their energy. That is what opinion polls indicate: most people say they think climate change is very important, but very few are prepared to sacrifice income now to address it.[2]

The ramp-up of oil and gas prices in 2022 led politicians in the US, the European Union (EU), China and India to roll back on measures to phase out fossil fuels. Joe Biden reverted to encouraging onshore and offshore US oil and gas production, Germany turned back to coal and nuclear, China and India both turbocharged coal, and the UK opened up drilling licences for North Sea oil and gas and even tried (and failed) to lift the ban on onshore fracking. Many countries cut fossil-fuel energy taxes and moved to subsidies of energy bills (funded

---

[2] See, for example, YouGov polling which asks what steps people are prepared to take. Note that none of these has an explicit cost attached to it: https://docs.cdn.yougov.com/hdemoi825d/Internal_ClimateChangeTracker_220720_GB_W.pdf.

by borrowing) on a scale that puts it into the category of the Covid interventions. As soon as the costs showed up on consumers' bills, the climate change measures took a back seat. At the first whiff of gunfire in Ukraine, net zero policies went into retreat.[3]

This is what discounting the future looks like in action. In 2022, US President Biden, German Chancellor Olaf Scholtz, Chinese President Xi Jinping and the then UK Prime Minsters Boris Johnson and Liz Truss all prioritised the present over the future. Burning coal now was prioritised over the consequences of the emissions to the climate later on.

A more sophisticated argument for acting on climate change is frequently advanced: that although there will be costs to decarbonisation now, these will be smaller than the costs of global warming that would be avoided. In other words, it is a good economic investment to head off something worse.

The obvious problem with this argument is that your actions (incurring the costs now) will have very little impact on global warming if others do not follow (and they are mostly not), with the result that you will pay *both* for the costs of mitigation *and* the costs of global warming. More importantly, the costs are very much now, whereas any benefits (if they materialise) are mainly later, accruing to the next generation. And this is regardless of whatever spin is made on every negative weather event being declared evidence of climate change now, without the balancing offset of the benefits now of warmer winters, long growing seasons and new ice-free sea lanes in areas of the world where most of the wealth (and quite a lot of the warming) is concentrated.

This climate change example illustrates why the question of whether to discount the future is anything but arcane and academic. It goes to the very heart of how to shape economic policies – with costs now to head off the damage (and hence costs) later on. Even at a very low positive discount rate, things that happen later this century to those students attending my recent lecture have little significance to decisions made now.

Let's illustrate this discounting issue with a much simpler example than the big picture of climate change. Consider nuclear

---

[3] See D. Helm (2022), 'The Retreat from Net Zero', 4 July, www.dieterhelm.co.uk/energy/climate-change/the-retreat-from-net-zero/.

power, one of the 'answers' to climate change that some advance. A new nuclear power station may take around a decade to build (most recent ones take longer). Once built it should run for say sixty years. All the while it produces nuclear waste in the form of spent fuel, and at the end of the sixty years there are a lot more radioactive materials to be dealt with as the power station is decommissioned. The costs of nuclear waste are large, but this is where discounting magics them away. Assuming an admittedly implausible low cost of dealing with the waste of £10 billion in 2090 when the station closes, if we discount at say 5 per cent, then £10,000,000 in sixty years' time is a minuscule £500,000 today. In other words, it is so small as to be irrelevant to the decision on whether to build the power station.

Lest you think this is a highly contrived and implausible outcome, let me disabuse you. This is very much what happens. Few countries have any serious plans to start dealing with the waste of existing nuclear generation, and even for already decommissioned nuclear power stations, other than to dig big holes at some future date and bury it. The analogy with climate change is obvious: all the waste that carbon emissions are putting up in the atmosphere from burning fossil fuels has been allowed to build up because this carbon waste is in effect discounted. The nuclear waste and the carbon waste are treated as future problems, and of little current economic value. This sort of discounting is at the heart of our environmental problems, mirroring our myopia, itself the reflection of our generational selfishness, our partiality.

Since whether, why and how the future is discounted is such a fundamental dimension of the sustainable economy, let's take a more forensic look at the underlying arguments for and against discounting. Is there any justification for this sort of discounting that lies at the heart of our neglect of the future? Are we just uncontrolled sinners, or is there more to discounting and our relationship and responsibilities towards the next generation than meets the eye?

There are at least three distinct arguments in play: (i) we *should not* discount future utility at all because future people are just as important as current people; (ii) we *should* discount because economic growth means that future people will be better off; and (iii) because of distributional reasons and a special concern about the poor, we *should* discount to make current poor people better off as the rising tide of economic growth, in theory, lifts all the boats.

The Pure Impartiality Argument

Let's unpack each bit in turn, concentrating on the first, about utility and consumption. It is the one that raises the most profound ethical questions. Whether to discount utility, our future happiness (if that is what we are worried about), and, if so, at what rate, is perhaps the most important single issue in designing the rules of the sustainable economy. The famous economist and mathematician, Frank Ramsey, remarked that to discount the future 'arises merely from the weakness of the imagination',[4] viewing the future through the lens of utility and implicitly the utilitarian ethic of the greatest happiness to the greatest number.

Let's see why this is so misguided. Just in case you are seduced by the argument that seemed so obvious to Frank Ramsey (and most utilitarians) that we should take pure utility impartiality as a central plank for the sustainable economy, making the future as important as the present, especially when it comes to environmental issues, think again. Recall that the ethical assumption, which pure impartiality relies upon, is that we should treat each and every individual equally, and hence any individual's utility is as important as anyone else's. This means that future people are just as important as current people, however far into the future they live, and all people now, wherever they live, are as important as each other.[5]

Superficially, this might sound good and reasonable, and, in particular, pretty environmentally benign. It might be something both economists and environmentalists could agree upon. But now think of a couple of consequences. You should not care about your own children more than about a child living in poverty in the slums of Lagos, for example, and you should not care about your neighbour, your town or your country more than about people in a Sudanese village, for example. It is a generic impartiality between individuals, and it includes the time dimension, but it also applies at any point in time. This moves us a long way away from maximising our own utility, our

---

[4] F.P. Ramsey (1928), 'A Mathematical Theory of Saving', *Journal of Economics*, 38(152), 543–59, at 543.

[5] This ignores the problem Jonathan Glover highlights of the determination of what sort of people there will be. Once the full consequences of artificial intelligence (AI) are taken into account, those people may be very different from us. It is not obvious why we should care about people in the future given these considerations. See J. Glover (1984), *What Sort of People Should There Be?*, Harmondsworth: Penguin Books.

own personal preferences (like our preference for our own children over others), to the requirement to care for all and everyone equally, anywhere and everywhere.

This demands too much of us and human nature. It is hopelessly idealistic and never going to happen. As we move away from our immediate circle of family, friends and those who share our localities, countries and cultures, we care less. We have different preferences about people *now* in our own countries than about people abroad, especially when they do not share our language and culture. Migrants from poor countries are often resented, borders are policed and it is even deemed appropriate by, for example, the UK government to send some of them to Rwanda. We care less about people not yet born whom we do not know, and even less about people in hundreds and thousands of years in the future. We do not care much about which people will live in this distant future. Our actions now may cause these people to exist, or not. We choose contraceptives and abortions in order to limit family size, changing the chances of being born.[6]

Discounting the utility of future people at a point in time is just a part of our human nature, open to modification, but not complete rejection. It is why we vote for politicians who will look to our immediate problems, preferring, in the above example, the short-term boost of coal burning in the energy crisis of 2022 over the longer-term impacts on the climate, and tax cuts and more spending, funding by debts that future taxpayers will confront as a result of our myopia.

We give very little of our income to those with less than us if they are remote from us. Foreign aid is very low, and even its low level is controversial. The maxim 'charity begins at home' appears to be politically popular. Aid budgets are soft political targets.[7] We spend great efforts on gender equality at home, but not so much in Afghanistan or Iran. At the 26th Conference of the Parties (COP26) in Glasgow in 2021, it was a struggle to get world leaders to commit to a climate fund of $100 billion per annum – a bit more than the annual dividend of the oil company, Saudi Aramco, in that year. Delivering even this sum has so far eluded the donors.

---

[6] Derek Parfit's non-identity problem gives an example of the choice between depleting and conserving natural resources. This choice affects who lives in the future. D. Parfit (1984), *Reasons and Persons*, Oxford: Oxford University Press, p. 362.

[7] The priority for home use of vaccines first, cuts in foreign aid and the small sums transferred to assist developing countries and address climate change are all such examples.

Advocating policies based upon pure impartiality when it comes to future generations runs into this brick wall of human nature. Any credible environmental ethic, and the policies that follow, is unlikely to have much chance of changing behaviours if it does so much violence to our basic human instincts, such as preferentially caring for your own children or deciding how many children to have.[8]

The pure impartiality approach runs into a further problem: since the future is open-ended and might go on to infinity, there may be an infinite number of people to care about in the distant future. It is a point that Stern noticed in his 2007 review on the economics of climate change, and he implausibly truncated his analysis by assuming a 10 per cent chance of extinction by 2100.[9] Otherwise, there is no limit to the demands on us of future people. For utilitarians from Jeremy Bentham onwards, it is even worse: they will want the greatest number of people if each additional person at the margin gains positive net utility.[10] Indeed, not only should you care about other children as much as your own, and probably even more so because a little extra income to poorer children would disproportionately increase their utility, but you should also have as many children as possible as long as they are expected to live a life with net positive utility, even if they are lives barely worth living. If that means that the average utility falls, then so be it.

The utilitarian's population is open-ended, until additional people are either net-negative utility machines, or they reduce everyone else's utility so much as to offset all their gains. This is the 'repugnant conclusion', as stated by Parfit: 'For any possible population of at least ten billion people, all with a very high quality of life, there must be some much larger imaginable population whose existence, if other

---

[8] When Jean-Jacques Rousseau took his children to an orphanage rather than raise them himself, or at least take responsibility for them, we are naturally appalled by his departure from what most would regard as the essential partiality of parents to their own children. See J.-J. Rousseau (1782), *The Confessions of Jean-Jacques Rousseau*.

[9] See also H. Greaves and T. Ord (2017), 'Moral Uncertainty about Population Ethics', *Journal of Ethics and Social Philosophy*, 12(2), 135–67.

[10] There are two separate justifications of utilitarianism given that are relevant here: the empirical and the purely ethical, and between the economists as they divide between them. The first is derived from empirical claims about human nature: utilitarians, from Bentham onwards, assumed that pain and pleasure are facts of human nature. When David Hume and Adam Smith grounded economics in the context of the wider search for a science of human nature, they were firmly in the first category. But when it comes to Stern's and Dasgupta's impartiality and not discounting future utility, it is obvious that this is not grounded in human nature. It is not a fact.

things are equal, would be better even though its members have lives that are barely worth living.'[11]

For environmentalists who worry that there are already too many people on the planet, it is the quality of lives well lived, not the quantity that matters. For them, having too many people may harm the quality of lives now and in the future. Better to have fewer people living better lives. It is for them 'repugnant' as well as inimical to sustainability.

In summary, the Ramsey view is wrong in so many ways – in its focus on utility and happiness (the sustainable economy focuses on assets); in its failure to come to terms with human nature and its limits (the sustainable economy takes citizens as they are, and not as utility-maximising consumers); and in its failure to make any distinction between different time horizons from now to infinity (the sustainable economy focuses on the next generation). It is another ethically 'repugnant conclusion'.

The Economic Growth Argument

The second argument advanced for discounting is economic growth. Future people will be better off because economic growth (in GDP terms) leaves them a bigger economy (a bigger pie) and hence the opportunity for more consumption. It is what lies behind governments setting GDP growth targets (as if governments can magic up specific levels of GDP growth). This might be called the 'Chinese model': set a target, make people better off in GDP terms, irrespective of the debts piled up on the next generation.

The argument runs as follows. You are almost certainly better off than your parents, and therefore, if anything, your parents should have consumed more to even up the utility between them and you. If the same happens for your children (and those school students in my lecture), you should get stuck into consuming more today to compensate for the fact that they will be better off.

The flaw in this argument is pretty obvious. It depends upon the assumption that economic growth actually occurs, that the next generation can be safely assumed to be better off, which in turn depends

---

[11] On the repugnant conclusion, see Parfit, *Reasons and Persons*, pp. 381–8. See also H. Sidgwick (1874), *The Methods of Ethics*, London: Macmillan and Co., Book IV, chapter 1, section 2.

upon whether it is *sustainable* economic growth. Where there is an enhancement of the core assets that we pass on to future people, and in particular growth in ideas and technologies, there may be a case for applying a positive 'economic growth' discount rate representing that expected economic growth, but only *after* allowance has been made now for the damage to the environment, and the investments to remedy some of the past damage. As will be explained in setting out the accounting for the sustainable economy, sustainable economic growth is likely to be significantly lower than GDP growth. Given the scale of the remedial damage that we need to address, it is likely to be at a very low rate. Using GDP economic growth to discount is wrong. Worse still, pursuing a GDP growth target, and in the process disregarding the environmental impacts, is incompatible with the sustainable economy. Discounting of genuinely sustainable economic growth is fine.

The Distributional Argument

A third argument for discounting, given particular importance by Dasgupta,[12] concerns the distribution of income at a point in time. If there is lots of inequality now, and if economic growth lifts the position of the poorest, this might be a reason to prioritise the poor now over the (assumed) less poor in the future (provided the economic growth is sustainable and actually happens). Dasgupta is of course right to recognise that concern for the next generation, and the current one, has a distributional dimension. If we should treat future people on the same utility basis as current people (and hence be purely impartial over time), we should also treat all people now as of equal concern in the (and his) utilitarian calculus.

There are great inequalities, and those in developed countries treat people in poorer countries very differently from those in rich ones, and within each country treat the rich differently from the poor. No amount of 'trickle-down' economics will provide an excuse. Turning away obviously very poor people migrating in small boats is witness to strong discrimination. As long as sustainable economic growth happens, and that it benefits the poorest, higher consumption now is justified at the expense of the next generation because the poorer in

---

[12] Dasgupta, 'Final Report – The Economics of Biodiversity', pp. 260–73; and P. Dasgupta (2019), *Time and the Generations*, New York: Columbia University Press, especially pp. 79–86.

this generation are poorer than the poor will be in the next. But only if these assumptions hold.

The above discussion tells us that what we assume about discounting goes to the heart of the sustainable economy and how it should be designed. It tells us that sustainable economic growth is the main reason why we can have higher consumption over time, and hence that this is a justification for discounting, because sustainable economic growth will make the next generation better off. It tells us that we will have to dig deeper into what causes sustainable economic growth, and later on we will see that this is overwhelmingly about new ideas and technologies. It tells us that not to discount utility is a demand for sainthood, but at the same time we should have rules that help us to be more than purely selfish when it comes to future people. Finally, the above discussion tells us that we should be serious about the poorest in any generation over and above the average, that social justice at any point in time matters in the sustainable economy.

Limited Realistic Impartiality

The sustainable economy harnesses *limited* impartiality, working with people as they are, and not with the utopia of pure impartiality. Opting for a more limited element of impartiality opens up the path to define the ethical foundations of the sustainable economy in a more practical, do-able and partial way. Looking forward through time, trying to make all the future people happy, stretches both our sympathies and our ability to predict what they will want. We need something less demanding and more achievable. A more parsimonious ethical assumption is to focus on the *next generation*, and to ensure that this next generation inherits a set of assets at least as good as we did.

There is, of course, nothing magic about the next generation, other than our direct connectivity with it. The next generation overlaps with us, and they are our children and grandchildren. They are those students in my lecture whom we met at the start of this chapter. It is easier to see why we might, as a matter of fact, care more for them than for subsequent generations.

By structuring our concerns in this way, a chain letter is created through the future generations, each concerned with its successor, giving something immediate and tractable to work with. We can be partial and at the same time take future generations into account, going with the grain of human nature. We can assume with the philosopher David Hume that, for our practical purposes of designing the sustainable economy, human nature is pretty invariant, whilst at the same time not closing off the opportunity to shape future human nature through the way we educate the next generation.[13]

It is true that some decisions we should take now will have less of an impact on the next generation, but rather more on much later ones, like what we choose to do with our nuclear waste in the example above. It is notable that we are very bad at taking these very long-term decisions: nuclear waste remains largely unaddressed.

Until recently, this category of longer-term decisions included climate change and biodiversity loss. But that is no longer true. Climate change is already happening, and although it might get worse for subsequent generations after the next one, in practice the damage by 2050 and 2100 will be very significant unless dramatic actions are taken now by this generation. It is very real and very immediate.

Similarly with biodiversity loss. The Amazon is drying and dying, as are most of the other great rainforests. The tundra is thawing and the great rivers and oceans are heavily polluted. The time horizon to really serious consequences is concertinaed back to us and the next generation. If we fixed all these things for just the next generation, think what a massive achievement that would be. Expecting more is utopian.

This shortcut of focusing only on the next generation fits with the approach to many of our current environmental problems, and more generally in the provision of education and health and making sure we properly maintain and enhance the physical infrastructures. It makes the 2050 climate change target for net zero more appropriate (even if badly defined and unlikely to be achieved), and it encourages twenty-five-year environment plans. It is a timeframe we can make a difference within, and hence gives grounds for hope that environmental progress can be made.

The focus starts at home, with the nation, and hence on what can be done on a unilateral basis, and for the next generation, closer to us and linked through family and children, rather than in, say, 100 generations' time. However much Frank Ramsey might think that it

---

[13] Hume thought our natural generosity was limited in scope. See J.A. Harris (2015), *Hume: An Intellectual Biography*, Cambridge: Cambridge University Press, pp. 126–7.

should not matter when or where an individual lives, in fact it does to us in this generation. It is not a lack of imagination, as Ramsey claims, to treat future people as less important. On the contrary, it is a lack of understanding human nature *as it is* and the possibilities and limits to influencing it. Trying to construct an ethical theory and, worse, to propose actions and policies on the basis of it, without regard to human nature, is a serious mistake. Utopia can wait whilst we sort out the legacy for the next generation.

Citizens and Their Capabilities

In narrowing the focus to the next generation, some things matter more than others. The utilitarian framework yields a narrow and simplistic vision of what makes people tick, and how they should behave, and underpins the consumerist approach to the economy and the environment. The sustainable economy treats people as *citizens*. Its citizens are not autonomous. Citizens are part of somewhere, of their specific society, and have entitlements, rights, duties and obligations from and to that society, now and in the future. Citizens have a location and a nationality. In democracies, they have an equal vote, and participate in political processes through some form of representative democracy. Consumers, by contrast, are 'agents' and have budgets, and income and wealth that define how much they can consume. They have these unequally.

Citizens' human nature may be given, but their outlook is conditioned by the society in which they are embedded and is reflected through its history, its education system and its institutions. Germans save more and worry more about balanced budgets than the British because they have the historical experience of hyperinflation, defeat and destitution before, during and after two world wars. Many Americans still carry the concepts inherited from their puritan ancestors, whether they realise this or not.[14] Citizens exist in time and the history that has gone before them. They are not abstracted from time and history. Attitudes towards the environment and future people are similarly conditioned.

Our behaviour is not best understood by abstracting from time, as science does. Economics, despite its science envy, is not a science.

---

[14] See G. McKenna (2007), *The Puritan Origins of American Patriotism*, New Haven: Yale University Press.

There are no genuine controlled experiments: counterfactuals are always hypothetical. Behaviour happens in historical contexts and citizens' reactions vary over time according to their culture and society. They are not abstracted from time such that they can match Ramsey's impartiality between any point in time, and the state cannot be fully impartial between citizens now and at any future time.

If the culture turns towards being consumer-oriented, as was encouraged in the 1980s and 1990s with 'greed is good', yuppies, Porsches and get-rich lifestyles, citizens are likely to behave in more short-term and selfish ways, and quite differently to how they would have behaved had they had recent experience of war, as for example in the 1940s and 1950s. Consumption is a fashion which thrives in the context of low social capital. Famously, the behaviours of the super-rich of the Gilded Age in the pre-First World War US led Thorstein Veblen to describe their behaviour as conspicuous consumption,[15] an echo of Adam Smith's comment on the pursuit of baubles in eighteenth-century Britain by the very rich.[16] Think of the differing attitudes to slavery and women's rights at different times. Culture, media and political leadership do shape our behaviour.

Context dependency shapes the choices people make, and social capital is the way this can be framed. The liberal tradition leaves it to individuals to choose how to live their lives, and keeps the state out of trying to make them happy. Happiness is one dimension of a life well lived, and it is for each of us to choose how to go about this. This is John Stuart Mill's *On Liberty* negative concept of freedom from the state.[17] The trouble with this classical liberal tradition is it leaves out the questions of the capability of its individuals to make these choices in the specific historical and cultural contexts they find themselves in, and hence is insufficient to underpin citizens in the sustainable economy. Citizens need the resources, including the social capital, to be able to enjoy their freedom. Enabling citizens to choose

---

[15] T. Veblen (1899), *The Theory of the Leisure Class: An Economic Study of Institutions*, New York: Macmillan.

[16] A. Smith (1776), *An Inquiry into the Nature and Causes of the Wealth of Nations*, republished 1976, Oxford: Oxford University Press. See especially A. Smith (1759), *The Theory of Moral Sentiments*, republished 1976, Oxford: Clarendon Press, Part IV: 'Of the Effect of Utility upon the Sentiments of Approbation'.

[17] Mill wrote *Utilitarianism* at around the same time as *On Liberty*. The former can contradict the latter, as famously demonstrated in A.K. Sen (1970), 'The Impossibility of a Paretian Liberal', *Journal of Political Economy*, 78, 152–7.

requires positive freedom, following Isaiah Berlin's distinction set out in his *Two Concepts of Liberty*.[18] This is further brilliantly developed by Amartya Sen in his concepts of capabilities.[19]

The basic idea of positive freedom (as opposed to an exclusive focus on economic efficiency) is that the state has to do stuff to facilitate the capabilities, but not go further to guarantee equality of outcomes, and in doing this, the state should not focus on utility alone.[20] In this it is parsimonious: what the sustainable economy should do is make sure that citizens have the capacity to live good lives, and not focus on trying to make people happy.

The feature that the sustainable economy adds is to try to sort out which are the most important capabilities citizens need and how they can be delivered. These are the primary assets: housing, heating, energy, water, broadband, transport and so on. All of these depend upon a combination of public and private initiatives, and all depend upon the environment. The environment is not just another provider of goods and services (eco-services), to be consumed to make people happy (in utility terms). Rather, it is the essential building block for the citizens' capabilities, and one that the state should ensure is protected and enhanced. It is ensuring an equal entitlement to all these capabilities, and hence the assets that deliver them, that defines the economic objective of the state, not GDP.

It would be a great advance to make sure that all citizens just have access to some basic minimum level of these primary assets. There would be a health service and an education system that grants all citizens basic healthcare and basic education. It requires equality of access to these minimum thresholds necessary to have the capability to function, and that does turn out to be incompatible with the sorts of inequality that have emerged in the last forty years. It is a strictly limited impartiality, focused on these basic capabilities, and thereby addresses inequality and social justice obliquely.[21]

In the sustainable economy, these assets need to be provided not just to the current generation but to the next one. Sorting out how

---

[18] I. Berlin (1958), *Two Concepts of Liberty*, Oxford: Clarendon Press, reprinted in I. Berlin (1969), *Four Essays on Liberty*, Oxford: Oxford University Press.

[19] A.K. Sen (2009), *The Idea of Justice*, London: Allen Lane.

[20] A.K. Sen (1980), 'Equality of What?', reprinted in A.K. Sen (1982), *Choice, Welfare and Measurement*, Oxford: Basil Blackwell.

[21] See J. Kay (2010), *Obliquity: Why Our Goals Are Best Achieved Indirectly*, London: Profile Books.

to do this is at the heart of the design of the sustainable economy, and what the subsequent chapters set out.

The Next Generation's Inheritance

Now that we have a focus on the next generation, and on citizens rather than consumers, we are in a position to set out what the underlying ethic of the sustainable economy is – what it is for and what it aspires to deliver.

A good starting point is the United Nations' (UN) 1987 Brundtland Report's definition of sustainability, which set the scene for the focus on sustainability and the great burst of UN activity on climate change.[22]

The Brundtland Report famously defined sustainability as: '[meeting] the needs of the present without compromising the ability of future generations to meet their own needs'.[23] As befits a UN report, this definition is wide-ranging and all-embracing. To drive the sustainable economy, it needs to be narrowed down. The sustainable economy focuses on the needs of the present without compromising the ability of the *next generation* to meet their own needs, and interprets the 'needs' as capabilities to choose how to live their lives. This first principle of the sustainable economy is what should be incorporated into its constitution.

This principle needs operationalising, to sort out what this all means for the design of the sustainable economy. Primary assets necessary to meet this requirement have to be identified, and especially the basic natural capital which underpins the economy. It is all about assets, not utility, as enablers for citizens by giving them the capability to choose how to live their lives, consistent with not undermining the opportunities for the generation that follows.

The place to start is with the assets that matter most, and upon which everything else depends. This is natural capital. Natural capital is what nature gives us for free. It is not practical or sensible to

[22] This activity included the setting-up of the Intergovernmental Panel on Climate Change and culminated in the UN Framework Convention on Climate Change (the UNFCCC) and all the COPs since then, from Kyoto (in 1992) to Glasgow (in 2021).

[23] United Nations (1987), 'Report of the World Commission on Environment and Development: Our Common Future' (the Brundtland Report), Part 1, section 3, para. 27, https://sustainabledevelopment.un.org/content/documents/5987our-common-future.pdf.

keep every bit of natural capital intact, and to do no damage. Humans' very existence involves doing damage. To date, we have pillaged and raped nature to our own short-run advantage, with little or no concern about the longer-term consequences. That will not do anymore. In the sustainable economy, we need to make sure that when damage is done, something else has to improve, so the overall state of the climate and biodiversity does not go backwards. Attaining zero emissions is implausible, and so is zero loss of biodiversity. It is the *aggregate* of natural capital that has to be protected.

As set out in detail in my book, *Natural Capital*, the rule that follows is that the aggregate level of renewable natural capital should be kept at least constant, and there should be *general* primary asset compensation for the depletion of non-renewables. Renewable natural capital is the stuff that is alive, and which reproduces itself, whilst non-renewables are things like minerals, which are dead and non-regenerative.

We could go further, demanding not only that the aggregate level of renewable natural capital should be kept at least constant, but also that the value of the economic rents from the depletion of non-renewable natural capital should be re-invested in renewable natural capital.[24] Aggregate natural capital rules require special attention to be paid to the maintenance and enhancement of renewable natural capital.

The two types of natural capital are crucial determinants of the assets that provide the capabilities of the next generation to choose how to live their lives. Without a stable climate and without lots of biodiversity, human life is going to be tough, and the next generation rule will not be met. But these two types of capital are not the only ones. They are necessary but not sufficient.

The next generation will need the other capitals too, all ultimately dependent on natural capital. These include energy systems, water and sewerage systems, transport systems and fibre and broadband communications systems. They will also require educational and health systems, a supporting research and development (R&D) infrastructure and human and social capital. Together with natural capital,

---

[24] Helm, *Natural Capital*, chapter 3, and especially p. 64. There is considerable overlap between these two rules and the concepts of strong sustainability and weak sustainability in the wider environmental literature. See R.M. Solow (1993), 'An Almost Practical Step towards Sustainability', *Resources Policy*, 16(3), 162–72; and J.M. Hartwick (1977), 'Intergenerational Equity and the Investing of Rents from Exhaustible Resources', *American Economic Review*, 67(5), 972–4.

these give the next generation access to participating in their society and economy. An economy is made up of these systems, and it is the sustaining of these systems that provides the main obligation on this generation to the next.

Combining the other capitals with natural capital makes the rules of the sustainable economy more comprehensive so that all the aggregate levels of all the primary capitals should be kept at least constant. Because it is about aggregates, it means that, where there is damage, it must be compensated for.

If these rules are met, the environment will be in a much better state, and the citizens of the next generation will have the main capabilities to choose how to live their lives. Yet even this is not enough: citizens of the next generation also need income to cover the necessities and a social infrastructure. Some element of basic income has to be added.

All of these capitals need to be properly defined, as does basic income, to turn these abstract requirements into practical economic policies. Subsequent chapters explain how the capital assets are selected, how they are accounted for and what it means to maintain them to meet our obligations to the next generation, and how a basic income can contribute to social justice.

A Radical Departure

The sustainable economy requires a radical departure from conventional economics. The approach is not based upon utility and utility-maximising agents, but rather on citizens. It is not based upon GDP and flows, but rather upon assets and capabilities. It is not based upon pure impartiality, but rather it is parsimonious in the assumptions it makes about the future. It is parsimonious too in its focus: it is not focused on all possible future people, just the next generation. It is this scaffolding upon which the components of what it takes to meet the first principle can be constructed, requiring us to ensure that the next generation has capitals at least as good as those we inherited, and especially renewable natural capital. The need to be parsimonious is further necessitated because of our uncertainty about what the future holds for us and the next generation, and this uncertainty reinforces the focus on assets and capabilities rather than on utility and happiness. It is this uncertain context to which we now turn.

3 TAKING PRECAUTIONS, BUILDING RESILIENCE

The focus of the sustainable economy is on the next generation, and that next generation can look after the one after them. Whether humans last another 10,000 years, or even 100,000 years; whether we go the way of all the other species, with extinction as our destiny; whether an asteroid hits, or a pandemic wipes us humans out; these are all interesting questions, but ones we do not need to answer. The geological record is littered with such calamities, punctuated by mass extinctions. There are lots of fossils, and ultimately that is probably our destiny too.

These potential catastrophes have got a lot nearer after the damage the twentieth century has wreaked on our environment. There might not be the luxury of waiting to find out whether these long-distant catastrophes happen. For most of human history, the answers to both the near- and far-term threats were thought to be in the hands of the gods. But increasingly humans think that they uniquely can avoid all these fates, and do so because of science, heading off asteroids and developing vaccines for viruses and antibiotics for bacteria, and fixing climate change by manipulating the atmosphere and biodiversity by genetically engineering life.

This 'masters of the universe' approach to our future depends upon the assumption that humans are benign, rational, and will cooperate to head off existential challenges. Such confidence gets quickly dented by the experiences of the twentieth century. In just a blip of time of human life on earth, and an indiscernible scratch on geological time, humans developed the capacities to destroy much of life on earth. Nuclear war could do the job very quickly, and for the second half of the twentieth century this was a very real possibility, casting its shadow of fear.[1] In 2022, Vladimir Putin put it back on the agenda again. So, too, could the escape of viruses from laboratories and biological warfare, raising the possibility of uncontrolled diseases and death, from anthrax to the twenty-first-century coronavirus.

These are all specific and very real threats, about which we can do a lot. The more general environmental damage is much more difficult, but at least this is no longer about ignorance of the causes or indeed the broad consequences. That much science has delivered to us. It is the inability to head off these very human-made threats to our existence that is the concern.

The Scale of Our Ignorance

If we were certain all these bad environmental things were going to happen, it would be about taking action, in the sure knowledge of the consequences of that action. But in most cases, it is less clear. Though we know a lot about the causes of climate change, we do not know what the precise global temperature increase will be by 2100. It might be limited to 2°C warming, or even 1.5°C. The increased concentration of greenhouse gases in the atmosphere means that we are already on a path towards 3°C, and it could be even higher. The range between a good and a bad outcome could be as much as 4°C.

We do not know how much biodiversity will be left by 2100. We do not know whether by then we will have wiped out half the species on the planet or stabilised biodiversity. Whilst we can at least measure the concentration of the greenhouse gases in the atmosphere, we do not even have an agreed measure of biodiversity and we do not even know how many species there are on the planet, partly because most biodiversity is beneath our feet.

---

[1] O.A. Westad (2017), *The Cold War*, London: Allen Lane. Thomas Schelling wrote that one of the most surprising things is that no major nuclear weapon has been used since Hiroshima. T.C. Schelling (2005), 'An Astonishing Sixty Years: The Legacy of Hiroshima', Prize Lecture, Department of Economics and School of Public Policy, University of Maryland, 8 December.

We do not know whether by 2100 the rivers and the coastal waters will be even more heavily polluted with yet more plastic, chemicals and agricultural run-off, or whether they will be cleaner and full of life. Will the seas be fished out and the sea floor scraped clean by trawlers, or will there be a recovery and vibrant marine ecosystems?

The pervasiveness of our ignorance is reinforced by our inability to forecast even a few years ahead. Economists' forecasts of GDP growth are notoriously inaccurate and there is no evidence that forecasting is getting better. Economists struggle to forecast a recession a few months in advance, and most did not see the financial crisis coming in 2007/8. It was not just the late Queen Elizabeth II in the UK who wondered why it had not been foreseen.[2] Forecasts of fossil-fuel prices are just as bad. Taking the projections of the International Energy Agency (IEA) since the 1970s, one study showed that at any point in this period it was better just to take the current price and extrapolate it, rather than to rely on the IEA's projections.[3] Up until 2014, the oil price was heading ever higher. Then it crashed. In 2022, there were lots of people certain it would carry on going ever upwards, and even more certain that the gas price would follow a rising trend. Possibly neither will.

Scarily, many are taken in by these sorts of forecasts and projections. Commentators hang on them, and behave as if they are true. The vogue in 2022 for believing that gas prices will go on upwards for the rest of the decade led opportunists to argue that, in these circumstances, all sorts of low-carbon technologies will be in the money. It reflected the pernicious influence of lobbying we will return to again and again, especially when it comes to systems and regulation. Wisely perhaps these same opportunists are not themselves completely fooled, for acting on such a forecast would be a powerful argument for the removal of many of the subsidies these technologies rely upon to keep afloat. Vested interests tend to take seriously only those forecasts that suit their purposes. They do not campaign to take away the subsidies upon which they depend.

It is not just the underlying trends that we are ignorant about; it is also the technologies. As soon as the timescale opens up beyond the next couple of decades into the second half of the century, our ignorance

---

[2] *Financial Times* (2008), 'Good Question, Ma'am', 14 November, www.ft.com/content/5b306600-b26d-11dd-bbc9-0000779fd18c.

[3] See D.R. Helm (2018), *Burn Out: The Endgame for Fossil Fuels*, updated edn, New Haven: Yale University Press, pp. 17–18.

about technologies starts to bite. If we knew what technologies would be around in 2100, we would already have invented them. A moment's reflection on the fact that the modern internet and the iPhone and laptop are all post-1990 tells us how profound technical change can be in just thirty years. Over a century, technologies can be transformational. Recent advances of quantum computing, AI, graphene and genome sequencing are already apparent, but we have less idea what precisely they mean for the prospects of the next generation. We don't know whether there will be negative unanticipated consequences, as there have been from DDT (the chemical compound Dichlorodiphenyltrichloroethane) and a host of chemicals spread over the land, and whether AI might unleash a whole new set of authoritarian controls and warfare.

To reinforce the critical nature of this uncertainty, and how the future usually turns out rather different to what we anticipate, consider a thought experiment. Think back to any date, and then think forward from that date five, ten and thirty years into the future. Five years ahead, there are always surprises. The coronavirus is the latest in a long line. Few foresaw the scale and destruction of the twentieth-century world wars. They were both widely anticipated to be 'over by Christmas'.[4] Few saw the fall of the Berlin Wall coming. The Soviet Union was thought to be a given.

As the time horizon opens up, science fiction takes over. That is another reason – beyond our limited impartiality discussed in the last chapter – for the single generational perspective. Many countries now have unilateral aims to be net zero by 2050, and the UK has added the aim, through a twenty-five-year environment plan, to leave the natural environment in a better state for the next generation.[5] Achieving these limited objectives would be a huge advance on where we are now. Thinking beyond a year is often a major political challenge. Hence the often-quoted remark by UK Prime Minister Harold Wilson in the 1960s: 'a week is a long time in politics'.

There are pretty immediate political uncertainties to frame what we do about the environment. Here are some things to ponder

---

4 On the First World War, see C. Clark (2012), *The Sleepwalkers: How Europe Went to War in 1914*, London: Allen Lane.
5 Defra and The Rt Hon Michael Gove MP (2018), 'A Green Future: Our 25 Year Plan to Improve the Environment', https://assets.publishing.service.gov.uk/government/uploads/system/uploads/attachment_data/file/693158/25-year-environment-plan.pdf. This is now embedded in the 2021 Environment Act.

in the quest to be sustainable even over the limited horizon of the next thirty years. What will happen in Ukraine and Russia, after the Russian invasion and the Ukrainian fightback? The fall of the Berlin Wall thirty years ago set in motion the current disaster. Will China invade Taiwan? The fall of the nationalists and Mao's Communist victory in 1948 set in motion the current threat by China to finish the business with Taiwan. Will China, the US and Japan go to war seventy years later? From a consumption perspective, will China's economy double or triple in size by then, with all the consumption that will bring? Or will it stagnate like Japan's has done since 1989? Will India and Africa grow fast, replicating the Chinese experience of the last thirty years?

These are just some of the uncertainties we face over the next thirty years. They are things that worry the young about their futures. They are more than enough to try to get a handle on, and indeed, if we do not, there might not be much left for the subsequent generations. Beyond 2050, the fog of uncertainty is even greater. Would anyone in 1920 have forecast an extra 1 billion added to the world population by 1950, and just under 6 billion by 2000? Or that temperatures would keep rising, in contrast to the concern in the 1970s, when global cooling and another ice age was thought by some to be the big threat?[6]

Try another thought experiment. Write down what you think now the world in 2050 may be like. Write down what you think the share of fossil fuels in world energy will be, relative to the 80 per cent today. Write down what you think the world population will be. Write down the main wars that you think will have happened by then. Write down by how much you think GDP in, say, the UK, the US, India, China and Nigeria may have gone up or down. Write down what technologies you think will dominate by then: electric cars, hydrogen, how you think quantum computing will go, whether you will be using cryptocurrencies. Then seal the envelope and lock it away ready for you to open in 2050, or leave it in your will for your inheritors to read. I would be amazed if you or they are not surprised.

All this matters because we are doomed to work in this murky world of uncertainty. Indeed, it is what makes human life so interesting. When it comes to thinking through how the bold objectives to limit climate change and protect biodiversity are going to be met, and how

---

[6] The concern focused on orbital forcing, and the return of the ice age, within which the current period can appear to be embedded, and on the emissions of aerosols.

we are going to get back onto a sustainable growth path, we should always start with the realisation that the gap between what we assume will happen and what might actually happen is very wide. We look out of the back window at our past to steer the car, assuming the future will resemble that past. When we close our eyes to many of the uncertainties, and what might lie around the bends in the road in front of us, we condemn ourselves to the certainty that our mistakes will commit us to. We treat the future as determined by the past, rather than open-ended, created by the decisions we make on the basis of the possibilities in front of us and our imagination.

How to Decide in Uncertainty

What should we do? How should we tackle these profound and deep uncertainties to save our planet? There are two very different approaches. One is to treat these circumstances as approximations to certainties, and to do all the sorts of forecasting and predictions that find their way into government budget forecasts, the Federal Reserve's and the Bank of England's forecasts of inflation, and the IEA's oil projections. This is what modern economics excels at. The other is to start with the assumption of radical uncertainty and work back by providing some stakes in the ground, in particular taking measures to make sure that the natural capital and the core infrastructures are maintained.

Modern economics makes the heroic assumption that we act as if we have probabilities over all future possible outcomes, allowing us as rational individual consumers to choose between the sure prospect of utility now as against the (discounted) expected utility at some future date to maximise our subjected expected utility.[7] It allows economists to go straight to future utility, and not to waste too much time on the underlying architecture of the economy. This is what lies behind many of the economic forecasts and economists' policy recommendations. It allows the clever planner to shape the future. It is a world for experts.

It is always possible to straitjacket behaviour into a probabilistic structure. Choices can always be rationalised as consistent with

---

[7] For a survey, see P.J. Schoemaker (1982), 'The Expected Utility Model: Its Variants, Purposes, Evidence and Limitations', *Journal of Economic Literature*, 20(2), 529–63.

you having subjective probabilities.[8] But that does not mean you do. Faced with the uncertainty unfolding before us, a better description of your behaviours is that you use the toolkit of behavioural psychology, to help deal with the reasonably familiar. Each of us relies on simple heuristics, often translating them into a series of mantras, passed down the generations. They are usually historically conditioned. Victorians believed in thrift and the avoidance of debt; consumerist societies embrace the opposites. 'Neither a borrower nor a lender be' is a heuristic that would be incomprehensible to most of the current US and UK populations, and to Keynesians in particular.[9] But it would not be to Germans, who prefer 'save now, have later'. These are all part of the shared and inherited social capital.

Environmental conservation is littered with such heuristics. One is to be precautionary, especially where the environmental damage might turn out to be irreversible. None is 'optimal', but then the very concept of optimality is challenged by radical uncertainty.

Such heuristics can work roughly well, until we hit the unknown unknowns, what in economics is known as 'Knightian uncertainty',[10] with the negative shocks and possible but highly improbable 'black swans'.[11] In these contexts, there are no heuristics to fall back on, no rules of thumb, because there has not been enough time to try to understand what is going on. Extrapolating from what has worked in the past is potentially very dangerous, given that the past has brought us to the current environmental cliff edge.

It is sometimes argued that the financial crash in 2007/8 and the coronavirus in 2020 are just such black swans. They came out of the blue, and most people had no obvious mental framework to comprehend what was going on. They left us very disconcerted. In time, people got used to these events, read and understood more about them, and then developed new rules of thumb about what to do if they happen again: using heuristics like 'keep social distance', 'open windows', 'wear masks' and 'take Vitamin D'. In the financial crisis case, it might be to save more to create a precautionary buffer, and in the virus case,

---

[8] See L.J. Savage (1951), 'The Theory of Statistical Decision', *Journal of the American Statistical Association*, 46(253), 55–67.

[9] In Act I, Scene III of *Hamlet*, William Shakespeare has Polonius saying 'Neither a borrower nor a lender be; / For loan oft loses both itself and friend.'

[10] After F.H. Knight (1921), *Risk, Uncertainty and Profit*, Boston: Houghton Mifflin.

[11] N.N. Taleb (2007), *The Black Swan: The Impact of the Highly Improbable*, London: Allen Lane.

to stockpile essential items. For climate change and biodiversity loss, it makes sense to do the capital maintenance, to build environmental resilience. Sadly, there is not much evidence that many of these heuristics are much more than passing enthusiasms. The next financial crisis will probably see us as exposed as last time around. On future viruses, public health measures taken now look precarious, and on climate change and biodiversity loss, so far little has been done.

Resilience

The curious and potentially dangerous feature of reactions to these sorts of possible shocks is that since we have no underlying deep causal explanations – since they are shocks – the most likely behaviour is indeed to carry on as before. The implication is that the greater the uncertainty, the more predictable our behaviour. Applied to climate change and biodiversity loss, this would be disastrous, yet it is a pretty accurate description of what has been going on for the past thirty years. Only as more information becomes available, and we are able to frame the events with a causal theory, do we adapt and change, but crucially *after* the shocks and in response to them, not in anticipation. Even when we do know more, we go on with our existing consumerist ways in a kind of parallel world, doing the same as yesterday even though we know it is not sustainable. Recall, the share of fossil fuels in the global energy mix remains at 80 per cent, the same as it was in 1970.

In the face of possible future shocks, we are not powerless to prepare, even if we do not know the format they will take or when they might appear and we do not have probabilities. In the two examples above, financial shocks do happen, and by studying past events, we can identify the main features. It is a bit like watching pre-earthquake tremors ahead of a volcanic eruption. Similarly, there have been lots of pandemics, and some of the consequences are known. Pandemics are part of the human condition. Climate change has happened quite a lot even in human times, and there have been great extinctions in geological history. Financial shocks, pandemics and climate change are all in this sense normal.

In these cases, the right response is to have the assets in place to cope as and when the shocks happen. It is about having the *capacity* to cope, about being *resilient*. The social care system could be capable of handling isolation caused by the pandemic lockdowns, and have had testing facilities. There could have been reserves to deal with the fallout from the credit crunch. It is not the uncertainty that is necessarily the problem, but rather having the assets capable of absorbing shocks. *Resilience*, not expected utility based upon probabilities, is the key requirement, so that future people are not left defenceless.

Take climate change. We have integrated assessment models (IAMs)[12] based upon probabilities, and hosts of energy models, and over time these are updated as new information becomes available. We have a schedule of costs for alternative low-carbon options, comprising a supply curve. Optimising the solution to climate change is, in these conventional models, about choosing the cheapest of these options against the damage that climate change is expected (probabilistically) to cause. Economists make the expected marginal costs equal to the expected marginal damages, and then come up with a social cost of carbon. Probabilities of marginal costs and marginal damages are then discounted back to the present. The expected utility approach simply multiplies the probabilities and the utilities together. This tells us how to go about tackling climate change.[13]

Except that this is not what we are actually doing and for good reasons. The 2°C target has no foundation in this sort of marginal analysis.[14] It is picked not because it is 'optimum' in an expected utility way, but because it is a rough guess at what we might aspire to achieve. We pick a target and then work back to thinking through how we might achieve it. We decide what it would be tolerable for the next generation to inherit, and what we might actually be able to achieve

---

[12] See DeCanio for what is still one of the best critiques of IAMs. S.J. DeCanio (2003), *Economic Models of Climate Change: A Critique*, London: Palgrave Macmillan. For a further discussion, see W. Nordhaus (2019), 'Climate Change: The Ultimate Challenge for Economics', *American Economic Review*, 109(6), 1991–2014.

[13] It is how, for example, Stern's critics, Nordhaus and Weitzman, go about it. W. Nordhaus (2007), 'A Review of the Stern Review on the Economics of Climate Change', *Journal of Economic Literature*, 45(3), 686–702; M.L. Weitzman (2007), 'A Review of the Stern Review on the Economics of Climate Change', *Journal of Economic Literature*, 45(3), 703–24.

[14] Various economists have tried to work out what the optimal degree of global warming might be. Of these, Nordhaus is perhaps the most prominent. In 2018, he suggested unabated climate change would reach 4°C warming, and compounded this with 3.5°C which would result from an optimal carbon tax. W. Nordhaus (2018), 'Projections and Uncertainties about Climate Change in an Era of Minimal Climate Policies', *American Economic Journal: Economic Policy*, 10(3), 333–60. See also K. Rennert, B.C. Prest, W.A. Pizer et al. (2021), 'The Social Cost of Carbon: Advances in Long-Term Probabilistic Projections of Population, GDP, Emissions, and Discount Rates', *Brookings Papers on Economic Activity*, BPEA Conference Drafts, 9 September.

for them, not how to optimise the expected utilities through time, and hence get the maximum happiness. Similarly, in working out how to tackle the coronavirus, we did not start with the expected utility and the life expectancy of people who might die, and compare the expected economic utility value of those lives that might be lost against the costs of saving them.[15]

The reason we do this is not just because we do not know the probabilities and the utilities of future people. That sort of climate change calculation cannot be made in any meaningful way. It is partly because we are uncertain about what the technologies are going to be even over the limited time horizon to 2050. Whether hydrogen will prove a key technology, whether there will be new forms of nuclear power, whether a new type of solar film becomes available, are all uncertain. So too is the effectiveness of future vaccines and antibiotics. None of these is amenable to probabilities. What we do know is that if future generations are to be able to live good lives, it is a good working assumption that they will need a climate that is no hotter than the 2°C target, and they will need a lot of biodiversity and protection against horrible viruses and bacteria, to give them some sort of resilience to these sorts of shocks. It is just conceivable that they might not need the resilience these things bring, but not remotely likely. The open-ended choices that make up the good life and conspire together to write the future history of our life on earth are more than the sum of expected subjective utilities.[16] There is so much more to life than economists assume. We should start the other way round to the conventional economists' approach: by defining the set of assets necessary for the sustainable economy, make sure they are resilient and then leave open how people choose to live their lives, safe in the knowledge that they will have inherited a world in which they can in fact do so.

The sustainable economy is one that starts with this polar opposite to the economists' models. It assumes that we are profoundly ignorant about the lives of future people and the environment they will inherit. That is why the focus is on assets to facilitate options and

---

[15] Some economists did: for example, R. Rowthorn and J. Maciejowski (2020), 'A Cost–Benefit Analysis of the Covid-19 Disease', *Oxford Review of Economic Policy*, 36(S1), S38–S55; and D.K. Miles, M. Stedman and A.H. Heald (2021), 'Stay at Home, Protect the National Health Service, Save Lives: A Cost Benefit Analysis of the Lockdown in the United Kingdom', *International Journal of Clinical Practice*, 75(3).

[16] In the coronavirus case, we did not know in early 2020 whether vaccines would work. Amazingly, we did not even know how badly testing and track-and-trace would work.

opportunities, rather than on trying to make future people happy in the utilitarian way. The added twist – the working heuristic – is to be precautionary about the fundamental systems that drive the economy, and the renewable natural capital in particular. Nature gives us natural capital for free, but we can so easily close it off from future generations by our destructive ways. Once gone, that will be it forever. The sustainable economy is parsimonious and risk-averse when it comes to assets, and especially natural ones. Precaution breeds resilience.

Asymmetric Risks

How much risk should we take with nature? Resilience and precaution are not free. They have costs. The key question is not whether we want to be resilient to future environmental and other shocks, but *how* *resilient.* What if we are wrong? What if temperatures level out, or even stabilise at a higher level, where there will be winners and losers? What if the costs of mitigation are too great on the current generation, and the future generations are just that much better off? What if there are new technologies that deal with the problems and at much lower cost? What if we can genetically engineer life in the future? For some, it is quite possible to accept conventional theories of climate change and at the same time argue that the urgency of action is overstated. They just assume it will all turn out fine, in the best of all possible worlds, as Candide did in Voltaire's famous satire.[17]

The 1992 Rio Declaration on Environment and Development takes a different stance: 'where there are threats of serious or irreversible damage, lack of scientific certainty should not be used as a reason for postponing cost-effective measures to prevent environmental degradation'.[18] This 'precautionary principle' is one of two secondary principles central to the sustainable economy, and relies upon the claim that there is *asymmetric risk*: be too cautious and there will be costs; be not cautious enough and the losses will plausibly be much greater.

Asymmetric risk is familiar in the development of modern medicines. Tests and trials and a demonstration that there will be no harm are required before permitting general use of a new drug. Even

[17] F.-M.A. Voltaire (1759), *Candide, ou L'Optimisme.*
[18] United Nations General Assembly (1992), 'Report of the United Nations Conference on Environment and Development', Annex I Rio Declaration on Environment and Development, Principle 15.

with the coronavirus vaccines, trials were required. That's why it took several months to get from the quick few days taken to develop vaccines to the authorisation of their deployment. In practice, the vaccine trials were rushed as the pandemic started spreading and people started dying. The goalposts were shifted a bit. The reality of precaution is that the decision to adopt vaccines is subject to a 'beyond reasonable doubt' test, and weighs up the importance of speed in saving lives against possible side effects.

In the case of genetic techniques, a similar precautionary approach is taken. Many countries have banned genetically modified organisms (GMOs) and, in the case of the EU, severely limited gene editing. Those campaigning in the UK for BREXIT regarded this last restriction on gene editing as a precaution too far, and saw BREXIT as a way of relaxing this constraint.

In the case of the natural environment, there is a class of assets that demand precaution because the consequences of a mistake can be irreversible, and hence the asymmetries are large. The 'cost-effective' caveat is very unlikely to be binding. These are renewable natural capital assets, the things that nature gives us for free, and which can go on reproducing themselves for ever, or until evolution catches up with them. Make a mistake, take a renewable natural capital asset, say a species, below the threshold above which it can reproduce and sustain its population, then all the benefits of the species to us and the ecosystems are gone *forever*. Extinctions are to be avoided for exactly this reason. We should take a very precautionary approach to the loss of biodiversity, especially where otherwise we are taking temporary gains for the current generation at the expense of *all* future generations. The current generation occupies the crease (in the cricketing analogy), but presides over the benefits to all that come after it.

In the case of the climate, it is less straightforward. It might be possible at some future date to geo-engineer the climate so that its composition can be altered. The damage may be partially reversible (already there are direct air capture technologies to extract carbon from the atmosphere), but it might not be entirely so. The climate might be tipped into a new equilibrium or into a vortex of ever-higher temperatures. The atmosphere might be lost, analogous to the way Mars lost its water.

Given the asymmetry between the costs of mitigating climate change now, and the open-ended destructive losses of these possible (and some would say even plausible) scenarios,[19] the precautionary principle tells us what to do. Time should not be wasted with the economists' cost–benefit analysis and the IAMs discussed above, but rather we should cut to the precautionary principle imperative, treat the atmosphere as a renewable natural capital asset and hold the line as best we can. Indeed, so important is this precautionary principle that it merits consideration of ways of embedding it constitutionally.

The question of whether 2°C is the right answer is at best an academic one, and one about which there is profound uncertainty. There is not the data to know the answer. The optimal climate cannot be defined. The precautionary principle tells us to try to keep below 2°C, just as it tells us to avoid extinctions and maintain the core eco-systems.

Austrian Economics and Entrepreneurs

Armed with the precautionary principle, and its imperative to maintain renewable natural capital, it is an obvious step to try to put in place detailed plans to achieve this. But again we should be aware of our ignorance and resist the temptation to assume that we know how the future will pan out. Scientists and economists too often just assume they know the answers or understate the uncertainties, and tell us precisely what we should do to head off climate change and biodiversity loss. They tell us how many wind farms should be built, how many nuclear plants and how fast the fossil-fuel industries should be closed down.

Detailed plans, ten point plans, carbon budget plans and spe-cific technology 'winners' are identified and then governments design subsidies, regulations, standards and institutions to impose them.[20] This is both seductive and dangerous. Our ignorance dictates other-wise. Ignorance is not abolished by pretending that we can accurately model future paths of technologies and investments. Such certainty about planning also creates a further downside: it is manna from heaven for all those lobbyists and vested interests who can capture

---

[19] There is a considerable literature on tipping points. See, for example, T.M. Lenton, J. Rockström, O. Gaffney, S. Rahmstorf, K. Richardson, W. Steffen and H.J. Schellnhu-ber (2019), 'Climate Tipping Points – Too Risky to Bet Against', *Nature*, 27 November, www.nature.com/articles/d41586-019-03595-0.

[20] The most inane of these is the UK's 'ten point plan', which boils action down to ten points. HM Government (2020), 'The Ten Point Plan for a Green Industrial Revolution', November.

the plans and their implementations, and the subsidies that so often go with them. The net zero strategies are littered with such capture. Worse, many are not working and some are counterproductive.

The nature and role of planning is a fraught topic, often debated by pro- and anti- camps, without regard to the subtleties of the different dimensions of planning, and it is a topic that recurs throughout considerations of the sustainable economy, its regulation and institutions. It is not just about scientific ignorance; it is about the way incentives work to get to the answers. This is where the Austrian school of economics comes in, largely ignored by conventional economists.[21] The Austrians start in the right place with radical uncertainty. It is not just that people have limited information; it is that this is all they can have to take decisions and create the future. It is about pushing out the boundaries of the ideas and the technologies people create, the primary source of economic growth. This is what is going on in the numerous start-ups around new climate change technologies. One new silver bullet after another is proposed: nuclear fusion, new types of batteries, new solar films. Each tries to capture governments but each is better tested in the climate change marketplace.

Hayek, the central figure in the Austrian school, argued that in order to get the best out of people, there needs to be a competitive market. This is not the perfect competition at the heart of the conventional economic theories; in perfect competition, Hayek pointed out that competition is dead, because the future is known and there are only normal profits, leaving no incentive for market entry or exit.[22] For Hayek and the Austrians, it is the *possibility* of profits that drives entrepreneurs, and the competitive market sorts out the successes and failures.[23] Markets are in Joseph Schumpeter's words 'a process

---

[21] The Austrian school is the name given to an eclectic group of mainly economists who emerged out of the broader Vienna Circle. The key figure was Ludvik von Mises. See L. von Mises (1949), *Human Action: A Treatise on Economics*, London: William Hodge. Hayek and Popper provided the main philosophical and political underpinnings, with Hayek developing its economics as well. Frank Knight and Joseph Schumpeter variously promoted some of the main ideas, and many were taken up by the Chicago school of economics, and more recently, in the policy context, Stephen Littlechild, the architect of RPI-X regulation and a powerful advocate of privatisation and competition in the UK, translated some of the key insights into practical policies.

[22] F.A. von Hayek (1948), 'The Meaning of Competition', in *Individualism and Social Order*, Cambridge: Cambridge University Press.

[23] See chapter 30 in G.L.S. Shackle (1969), *Decision Order and Time in Human Affairs*, 2nd edn, Cambridge: Cambridge University Press, and (1972), *Epistemics and Economics*, Cambridge: Cambridge University Press.

of industrial mutation that continuously revolutionizes the economic structure from within, incessantly destroying the old one, incessantly creating a new one'. The possibility of profits lures in rivals, and their ideas and innovations are tried out in the hard reality of competitive markets.[24] Economic evolution follows a path of market selection.[25] Right now new hydrogen technologies are being tried out and will have to compete with alternative ways to decarbonise unless, of course, they are permanently protected by subsidies.

The point about this Austrian competitive process is that the future cannot be defined in probabilistic terms. It is radical Knightian uncertainty that makes the case for markets and competition. Scientists, intellectuals and business entrepreneurs advance knowledge, making the future up as they go along, on the basis of conjectures and their refutations, to use Karl Popper's terms.[26] They scan the possibilities, and then use their imagination to make decisions across a range of possible future scenarios. All knowledge is tentative, and the way to build it up is to try to knock down the conventional wisdoms. Many entrepreneurs and innovators are fixated with particular possibilities, often displaying beliefs that go well beyond the rational. This is the world of Elon Musk, Bill Gates and Jeff Bezos, and the inventors of innumerable new digital businesses. All are flawed, all take big risks and most fail. Many are led by highly egoistic, dyslexic and irrationally optimistic individuals. For new ideas and inventions, there are no probabilities, because they do not exist until they are created.

Open Societies

The sustainable economy creates the space, through assets, to encourage trying out the conjectures, so that the new technologies can unfold. It puts entrepreneurs, researchers, mavericks and eccentrics centre stage in finding practical solutions to climate change and biodiversity loss.

[24] J. Schumpeter (1942), *Capitalism, Socialism, and Democracy*, New York: Harper & Bros. It is very much borrowed from Karl Marx. See K. Marx (1951),*Theories of Surplus Value: A Selection from the Volumes Published between 1905 and 1910 as 'Theorien über den Mehrwert'*, ed. K. Kautsky, taken from Karl Marx's preliminary manuscript for the projected fourth volume of *Das Kapital*, translated from the German by G.A. Bonner and E. Burns, London: Lawrence & Wishart.

[25] R.R. Nelson and S.G. Winters (1982), *An Evolutionary Theory of Economic Change*, Cambridge, MA: Belknap Press.

[26] K. Popper (1963), *Conjectures and Refutations: The Growth of Scientific Knowledge*, London: Routledge & Kegan Paul.

The Austrian approach to competition and markets, and to capitalism more generally, has always had a political economy underpinning. Popper was interested in creating a society (and a supporting economy, though he did not much interest himself in economics) in which this critical process of attempted refutation would have maximum scope, and where individuals could keep throwing up bold conjectures to be knocked down. The sort of society he had in mind was an open one, and one free of determinism and certainty.[27] Piecemeal corrective measures to market failures could fall into a trend – a slippery-slope argument.

The Problem with Planning

Hayek and the Austrians have a further insight which helps to explain why the many policies and interventions in support of detailed plans and picking winners will fail, and indeed have done so far, given how little progress there has been to stop the increase of carbon in the atmosphere over the last thirty years or to halt biodiversity loss. Hayek generally prefers competitive markets to state planning because the planners do not really know what they are doing. They think they do and, certain of their knowledge, they try to 'nudge' us towards what they think is in our best interests and even evoke the dark arts of behavioural economics to help to get us to do what they want. But they don't know. Planners have to put themselves in our shoes, know all the underlying preferences and motivations of the consumers, and all the production costs, and all the (exogenous) technologies, now and into the future by knowing the probabilities too, to pick the 'right' allocation of resources.[28]

---

[27] K. Popper (1945), *The Open Society and Its Enemies*, 4th revised edn, 1962, London: Routledge & Kegan Paul. He accused them of 'historicism', and with Hayek's *Road to Serfdom*, the two books set out not only the critique of Marxism and the Soviet variant in particular at a time when many of the intellectuals in the West were being seduced by both, but more generally Popper and Hayek claimed that state planning was a stepping-stone towards these more totalitarian forms of government. Social democracy and welfare states were the slippery slopes to 'serfdom'. F.A. von Hayek (1944), *The Road to Serfdom*, Chicago: University of Chicago Press. See also G. Orwell (1944), 'George Orwell's Review of Hayek's The Road to Serfdom', in G. Orwell (1988), *The Complete Works of George Orwell*, vol. XVI: *I Have Tried to Tell the Truth 1943–44*, London: Secker and Warburg.

[28] See F.A. von Hayek (1948), *Individualism and Economic Order*, Chicago: University of Chicago Press.

This is the sort of thinking that lies at the heart of great plans for tackling climate change, with a certainty that is often staggering. Past energy strategies, energy plans, specific technology supports and a remarkable number of speeches that purport to provide us with a silver bullet are littered with this sort of thinking. The UK's Climate Change Committee (CCC) produces five-year carbon budgets, and sets out, technology by technology, the route to the 2050 targets. There are elements of Soviet-era 'tractor plans' here.

For this to work, government ministers have to be very clever, and avoid capture by vested interests and corruption. They need to be sceptical and have doubts, rather than the sorts of naive certainties many politicians echo. Even where well-intentioned, the track record is often appalling, before we add in such capture.[29] Whereas the markets punish the mistakes of businesses, the state faces only weak sanctions, if any at all. Think of the UK example of Boris Johnson and his garden bridge, bendy buses, the bridge to Northern Ireland, faith in 'sustainable' aviation fuel and his 'ten point plan'. Think of all the jobs in these vested interests that ministers and their advisers take up upon leaving office or even come from. It is no wonder that the path to the sustainable economy remains elusive. It is elusive by design. This ever-present risk of capture and the distortions caused by lobbying is a cancer at the heart of attempts to tackle the great environmental problems of our time and to get to the sustainable economy.

In Hayek's world, the beauty of the competitive market is that each of us only needs to know the current prices and have the liberty to choose and experiment. It is a stark warning against making the jump from the recognition that we face existential challenges in climate change and biodiversity to the assumption that the state (or the CCC in the UK case) knows best and that, if only we can move to state planning, all will be well. Experts can fix climate change if only stupid politicians and us the voters would pay attention. The lazy and easy jump from recognising the environmental challenges to state planning turns out to be, if not Hayek's *Road to Serfdom*, at least a hazardous and often very costly approach.

A Hayekian economy is one with a constitution of liberty, keeping the competitive markets open.[30] The economy of conventional

[29] See D. Helm (2006), 'Regulatory Reform, Capture, and the Regulatory Burden', *Oxford Review of Economic Policy*, 22(2), 169–85.
[30] F.A. von Hayek (1960), *The Constitution of Liberty*, Chicago: University of Chicago Press.

economists tries to pick the equilibrium path on the basis of assumed exogenous preferences, probabilities and exogenous technologies. This Austrian openness in the presence of fundamental uncertainty constrains the role of the state because it recognises that not only are market participants ignorant about the future, so too are governments.

What Hayek (and many neoliberals who have followed his lead) understates is the need to ensure that the assets – the core infrastructures – are in place to set the *context* within which the choices are made, and the need for the state to force polluters to face up to the costs of their pollution: the polluter pays (a key secondary principle of the sustainable economy). It is the difference between the negative liberalism of John Stuart Mill, and the positive liberal approach of Isaiah Berlin and Amartya Sen we met in chapter 2. *Some* planning and *some* state provisions are essential, and they will turn out to be quite a lot bigger than Hayek had in mind. It will also turn out to be essential for competitive markets to work as Hayek wants them to. Markets and *system* planning (and support for R&D) turn out to be complements, not substitutes. It is not a simple choice between planning or competitive markets, but rather about what kind of planning is essential for the sustainable economy and its markets to prosper.

Technical Progress and the Sustainable Economy

Technical progress has a starring role in the sustainable economy. There is no plausible explanation for why and how technical advance actually takes place. This is another of the great insights of the Austrians, who put innovation and specific technological progress as central to the way they think about the architecture of an economy, full of individuals free to create history, and, with it, creatively destroy what went before, to make bold conjectures and then face the music of their refutations. But what the Austrians neglect is that they do this within the framework of both support for science and state provision of many of the great system public goods. The problem with R&D and innovation is that ideas once discovered are public goods, and private markets have a big incentive problem with public goods. They are not rivals – we can all benefit simultaneously, and it is hard to exclude people from their benefits. Entrepreneurs cannot capture all the profits, nor should they. We can – and should – benefit from Darwin's theory of evolution. They need public support and patents to create private property rights. It is the market *and* the state, not the market *or* the state.

Technical progress of the sort needed in the sustainable economy to address climate change and biodiversity loss rests upon *fundamental* research, and this tends to be done by universities and research laboratories supported by the state. Private charities and rich individuals may contribute, but altruism is unlikely to be even remotely adequate. These research institutions are core assets necessary for the sustainable economy to have the capability to innovate. They are an essential part of building in resilience to unknown unknowns that may cause shocks to future people. Fundamental climate science relies on fundamental physics, and fundamental genetics research helps us to understand how to protect biodiversity.

The Austrian economists are right about the dangers of direct state support for a specific technology and the legions of lobbyists that lie behind each one. But they go too far. The core infrastructure assets, and natural capital in particular, will not spontaneously be created and maintained. The generational ethic, the key principle of the sustainable economy, will not be met solely by reliance on competitive markets. Whilst Hayek is neither a conservative nor a *laissez-faire* economist, and recognises the need for a constitution of liberty, and hence a state, and he does mention public goods, he does not put these infrastructures at the core of his ideal economy. This is where he and I part company. In many infrastructures, as systems, there is no choice but to do some planning for all the faults that Hayek identified. The question is about what sort of planning is appropriate.

In the sustainable economy there would be lots of fundamental research. This is not only further from the market, but open-ended. All sorts of research projects have no obvious use and application – until one turns up. Einstein's theory of relativity transformed science, and this has fed into lots of things we now consume and take for granted. Darwin's theory of evolution is the foundation for modern genetics; quantum physics may deliver quantum computing. Our modern world is defined by the unexpected results of such fundamental research.

The sustainable economy would allow for lots of potentially wasteful R&D. It might bring us new materials for capturing solar power, new ways of using nuclear power, new materials for building and new ways of capturing carbon. It might also bring new ways of protecting the genetic variety of plants and animals, and new understanding of how ecosystems work, and their capacity to sequestrate carbon. Or it might not. Mostly it will fail. The key point is that a scientific research basis is a critical part of resilience in the face of fundamental uncertainty.

The Sustainable Economy Based upon Uncertainty

To sum up. The Austrians have the right idea: start with an assumption of radical uncertainty and then work out how best to organise the economy and the wider open society to embed trial and error, human ingenuity and entrepreneurial forces. Forget about probabilities and exogenous and given preferences, exogenous technical progress and rational consumers maximising utility. Allow the Amazons, Apples, Microsofts, Googles and Facebooks to innovate and have their products and services tested in the markets, even if the subsequent monopolies need breaking up and regulating. The planners have the wrong idea when they start with the assumption that governments and their committees and advisers are better than markets, replace competition with the state picking the winners and try to nudge and persuade us that they are right. Typically it is losers who pick governments.

We need to be clear about what we don't know. We don't know what future people's preferences will be. We don't know what technologies they will have. We don't know what their options would be if they were deprived of primary assets, such as natural capital. We don't know what would make them happy, even if we wanted to make them happy. Ignorance is the pervasive context of human endeavour, and it is what makes life interesting. A perfectly competitive general equilibrium is not only one where, as Hayek rightly pointed out, competition is dead, but it is also profoundly boring. It is not the human condition.

What we can do is provide future people with the capabilities within which to make their choices. To do this we want to transfer to them lots of ideas and technological opportunities, and we want to have an economic system that promotes and encourages that technological advance. We also want to make sure they have the infrastructure systems within which to function.

The main foundation to face uncertainty is the set of sufficiently well-maintained primary assets, and then citizens can better accommodate the shocks that may come. This is about resilience, notably in the face of asymmetric risks. It is hard to think of any shock that is unforeseeable *in general*. Tsunamis, pandemics, asteroids, sudden methane escapes from the tundra, volcanoes, severe weather – these would all be shocks, but they are also shocks we could prepare for. In each case, having the resilience that the primary assets provide in place and properly maintained is a good starting point. We do not know with any precision what will confront the next generation, but we can enable future people to better cope by ensuring that they have the assets so that they have the capabilities to respond. The sustainable economy has a good chance of sustaining itself in the face of the known unknowns, and most of the unknown unknowns are in fact known in outline. Donald Rumsfeld's famous triad should be rewritten: knowns, known unknowns and known shocks.[31]

Uncertainty is pervasive, fundamental and it requires that the sustainable economy is designed around it. Assets are the essential building blocks, to which we now turn.

---

[31] D. Rumsfeld (2002), US Department of Defence news briefing, 12 February.

4 THE CAPITALS

Imagine you visit Russia. Someone asks you what it is like, and in particular about its economy. You might google its GDP. It is about 80 per cent that of Italy.[1] Would this be a good answer to the question? What about its vast oil and gas reserves, its northern forests, the great Lake Baikal, the Arctic resources? What about the cities, the roads and railways? And then there are its military and its reliance on the commanding heights of the state and the oligarchs who loot them – Gazprom, Rusal, Rosneft and so on.

A better answer would highlight the fundamental difference between Russia and Italy. Russia is overwhelmingly dependent on its natural capital. It has been exploiting and using up its natural capital since its early origins – first timber and animal furs, then coal and now oil and gas. Oil and gas now make up around 40 per cent of government revenues and around 20 per cent of its GDP. All natural resources make up about 60 per cent of its GDP, and whilst its GDP is quite small, Russia is the world's fourth largest carbon polluter.

This answer reveals something very different from Russia's GDP. It is focused on the core assets of the economy, and in particular its natural capital endowments, and their exploitation. These are what matters,

---

[1] https://data.worldbank.org/indicator/NY.GDP.MKTP.CD?locations=RU. See for a variety of economic data on Russia: https://datacommons.org/place/country/RUS?utm_medium=explore&mprop=amount&popt=EconomicActivity&cpv=activitySource per cent2CGross DomesticProduction&hl=en.

though assets and the systems they are embedded in hardly feature in economics textbooks. These are all critical for pollution and its control.

There are four core capital asset classes that matter for the sustainable economy: natural capital, physical capital, human capital and social capital. These differ from the rest of the capitals in the economy because they mostly come as systems, and are necessary for the economy to function, because all economic activity goes through them. These systems, in which the capitals are embedded, are mostly highly capital-intensive with low to zero direct usage costs (near-zero marginal costs), and the infrastructures they comprise are best regarded as assets-in-perpetuity, and all span the obligations to the next generation. The contrast with the conventional economists' approach is stark: economics is all about the margin and marginal cost, and about flows of outputs, discounted back to the present. The focus of the sustainable economy could not be more different. This is a world far away from short-term use and throw-away consumerism.

The key feature of a system is that everything depends upon everything else. Systems do not come in marginal bits. Each bit that is added has an impact on the system *as a whole*. Add a new motorway to the road network and it will change the traffic flows throughout the system and change the road system's resilience to closures. Add a nature-based flood alleviation scheme upstream in a river catchment, and it will affect water quality and biodiversity all the way down the catchment to its estuary and beyond. Connect up a rural area to broadband and mobile phone networks and every household and business will be able to fully engage in the digital economy, and the structure of that rural economy will be open to new businesses and enterprises relying on a digital marketplace. Take away a keystone species, and the whole ecosystem shudders.

Not only does everything in each system depend upon everything else in that system, but each system depends upon the other systems too. The energy network depends upon the communications system, and the transport and water systems depend upon energy, and so on. All of them depend upon natural capital.

Natural Capital – the Primary Asset

Natural capital is the primary building block of the sustainable economy. It is what nature gives us for free. It is our inheritance, which has evolved and developed over the last 4 billion years. Everything we are and have is ultimately derived from this natural capital inheritance. Temporarily in our specific geological time, it has given us our specific lives and the lives of all the other creatures on this planet: the fungi, the plants, the mammals and the invertebrates. In a state of constant flux in geological time, climate change is normal. Extinction is normal. Both have been necessary to produce us. Over aeons of geological time, or perhaps much sooner, we too will go from ashes to ashes. But just not right now. We need the stability to let the world roughly remain as it is, not because it is in any sense 'optimal', but because it is the one we have evolved in and are adapted to.

To recap, natural capital comes in two types: renewable and non-renewable. Renewable natural capital renews itself. It is alive and it reproduces and keeps on giving until evolution catches up with it. Most of our food comes from life that has this characteristic, whether we think of the renewable natural capital as species, genes or complete ecosystems. Once we drive it below the critical thresholds, it stops being renewable, and goes towards extinction, thereby extinguishing its benefits forever. That is at the heart of our current environmental crises. It is first and foremost about fixing renewable natural capital.

There are lots of conservation projects to save individual species that are still hanging on from extinction, usually focused on big mammals, birds and reptiles with human-friendly faces and images. It helps too if tourists like them. Saving the tigers, the Galapagos tortoises and the Andes condors comes to mind. At often very great expense, some of these projects are successful, at least temporarily. Attempts are also made to protect key habitats, often very late in the day. Stopping fishing the once superabundant cod on the Canadian Grand Banks preserves a remnant population that might, at some distant date, make it back to abundance.[2] Some 'rewilders' believe that, humans having modified the entire planet, nature will bring lots of species back from the brink if only it is left to its own non-human devices, creating an apartheid between places where we live and places we are excluded from. This is largely a delusion – indeed, in almost all rewilding projects, active conservation is being practised rather than nature being left alone. Reintroducing wolves, beavers, sea eagles, tigers and cheetahs to old habitats is about as intensively interventionist as it gets.

---

[2] Even if it is too late for the Great Auk the fishers plundered, the last pair to be shot in Iceland in 1844.

These sorts of specific interventions have their place, but the really big challenges for the sustainable economy are to maintain whole ecosystems, like the Amazon, to protect the oceans as a whole and to keep the balance of greenhouse gases in the atmosphere. These big systems are what really matter in the scheme of renewable natural capital and hence the future of life on earth. They are the assets which we have a duty to bequeath to the next generation in good shape. The biodiversity crisis is not about individual species, but rather about whole ecosystems on a global scale within which the biodiversity of life functions and reproduces itself, and the climate crisis is not about just the emissions and sequestrations of one of the greenhouse gases in a specific location, but the concentration of all of them in the global atmosphere.

Life also depends on the earth's mineral-rich crust, which contains our non-renewable natural capital, and all the minerals that we rely upon. These, together with the impacts of what we do, determine the atmosphere, the landforms and the oceans. Our natural capital includes the legacy solar (and therefore ultimately legacy nuclear from the sun's nuclear fusion) energy packed into the fossil fuels that still make up that 80 per cent of our energy, and our petrochemicals and plastics. It includes the iron ores out of which we make steel, and all the chemical elements which we combine in ever more ingenious ways, and all the limestones and chalks to make cement. It holds the cobalt, lithium, nickel and copper essential to the development of electric car batteries and wind turbines. There is no decarbonisation without digging up lots and lots of these minerals. Next time you see claims about 'clean energy' and 'zero-emissions cars', ask where the minerals come from, ask how they are mined and then ask how they are refined to make the batteries and the turbines.

This non-renewable natural capital is the stuff that does not have that property of life to reproduce itself. We have a rich endowment from which we have created our modern world. Non-renewable natural capital does not go away because we transform it into something else. Energy cannot be destroyed, and hence we do not strictly consume it. Rather, we transpose it into some other form, for example into heat, creating pollution in the process. This is true for all the other minerals too, and it is why we have lots of landfill sites full of the waste products. In theory, much non-renewable natural capital can be recycled, using other non-renewable natural capitals to help recover and reformulate. But recycling always needs more resources and it is never a closed-loop cycle, as some advocates misleadingly claim.

Because we tend to use stuff once and throw it away, it is helpful to call this non-living and non-renewable stuff. Even if it is recyclable, it cannot reproduce itself. One day, someone might start mining landfill sites, but for the time being most of our wastes are buried. It is one of the reasons why it is possible to talk in theory about running out of certain minerals, and in particular depleting mines and oil and gas wells. Yet even here, the bounty that is our non-renewable natural capital inheritance is so great that there is little we are in fact in danger of running out of, despite the repeated dire warnings. There is enough oil, gas and coal to fry the planet many times over, lots and lots of iron ore, and we are never going to run short of the key building blocks of our modern economies, the cement, steel, petrochemicals, aluminium or fertilisers made from these minerals.

Abundance has in the past meant that non-renewable natural capitals are treated as free (and renewables too, like the cod on the Grand Banks). They have been plundered at will, safe in the knowledge that their supplies are practically inexhaustible. As a result, at near-zero resource cost, natural capital has until very recently rarely seen the inside of an economics or management textbook or been part of finance ministers' economic policies. Without cost, there was assumed to be no resource allocation question that needs answering, and economics is all about the allocation of scarce resources. For the non-renewables, it is not that the resources are limited; rather, it is that their extraction and use can have serious and sometimes dire environmental consequences, and the environment is the ultimate scarce resource. There is, as often remarked, only one earth. These associated costs should be priced – polluters should pay. It will require restraints in the face of abundance to reduce the environmental damage.

Physical Capital, Network and Infrastructure Systems

Out of the non-renewables, vast amounts of physical capital have been created, using bricks, cement and steel made by the application of fossil-fuel energy. The stock of houses has a value in conventional accounts way in excess of natural capital. Houses are the ways many of us hold our wealth. In the UK, for example, the housing stock is valued at £7.56 trillion ($8.7 trillion) as at March 2021. This compares with the implausible value placed on UK natural capital by the Office for National Statistics, at £1.2 trillion in 2019.[3] The US housing stock comes in at about $43 trillion (£36 trillion) by comparison. Factories, other buildings, machines, vehicles, power stations, wind farms and solar panels all form part of human-made physical capital. Most of these assets have limited lives, and some very short ones. Much of the physical capital stock turns over on aggregate inside a decade.

There is however one special form of physical capital that lasts much longer. It comprises the core physical system network infrastructures. Think electricity networks, water and sewerage works and pipes, rail and road networks and communications networks. Whilst little effort has gone into protecting and enhancing the natural capitals, government efforts have gone into these physical infrastructures, with most ending up as natural monopolies regulated by, and often owned by, the state. Ensuring their provision has become a core state responsibility. They are crucial assets in the sustainable economy.

They don't usually start off this way. There are very few examples where a state decides that it needs a new system infrastructure and sets about creating it. Typically, instead there is an initial 'wild west' free-for-all, driven by start-ups, entrepreneurs and very much in the Austrian spirit of creative destruction. The most recent examples are fibre networks and electric car charging networks. It starts with invention, followed by local developments and with full integration at a later stage as monopolies form and the state steps in.

Early systems included transport, from roads to canals, ports and railways. Until the late nineteenth century, roads were notoriously bad, and travel involved much time and discomfort. Getting from London to Edinburgh took several days by horse and carriage, and involved overnight stops at coaching inns. Roads had from an early time been provided by military states, the Romans being the stand-out example. Turnpikes, bridges and private roads developed, based upon local monopoly. Modern roads are mostly state roads, though there are many examples of tolled private motorway concessions from the state.[4]

---

[3] For details of how the accounts are constructed, see www.ons.gov.uk/economy/environmentalaccounts/methodologies/naturalcapital.

[4] For example, after the Battle of Culloden in 1746, the military built roads across highland Scotland to maximise control over the defeated clans.

Railways grew after the invention of the steam engine, and initially they provided single links between population centres and gradually developed into a mania as investors sought permissions and monopolies over specific routes.[5] As with roads, military considerations were an important influence, notably in the First World War to get the troops and munitions to the front lines. The opening up of the American West was driven by the coming of the railroads. The resulting railways, put together by different and sometimes competing companies, still haunt the rail sector of many countries today, comprise a patchwork of gauges and connectivity, and in many countries have been nationalised.[6]

The absence of adequate systems has led in some cases to the state deliberately stepping in to plan and provide public infrastructure. The London sewers were built in the nineteenth century after the Great Stink.[7] Municipal authorities took the lead on health grounds. Manchester and Birmingham secured water supplies from reservoirs in the Lake District and the Elan Valley in Wales respectively, and all took on waste as a municipal function.[8] To these were added streetlighting and then electrification. For most of Europe these remain a local or regional function today. The exceptions in electricity are France and the UK, both of which nationalised their electricity industries after the Second World War, and created powerful large, integrated companies to plan and deliver the networks to meet the growing post-Second World War demand for electricity. France has renationalised EDF. Water remains publicly owned and locally controlled in most of Europe and the US. The exception is England and Wales, but still at the regional rather

---

[5] See G. Campbell (2014), 'Government Policy during the British Railway Mania and the 1847 Commercial Crisis', in N. Dimsdale and A. Hotson (eds.), *British Financial Crises since 1825*, Oxford: Oxford University Press.

[6] William Gladstone's attempt to create an integrated railway institution failed. See W. Quinn and J.D. Turner (2021), *Boom and Bust: A Global History of Financial Bubbles*, Cambridge: Cambridge University Press.

[7] There was an intense debate, in which John Stuart Mill took a very active part corresponding with the Metropolitan Sanitary Association, about ownership and the integration of the multiple private water companies in London. This correspondence was published in 1851 as 'Public Agency v. Trading Companies. The Economical and Administrative Principles of Water-Supply for the Metropolis' and is partly reprinted in A.L. Harris (1959), 'J.S. Mill on Monopoly and Socialism: A Note', *Journal of Political Economy*, 67, 604–11. See also N. Tynan (2007), 'Mill and Senior on London's Water Supply: Agency, Increasing Returns, and Natural Monopoly', *Journal of the History of Economic Thought*, 29(1), 49–65.

[8] J.A. Hassan (1983), 'The Impact and Development of the Water Supply in Manchester, 1568–1882', *Historic Society of Lancashire and Cheshire*, 133, 25–45.

than the national level. In all these cases, cities around the world have taken on many of these responsibilities, and especially for water and sewerage.

This piecemeal and bottom-up development of new system infrastructures was repeated for the new communications from the 1980s onwards. The internet developed in an anarchistic and very Austrian way, but gradually the services concentrated around a small number of very large companies, known as 'Big Tech'. What started out as new and exciting technological innovations gradually became general-purpose technologies,[9] and in due course access to the web, email and modern broadcasting became essential. As banking, shopping and government services and welfare support went online, not having access to these new systems became a competitive disadvantage to businesses and led to social exclusion. As with electricity and the railways, the state is now stepping in to complete the new networks and ensure that they are universally available. They, like access to transport, water and electricity, are critical to decarbonisation, and protecting and enhancing natural systems: so important are they, that all have become universal service obligations (USOs). Citizens must have access to them, and the sustainable economy cannot do without them. They are key capabilities and critical to social justice.

Once the initial burst of enthusiasm and entrepreneurship is over, and the systems consolidate, they need a plan, and a set of institutions, private and public, to deliver the plan. Despite the critique of the Austrians and Hayek against the very concept of planning noted in the previous chapter, the infrastructures require a plan for two separate reasons. The first is that these systems are mostly natural monopolies, so there is no competition to discipline them in the Austrian trial-by-markets. The second is that because the rest of the economy depends upon them, there needs to be a precautionary cushion of excess capacity in each system to handle shocks. The precautionary principle starts to bind. The systems have to be resilient, beyond the normal market equilibria. This resilience extends to the protection of citizens, who need to be able to rely upon these systems for their own personal resilience. It is a public good, and will not be adequately provided without intervention.

---

[9] N. Crafts (2021), 'Artificial Intelligence as a General-Purpose Technology: An Historical Perspective', *Oxford Review of Economic Policy*, 37(3), 521–36.

To these two there is now a third reason for some planning, because the systems are all highways for most of the pollution in the economy. This means that unless the overall environmental objectives of the sustainable economy are designed and developed in ways that facilitate low-carbon activities and the protection of biodiversity, they will not be met. Providing electric car charging points and a grid capable of handling the new electric transport demand and the decentralised, intermittent and low-density wind and solar generation is necessary (but not sufficient) to achieve the overall net zero targets. Providing adequate sewage treatment is necessary for maintaining biodiverse rivers and lakes. The plan may be as simple as a target for fibre coverage, or it may be as complicated as the detailed decarbonisation of energy and transport systems.

Ideas, Knowledge and Human Capital

The third type of capital is human, which has largely replaced manual labour as the stuff that is combined with physical and natural capital to produce economic output. This transition was driven by fossil fuels. The tractors and artificial fertilisers transformed agriculture away from both manual labour and horse power, and digitalisation and robotics are about to take it one stage further, to the point where there are 'hands-free hectares'.[10] This transformation of agriculture, which once dominated employment in most pre-industrial economies, allowed workers to flood into industry and cities, and now as these factories are digital too, labour in the old-fashioned manual sense is increasingly being marginalised.

What people now mostly do at work is apply ideas, science and the technologies these bring, in an increasingly digital way to guide the paths of physical and natural capitals towards the economic outputs. They don't even have to physically go to a workplace to produce outputs. They can work from home, as realised during the Covid lockdowns.

Each generation inherits a body of knowledge and the technologies that go with it, and in the sustainable economy this is one of the capital systems that are passed on. It is typically better than

---

[10] 'The Hands Free Hectare Project', Harper Adams University, 30 June 2019, www.harper-adams.ac.uk/news/203518/the-hands-free-hectare-project.

this: each generation gets a better stock of knowledge and technologies. What facilitates the transition from one generation to the next is the provision of education, which has to be continuously passed on because people die.

The stock of ideas and technologies exists independently of any individual, just as natural capital does. It has a life of its own. Passed down through the monasteries and religious schools through to secular schools, universities and now a host of other institutions and websites, it is a key enabling asset to address our global environmental crises. Science allows humans uniquely to understand what they are doing to our planet, and gives them the ideas and technologies to protect it.

Though it is often claimed that it is 'pure' research that does exactly this, and has produced lots of surprises for the benefit of humans, the actual evidence is more nuanced. There is a case for letting scientists come up with whatever they do when left to their own devices, as long as they are provided with incomes and funding for their research and experiments. That is what many of my colleagues at Oxford do. But even that research, pure or otherwise, starts with *questions*, and these questions arise out of two related contexts: the existing body of theory and knowledge; and the specific actual challenges of the sustainable economy.

Take the example of climate change. Current theories and models are the product of centuries of research into fundamental physics, research into the greenhouse gases, research into the atmosphere, data on long-term temperature records going back thousands and millions of years, all to give us the current conjectures on the determinants of climate change. To these physical theories and empirical evidence, centuries of research into energy is added, the innovations and inventions that gave us the Industrial Revolution, and detailed work on specific ways of measuring, capturing and substituting away from carbon-intensive production. Then there is the emerging science and understanding of sequestration of carbon by the seas, and by forests and soils, based on the biological sciences.

The questions that are addressed and which motivate this research are multiple. Climate change brings them together, and the Intergovernmental Panel on Climate Change is a remarkable example of attempting to provide this synthesis and, in the process, throw up new questions and challenges.

Karl Popper, whom we met in the previous chapter, described this approach to knowledge and ideas in a remarkable series of books and papers, most notably in the *Logic of Scientific Discovery* (1934), *Conjectures and Refutations: The Growth of Scientific Knowledge* (1963), and *Objective Knowledge: An Evolutionary Approach* (1972). This body of work is more respected by practising scientists than it is by mainstream philosophers.[11] Be that as it may, the main part of his description of how science works and how the body of knowledge is built up remains revolutionary, and it lends itself to our assets-based and systems approach to the sustainable economy. Consequently it is worth exploring in further detail.

Popper regards the scientific process as starting with the posing of specific conjectures. He does not think that there is any deterministic model of how these come about nor where they come from. In this respect, his approach is very Austrian. Scientists are rather like entrepreneurs, motivated by all sorts of things.

Now Popper's radical bit. Scientists do not try to establish truths; they try to refute conjectures made by others (and by themselves). They are engaged in falsification. All knowledge and ideas are tentative. The task of the scientists is a continuing one of knocking down the old, and making new conjectures that can better capture our empirical world, until they in turn are rejected. It is a scientific version of Schumpeter's creative destruction.

Whilst science does not quite match up to Popper's stringent requirements, and scientists often end up defending existing paradigms, the threat of empirical testing remains powerful. Paradigms can resist, and it takes time to change them and allow for what have become known as Kuhnian revolutions.[12] Whatever the actual processes of scientific discovery, and partly due to the resilience of established paradigms, at any point in time there is a body of knowledge that is still standing, yet to be refuted. That is our current knowledge. It includes the theories of Einstein, after Newton had been found wanting. It

[11] P. Godfrey-Smith (2016), 'Popper's Philosophy of Science: Looking Ahead', chapter 4 in J. Shearmur and G. Stokes (eds.), *The Cambridge Companion to Popper*, Cambridge: Cambridge University Press, pp. 104–24. Popper did not help his philosophical reputation by claiming to have solved Hume's problem of induction. See also A. O'Hear (1980), *Karl Popper*, London: Kegan & Paul.

[12] T. Kuhn (1962), *The Structure of Scientific Revolutions*, Chicago: University of Chicago Press.

includes Darwin, after the creationist theory had been knocked away. And so on.

This body of knowledge is a primary asset, the basis for the economies and societies built up over the centuries. It is the best we have, and it will change over time. It should grow, and hence provide further underpinnings to sustainable economic growth. It is what we inherit and what should be bequeathed to the next generation. It is the chain letter down the generations. We do not need to worry about the generation after next; we simply need to make sure we pass the baton on in good shape. If and as it grows, sustainable economic growth can take place.

There have been dark ages in the past. There have been closed societies, totalitarian ones, which prescribe and try to destroy bits of the knowledge systems, even burning books. The Taliban regime in Afghanistan again reminds us that dark ages are not purely history. Women are denied education. This is the link between Popper's theory of science and his theory of the open society discussed in the previous chapter, and it is a link that Hayek would hold to as well. It is one of the reasons why there needs to be a constitution of liberty, and why totalitarianism is such a terrible threat.[13] It is why many totalitarian societies find it hard to match the innovation and scientific progress of the democracies, and why they are typically so environmentally awful.

You might think that one difference with the approach to natural and physical systems is that the protection and enhancement of the knowledge system and its intangible assets exist in the ether, independently of states and public interventions. On the contrary, without some supporting framework, they will fragment and perhaps fall apart. This is because the knowledge system, and the infrastructure within which new ideas are generated, is a public and not a private good. Private markets do not do much to add to the body of knowledge: they tend to exploit the public goods for private ends, applying ideas in practical businesses. Our understanding of climate change and the ecosystems within which biodiversity is embedded comes from public institutions rather than private companies. Universities tend to be state-driven, as is the funding of much research, even if augmented by private donations. There are examples of maverick, brilliant individual

[13] Hayek sets this out in *The Constitution of Liberty*.

scientists outside this mainstream framework, but they are isolated exceptions.

For the knowledge *system*, recent attempts to apply the economists' cost–benefit analysis to research grant applications is an example of using inappropriate disaggregate techniques. Very few bits of research are separable from the general research endeavour. Whilst there are specific questions which, if we answered them, have specific benefits, most problems are not like this. For example, the development of vaccines for coronavirus led to the new mRNA (messenger ribonucleic acid) techniques, using gene editing, which may translate into specific targeted methods of addressing cancers and help develop a form of personalised medical interventions. They may change crops too. It is very hard to keep any specific bit of research in its box. Because the potential benefits are open-ended, it is particularly damaging to apply crude discounting to them, and hence create a bias towards shorter-term near-market progress. With research, it is rarely clear what the benefits will be, and which to discount. The benefits of scientific advances are forever, open-ended and hence of much greater value than specific projects subjected to cost–benefit analysis. Scientific knowledge is best considered as an asset-in-perpetuity and shares with sustainable natural capital this open-ended property.

Popper described these assets as his *World 3* of objective knowledge, as distinct from the physical universe of World 1 and the human consciousness of experience and thought of World 2.[14] This World 3 body of knowledge could be regarded as the outcome of a process akin to natural selection: the theories which have so far survived the competitive challenge of empirical testing. It is a neat way of encapsulating the system asset which needs to be maintained and enhanced for the next generation, and the source of sustainable economic growth, and hence a critical bit of the architecture of the sustainable economy.

Now contrast this with the economists' approach to human capital. Gary Becker, the great Chicago school economist on all this, described human capital as essentially a discrete investment activity with marginal costs and damages. Each of us 'chooses' how much human capital to acquire on an autonomous basis. We invest as if we are entrepreneurs, looking for profit. We are personal 'factories' built

---

[14] K. Popper (1979), *Objective Knowledge: An Evolutionary Approach*, revised edn, Oxford: Clarendon Press, chapter 3.

out of this investment, and our acquired knowledge has a capital value, which yields a flow of income, in the form of higher wages. It is an individualised hyper-capitalism in which we are all little capitalists playing out our lives in the competitive marketplace.[15]

As an economic theory, it goes some way to explaining the differential returns in wages to those with university education over those without, and why unskilled and poorly educated people have done so badly in recent decades, notably in the US. Not surprisingly, more education tends to lead to higher productivity and higher wages.[16] But this rather obvious claim only gets us so far. It may be that it is also social position that counts, and educational attainment is the outcome of inequality as much as university degrees. Education can be a screening device. But in any event, it does not deal with the wider benefits of education to society as a whole, or to the incentives to invest in Popper's World 3, which is primarily a public rather than a private good. The body of ideas, knowledge and technologies exists independently of the bits of it that are acquired by individuals. Becker's human capital is really about specific aspects of education and educational choices, not the public good of science. As long as human capital is assumed to be just a set of discrete atomistic investments, human capital decisions are examples of forgone consumption now for more consumption later, in effect part of the allocation of time (the ultimate personal asset).[17] In contrast, the systems public goods approach sees education enhancing not just for the narrow investment decisions but also wider sustainable economic growth because it helps to apply science, and it is the science that is the primary cause of that sustainable growth. Universal education and the development of the primary asset of science are both necessary parts of the sustainable economy.

For both narrow economic reasons and because education provides a core capability, it is not surprising that governments have taken on the duty to provide education, and to largely fund it too. Where it

---

[15] This is the model Becker developed and which has dominated the economics of education ever since. See G. Becker (1964), *Human Capital*, 2nd edn, New York: Columbia University Press; and D.J. Deming (2022), 'Four Facts about Human Capital', *Journal of Economic Perspectives*, 36(3), 75–102.

[16] See the survey of empirical evidence on human capital in K.G. Abraham and J. Mallatt (2022), 'Measuring Human Capital', *Journal of Economic Perspectives*, 36(3), 103–30.

[17] See Becker's brilliant 1965 paper 'A Theory of the Allocation of Time', *Economic Journal*, 75(299), 493–517, and more generally his *A Treatise on the Family*, Cambridge, MA: Harvard University Press, 1981.

does not, in particular in higher education in the US and increasingly in the UK, the results become highly skewed to the elites who can buy access to human capital and then exploit the benefits.

Social Capital

The fourth type of capital that comes in systems is called 'social capital', the hardest to define, being intangible, and the most difficult to advance. It has long been observed that societies function best when the citizens share a common outlook, a common set of beliefs and a focus on the good of the whole community, as well as on their own short-term self-interests. The sustainable economy cannot work without a fabric of social capital, and one that is well maintained. Religions, national identities and shared cultural histories, with their associated rituals, bind societies together.

There have been many attempts to explain, for example, the coming of capitalism by religion, and to identify the Protestant religion as especially sympathetic to industrialisation and market economies.[18] Correlation – Protestantism and economic growth – does not in itself provide a causal explanation, and social capital is one of those very slippery concepts that tends to get defined in ways that suit those doing the defining. Of the characteristics of a society that might contribute to a successful economy, trust and the respect for the property of others stand out. There are lots of paths in different societies to establishing these core social assets. Contrast Iran with the US, and the US with Germany: very different cultures, but all built into their specific social capital.

Exchange and transactions between individuals always depend upon an element of trust. Markets cannot function without it. Parties engaged in trade must ask themselves: why is the other party selling this to me, or buying it from me? What do they know that I do not which makes the price we agree one each wants to accept? If I sell my house to you at an agreed price, is that because I know it is worth less? The answer is that trade tends to open up possibilities to each of us of

---

[18] M. Weber (1905), *The Protestant Spirit and the Rise of Capitalism*, reprinted 2002, London: Penguin Books; R.H. Tawney (1926), *Religion and the Rise of Capitalism: A Historical Study*, London: J. Murray; and M.J. Wiener (1981), *English Culture and the Decline of the Industrial Spirit, 1850–1980*, Cambridge: Cambridge University Press. See also B.M. Friedman (2021), *Religion and the Rise of Capitalism*, New York: Alfred A. Knopf.

exchange, specialisation and comparative advantage, and is a vital part of our ability to function and thrive. Comparative advantage suggests that each of us specialises. Some are better at growing and making food than others because they have acquired specific human capital skills, and some have better climates and better access to natural resources than others.

In the case of the house, quite detailed contracts are written to certify what exactly the house is that I am selling. But even when it turns out that the roof is in a poorer state than you were led to believe when you bought the house, enforcing the contract terms is quite difficult. You have to carry an element of trust in the seller, otherwise the contract is going to be immensely complicated. It turns out that most transactions are overwhelmingly based upon trust, built up through repeated transactions. This trust is also based upon the other person being part of a culture in which untrustworthy behaviour is frowned upon, and social conventions ostracise those who behave in untrustworthy ways.[19]

Societies without these shared cultural norms find trade and exchange harder and thus are worse off. Where greed, short-termism and narrow opportunism are encouraged, such as in the yuppy culture of the 1980s, and the 'greed is good', 'loads of money' mentality is promoted politically, productivity suffers. Think of the post-pandemic working-from-home issue. It is harder for employers to monitor what you are doing at home rather than in the office, but working from home cuts your commuting costs and has other benefits. Does the employer trust the employee to be working 9 to 5? If trust is present, there is great scope for high outputs because there is less stress and costs are lower. If not, then working from home is less prevalent than it could be. Cultural norms, such as the German attitudes to savings, are more likely to create (and reflect) social solidarity and understanding.

A second aspect is trust and the limiting of crime (including environmental crime). Markets rely on a prevalence of honest transactions. They rely on us not stealing most of the time, and societies with a greater degree of social capital tend to have lower crime rates and hence have lower costs. Think of how much economic activity is spent on crime prevention. Think of all those locked houses, those passwords

---

[19] J. Son and Q. Feng (2019), 'In Social Capital We Trust?', *Social Indicators Research*, 144, 167–89.

and protective measures on the internet. In this latter case, the intriguing possibility is that the more remote and anonymous trade is, the less trust and the more scope there is for crime and the higher costs. As the world gets more virtual, this may lead to higher levels of crime. Inevitably, the sustainable economy will be undermined.

At the country level, low social capital helps to explain the economic difficulties of Russia, with its political corruption and the short-termism this induces in its population. It explains why Putin has tried to cultivate the Russian Orthodox Church, to buy into its social capital.

Social capital is a key part of the inheritance of the next generation. There is a reason for the protection and enhancement of the institutions that nurture this form of capital, including education. Social capital is especially important when it comes to climate change and biodiversity loss. The reason is the powerful incentive to free-ride on the provision and protection of these great environmental assets. Whether you do anything to reduce your emissions will have almost no effect on climate change, just as if you vote it will not determine the outcome of an election. The reason is that we are all too insignificant to make a difference. Climate change requires the Chinese, the Indians and the Africans, and your neighbours next door all to simultaneously take steps to reduce their carbon footprints. If any of these people take active steps, you get the benefits (less climate change) and no costs if you make no effort yourself. You have a powerful incentive to free-ride. Social capital leans into the wind of free riders, limiting their impact.

Thinking as a greedy, self-interested individual, why not party whilst others take on the costs of reducing emissions? This scares environmental activists a lot, and for understandable reasons. If each of us realised that this free-riding incentive is sufficiently serious such that it is very unlikely that we will collectively head off significant climate change, and if it turns out to cost us individually quite a lot to do our small contributing part, then even if we are not ourselves selfish, it is not hard to conclude that we should not bother to act in a hopeless situation. Why bother either if some others are not, or if no one else is bothering? In neither case will your action make any difference. This gives environmentalists an understandable urge to tell an optimistic story, to say we can each make a difference and that it will not cost much, even if it is not true. Indeed that is what is going on.

But it is not working, though the manipulation of the media has led to many actually believing they can make a difference and that the costs are low, despite the evidence to the contrary. The alternative is to fall back on social capital and in particular the shared ethical outlook, to stress that 'we are all in this together' and we have to act collectively in the collective interests. This demands that we both recognise the free-rider incentives and yet suppress our narrowest self-interest for the greater good. Getting people to do this depends upon whether they do in fact see the world this way and see themselves as part of a cohesive society, and hence whether there is enough social capital. It is the sort of 'togetherness' that enables countries to fight wars, for the young (predominantly men) to sacrifice their lives. It is the social equivalent of 'team spirit' that motivates a group of sports players to work together, even if it reduces their own personal chance of scoring a goal.

Social capital is acquired from parents and schools, and from the media. All of these in turn grow out of the history and culture of the society, and it is for this reason that these parts of education are especially important aspects of the capital assets we should pass on to the next generation. What matters in the absence of religions is that there are rules which govern our behaviours and the way we treat each other and the wider environment. In the sustainable economy, the overriding rule is set by the first principle, that it is our duty to pass on a set of assets at least as good as we inherited, and that this is embedded in institutions. It is a reason to treat radical institutional reform with scepticism, especially since such institutions (and any radical new ones) take generations to build up. Institutions, like social rules, need to evolve.

The sustainable economy is made up of the four capital systems: natural, physical, human and social. These systems are what we should pass on to the next generation. They are what the aggregate rules derived from the first principle require us to maintain and enhance.

But how to do this? The next step is to shine the torch on the state of these assets, to understand the sorry state some of them are in and work out how to maintain and enhance them where appropriate. To do this we need a balance sheet and some accounts.

5 SUSTAINABLE ACCOUNTING AND THE BALANCE SHEET

William the Conqueror is famous for at least two things: winning the Battle of Hastings, thereby conquering England; and commissioning the Great Survey, better known as the Domesday Book. Remarkably, neither exercise has been repeated since then: England has not been successfully invaded and there has been no 'Great Survey' of the assets of the country.[1] To meet the first principle of the sustainable economy, a somewhat similar survey is now required, howbeit for a very different purpose. To be good stewards of the capitals, and the systems they are embedded in, especially the natural capital, requires accounts that answer the question: how well is this generation looking after them? To fill these accounts in, a baseline is needed.

The assets and systems approach lends itself to balance sheets and national accounting that are very different from the way the current GDP accounts are put together. The current national accounts answer a different question: how well is the economy doing in terms of flows of consumption, production and income? And, more narrowly, is the government balancing its books in cash terms? Neither of these questions addresses the stewardship of the sustainable economy, and in particular the primacy of maintaining its capitals, so that the

---

[1] Although there was a '1873 Return of Owners of Land'. Local Government Board (1873), '1873 Return of Owners of Land', presented to both Houses of Parliament by Command of Her Majesty, Volume 1, HMSO 1875.

consumption is sustainable and we are not living beyond our sustainable means. Neither provides an assessment of the liabilities, environmental or otherwise. Getting the question right is the most important thing for accounts, telling us what the accounts are *for* and hence whether they tell us anything useful.

To construct the national accounts of the sustainable economy, the starting point is the capital maintenance of the core systems. This is all about making sure that the assets are not in decline. It requires a baseline of the set of assets the current generation inherited. Remedial investment may be required to bring the baseline up to scratch. Next come enhancements and improvements to these assets. With maintenance and remedial investment and enhancements properly incorporated, the sustainable economy balance sheet can be constructed. This sets the frame for the macroeconomics and how the aggregates for investment, savings and consumption should be determined. These are the accounting issues for the sustainable economy: the maintenance of all the main capitals (natural, physical, human and social); plus remedial investments; plus enhancements.

Capital Maintenance

Renewable natural capital is an asset-in-perpetuity, provided the stocks do not fall below their critical thresholds. For practical purposes, key physical system network infrastructures can also be treated as assets-in-perpetuity, as are ideas and new technologies. So too is social capital, built up over past generations. These are all assets the first principle requires us to protect and pass on to the next generation. Within this wider context, there are also many limited-life assets, like vehicles, many buildings and equipment that depreciate through use and hence the capital is used up, and there are many borderline cases. Cathedrals are best thought of as assets-in-perpetuity; modern blocks of flats are not.

Almost any asset can be maintained in perpetuity if enough is spent on its maintenance. A car could be kept in pristine condition if it is continually repaired, and its parts replaced. There are many examples in museums and collections of very old vehicles that work just as well as when they were manufactured, and sometimes even better. The reason we do not maintain all but the museum trophies is not that we cannot, but rather because of the advances in technology. A 1930s Model T Ford car is very inefficient compared with a current Ford model. The new models are faster, more comfortable, vastly more fuel-efficient and much cheaper. In due course, with decarbonisation, new electric models should be much less polluting and therefore it will be better to replace the current petrol and diesel models with these.[2]

These simple examples illustrate the two ways the value of assets can be kept intact: existing physical assets can be maintained; or a set of assets necessary to deliver the services can be maintained, recognising that the physical configurations might change. In the latter case, different types of pipes and wires, different materials and different ways of coordinating can replace existing assets to deliver the services, as technical change comes along.

In the case of renewable natural capital, physical preservation is the correct and only way to keep the benefits to future generations open-ended. To maintain renewables, we have to both limit our consumption of them and engage in spending to protect the environmental systems within which they can reproduce. Although there are many environmentalists who think that the cost of capital maintenance would be close to zero if only we left the environment alone, and that the best way to do this is to rewild, the reality is that humans have changed the natural world so profoundly that there is no wild to get back to. As a result, as managers of the land, sea and air, the protection of renewable natural capital, and maintaining its value at least constant, typically requires proactive capital maintenance spending. If renewable natural capital is allowed to depreciate, as assets in mainstream economic and business accounting are, then it eventually ceases to be renewable, lost forever.

Since capital maintenance is a cost of delivering the services, not an investment, it should be a first charge on the revenues of the country, municipalities or businesses. For assets-in-perpetuity, it should be deducted from the profit and loss account and should not be a balance sheet adjustment through depreciating the asset. This simple point has very radical consequences, rewriting our national accounts and restating how well we are doing and what our sustainable consumption can be. Depreciation is a repayment of capital, and hence capital consumption. It requires capital investment to replace

[2] M. Scott (1991), *A New View of Economic Growth*, Oxford: Oxford University Press.

what has been consumed. Maintenance is just a running cost, a cost of operations.[3]

Capital maintenance might be to clear up pollution, create and enforce protected areas, protect peat bogs, and for other land conservation measures. In particular, since the biodiversity that remains is the biodiversity that has evolved and adapted alongside humans, many of the human landscapes need to be maintained to protect what we have shaped. Alpine meadows work because of the grazing routines; water meadows function as specific farming techniques, and their plant, insect and animal lives are dependent on this being maintained. Hedges require laying. Simply rewilding means setting capital maintenance to zero and will often be detrimental, especially so where it causes a reversion to a uniform ecosystem. Much rewilding is actually a type of asset depreciation. It cannot be repeated too often that the sustainable economy is not an economy with only nature, and without people and human interventions.

It has begun to be appreciated how great the cost of capital maintenance of the atmosphere is, to prevent further damaging climate change. Let's assume that our first principle includes the duty of the current generation to bequeath to the next at least as good an atmosphere, and hence a climate, as it inherited. Though there are some interesting arguments about whether the current climate is optimal, it is nevertheless the one we and nature have adapted to. Over a period of more than 10,000 years, there can be ice ages and warm periods, but for now, the current climate is what we should concentrate on maintaining. It is the climate most suited to the needs of the next generation. The simple fact is that we are failing to do so because the required capital maintenance is not being carried out. Indeed, we have already given up on anything better than a 2°C warming, and remedial action back to 0°C warming is not contemplated.

Suppose we now decide to maintain the climate, and stop global warming beyond 2°C. The costs of doing at least this should come from current revenues and not from borrowing. It is maintenance not investment. Imagine if this sum was deducted from the national current accounts. The fiscal position would be radically worse, and this is a measure of how far we are living beyond our environmental

---

[3] See 'Concepts of capital and capital maintenance', https://annualreporting.info/intfinrep stan/8-concepts-of-capital-and-capital-maintenance/, accessed 23 December 2021.

means just in respect of the climate. The sustainable economy would have a revenue-raising charge on pollution of the atmosphere and an expenditure on the capital maintenance of the energy, transport, water and other core physical infrastructures to render them net zero. It is a very big and radical ask.

Nature gives us our climate for free. Natural ecosystems are made of carbon and they sequestrate it.[4] The green biomass on land and in the seas, plus the natural absorption of the seas and the weathering of rocks,[5] all combine to soak up the emissions and have helped to create our current climate. This has changed over long time periods. Nature gave us the carboniferous periods when the fossil-fuel deposits, and especially the coal, were created in a giant sequestration burst. At other times, there has been a very different balance.

The capital maintenance of the atmosphere requires not just stopping the emissions, but enhancing the ability of the earth's ecosystems to take back the carbon we emit. Restoring peat bogs, protecting the great rainforests, and returning to a greater tree cover are all examples of capital maintenance. The units for capital maintenance should be ecosystems, not individual species, and these great ecosystems include the catchments of rivers, large and small, the coastal fringes, marshes and mangroves, and of course the oceans. A glimpse at how far we are from the sustainable economy is provided by recalling the observation that parts of the Amazon are now net emitters of carbon.[6]

For man-made physical system infrastructures, capital maintenance is to protect the services that the assets enable, without undue pollution. The bundle of assets-in-perpetuity which deliver the services (such as electricity, clean water, sewerage, transport and communications network systems) may change over time. Lead pipes were once widespread for water supply; now they tend to be plastic. Once the electricity networks used oil-filled cables; now they use modern wires. Telephone calls used to be made via copper wires; now internet access and calls are made possible with smartphones and fibre.

---

[4] This is reflected in the division in chemistry between organic (carbon) chemistry and non-organic (inert) chemistry.

[5] The weathering of rocks, the chemical breakdown of minerals in mountains and soils, sequestrates carbon from the atmosphere and transforms it into stable minerals. This notably includes the creation of carbonic acid as carbon dioxide and water combined in soils and oceans.

[6] L.V. Gatti, L.S. Basso, J.B. Miller et al. (2021), 'Amazonia as a Carbon Source Linked to Deforestation and Climate Change', *Nature*, 595, 388–93.

The extent of these changes can be overstated, but neverthe-less the general rule is for *operational* capital maintenance rather than setting the physical capital assets in stone. In some cases, like communications, this has mattered a great deal over the last thirty years, but now the fibre-optic cables may last fifty or even a hundred years. The natural gas pipes have been used for the last forty years, but now many need to be upgraded and altered to take hydrogen. The water pipes, reservoirs and sewers may last fifty or a hundred years.

Technical change demands pragmatism in considering what exactly capital maintenance means in terms of the asset composition. For natural and social capital, capital maintenance is tied to the configuration of assets as they currently stand, and for human capital, ideas and technologies it is built on the current theories and hypotheses (Popper's World 3). For physical system utility infrastructures, it is a moving feast.

All this has very radical implications for us and what we need to do to live within our sustainable means. Consider the implications of charging capital maintenance for just the main physical infrastructures to us as citizens and taxpayers and what it means for national accounts. When your bike or car hits a pothole, you know that it is because the roads are not being properly maintained. This sort of neglect tends to result from political considerations and expediency. When governments and local authorities find they need to placate their voters, the roads may be given less priority over other consumption spending. In the early 1980s and in the post-2007/8 austerity, the pot-holes got bigger and more numerous in the UK, however 'shovel-ready' the maintenance might have been. They are generally worse now after the pandemic. Across the EU and the US, the state of roads, railways and bridges is widely acknowledged to be poor and they cope very badly with droughts, floods and heatwaves. They have little resilience. For the climate, the rise in oil and gas prices in 2021/2 led to a political downgrading of the relative importance of the capital maintenance of the climate, inducing a retreat from net zero.

Suppose that national accounts prepared by the national statistical offices were required, with regular audits, to set out the state of the infrastructure systems, report the capital maintenance requirements and any shortfalls, and set these against the current revenues. There would be no more capital consumption subsidising current consumption. Capital maintenance would be on a pay-as-you-go basis.

The scale of the adjustment would be enormous, showing that, in addition to living beyond our wider environmental and social means, we are also living beyond the means of our physical infrastructure systems. These are examples of our excess consumption now at the expense of future generations. The physical manifestations are reflected in power cuts, hosepipe bans, potholes, defective bridges and broken rails. The accounting manifestations are in the depreciation numbers.

Capital maintenance of human capital focuses on the transmission of knowledge between the generations. Each generation must be educated in a continuous process. The calculation here is in one sense easier. We could simply take it as the cost of education and charge it against current revenues. Indeed, this is roughly what is done. Attempts to fund education through borrowing and hence finance it through debt have not been a great success anywhere for school education, and have had at best mixed results at the university level.[7] Pay-as-you-go by each generation funding the education of the next has been the norm for good reason. We gained our education for free and we should provide it to the next for free, so that the basic human capital assets are passed on at least intact to the next generation. The sustainable economy does not rely on student loans, or a specific graduate tax. Education is not primarily an investment in asset enhancements, but a capital maintenance generational necessity. Capital maintenance in education is the steady-state charge. (The really interesting questions are about *who* should be educated and *how* the human capital should be spread across the population. Not everyone needs to understand nuclear physics for the knowledge assets to be maintained.)

On top of education, there is the research base. Much of this is enhancement not capital maintenance, adding to our stock of ideas and technologies. The research base needs protecting, but the output of the research adds to the knowledge and hence improves the prospects for the next generation. This is investment not capital maintenance.

Maintenance of social capital focuses on the provision of a wider social cohesion and hence on cultural values and communities. New methods of social interaction, such as WhatsApp, Twitter (now X), Instagram and TikTok, emerge alongside older local networks based on

---

[7] L. Dearden, E. Fitzsimons and G. Wyness (2011), 'The Impact of Tuition Fees and Support on University Participation in the UK', IFS Working Paper W11/17, 5 September, Institute for Fiscal Studies.

books, magazines and religions. The set of assets is largely intangible, and while many of them can take a long period of time to build up, they can be quickly dissipated. Shared history makes social capital location-dependent, and much social capital maintenance is about the support for voluntary organisations and charities. Though more diffuse and harder to measure, capital maintenance is not zero cost. Each generation should provide for the maintenance of social capital.

Taking each of the capital assets in turn, and working through the capital maintenance for each, provides an economy-wide estimate of the overall aggregate baseline against which sustainable consumption can begin to be defined. Even though this would be a radical departure from the status quo, holding the line, particularly for renewable natural capital, is hardly a great achievement. This aggregate baseline is already greatly depleted. Given the damage the current generation has done, and is responsible for, there are many aspects of core systems where remedial action to repair the damage is required to improve the inheritance of the next generation. Education and social capital are just a couple of examples. But only after we have properly accounted for and carried out the capital maintenance.

Remedial and Enhancement Investments

The scope for improvement over and above the capital maintenance for our system assets and this generation's remedial responsibilities is considerable. We could have a much better natural environment, better communications, a decarbonised electricity system and much better water and river catchments, and bequeath these better assets to the next generation. We could have even more ideas and technologies and greater trust and social cohesion. This is where investment comes in, on a systems basis.

These considerations provide a distinction between two sorts of investment, both of which are advances on the current baselines. *Remedial investment* makes good damage in this generation relative to the assets it inherited; *new investment* enhances the overall stock of assets. In theory, we could go back iteratively through the damage past generations have caused too, but for pragmatic reasons, and because the sins of past generations are not our fault, we should pragmatically stop the analysis at our generation. The results would be so radical anyway, even from this limited within-generation perspective, that anything over and above this would be politically extremely difficult. There is a symmetry here too: we should care about the next generation because we are closely connected to it; we should address the pollution and the damage this generation has caused to natural capital because we are the responsible party.

Let's start with remedial investments. Take renewable natural capital. We need a baseline, and we have a rough idea of the state of the natural environment in the years immediately following the Second World War and increasingly detailed data since then. In the UK, natural historians have painstakingly documented the decline of our natural fauna. It is a very sad story, punctuated by some successes which need to be balanced off. Much of the total loss of the 97 per cent of water meadows,[8] and 50–75 per cent of the insects,[9] has happened since that war. The asset deficit is clear. It would be impractical to put them all back. But that is no excuse for not recognising the damage in the accounts and not doing at least some remedial works.

Biodiversity has been hammered by modern agriculture, plastic pollution and atmospheric pollution. Capital maintenance requires that we do not make matters worse, that for the carbon content of the atmosphere we hold the current line, now over 420ppm (as at the time of writing). But what about the 100+ppm we have added since before the Industrial Revolution? That baseline might be somewhere around 275ppm.[10] Should investment be made as *reparations* for all the damage done, just as it is often demanded from perpetrators to compensate for the destruction wrought during wartime, and notoriously so in 1918 after the First World War, and now in respect of Ukraine? The point here is a fundamental one: there is no 'optimal' baseline to get back to.

If we were to put right all the environmental damage done in just this generation and choose as a baseline the state of assets which we inherited from the last generation, it would require an enormous correction and would seriously reduce our standard of living. This

[8] Environment Agency (2022), 'Working with Nature', Chief Scientist's Group report, July, https://assets.publishing.service.gov.uk/government/uploads/system/uploads/attachment_data/file/1094162/Working_with_nature_-_report.pdf.

[9] C.A. Hallmann, M. Sorg, E. Jongejans et al. (2017), 'More than 75 Percent Decline over 27 Years in Total Flying Insect Biomass in Protected Areas', *Plos One*, 18 October, https://journals.plos.org/plosone/article/file?id=10.1371/journal.pone.0185809&type=printable.

[10] 'CO$_2$ and Greenhouse Gas Emissions – Our World in Data', https://ourworldindata.org/co2-and-other-greenhouse-gas-emissions.

would be the case even if all the investment made in new ideas and technologies and in some new physical assets was subtracted. China, for example, might set all its new hard infrastructure and educational gains against the destruction of its three main rivers, the widespread land pollution, the massive coal-related emissions and the pollution of the South China Seas. If the true economic costs of China's expansion over the last thirty years were properly accounted for, the balance might even be negative.[11]

The key point about the accounting for remedial investments is that they have to be paid for by the current generation. Using debt finance, with debt falling on the next generation, is only consistent with our intergenerational rule, the first principle, if it is a positive *improvement* above the baseline back in the early post-Second World War context we might have arbitrarily chosen, but practically, selected as the start line for the current generation. (We could have simply set it at say 1970 or 1990 or even 2000 – any one of these would create a major remedial requirement.) We did the damage and we need to repair and enhance the environment back to where it was. That is why it should be charged to our current account as a repair to our balance sheet.

In the case of genuine new enhancements, the *additional* assets are created which the next generation will benefit from. While, on the environmental front, it has largely been a downhill path, in other dimensions of the economy there have been positive advances in this generation which the next generation will benefit from. The next generation will get a full fibre network and communications system on a whole new level. In the UK, they may (or may not) get HS2 whether or not it is value for money.[12] They may also inherit a significantly decarbonised energy system. Some of this will be an operational way of maintaining the system services, and some, like fibre, will be a considerable enhancement over and above the copper wires it replaces. The

[11] See, for example, K. Arrow, P. Dasgupta, L. Goulder et al. (2004), 'Are We Consuming Too Much?', *Journal of Economic Perspectives*, 18(3), 147–72, especially Table 3. In so-called inclusive wealth type calculation, China escapes the negative numbers because very high values are ascribed to educational advancement and the relief of poverty. See also E.C. Economy (2010), *The River Runs Black: The Environmental Challenge to China's Future*, Ithaca: Cornell University Press.

[12] S. Glaister (2021), 'HS2: Levelling Up or the Pursuit of an Icon', Institute of Government, July, www.instituteforgovernment.org.uk/sites/default/files/hs2-levelling-up-stephen-glaister.pdf.

service provided is vastly enhanced compared with that which could be provided by copper.

It is in the new and additional human capital and the ideas and technologies where enhancement is likely to be most apparent. Each generation inherits a *better* body of science and its applications than the previous one, making future generations better off. It is what constitutes genuine economic growth and hence allows for an element of discounting. Enhancements in the arts are harder to identify and very hard to evaluate. It is not clear that there is 'progress' in literature. These arts cases are best regarded as capital maintenance only. Enhancements in social capital are at best aspirational. Maintaining trust is a huge ask, before thinking about how to create a more socially cohesive society.

The first principle of the sustainable economy suggests that these genuine enhancement benefits should be charged to those who will benefit from them, and hence the new enhanced assets should come with the debt liabilities. This, and not remedial investment or capital maintenance, is where borrowing is justified, and the total borrowing should reflect the enhancement investments that are being made. Debt on the balance sheet should be equal to or less than (if the investments have high returns) the new asset enhancements it facilitates.

The Contrast with Existing Accounts

We now have a conceptual framework that enables us to construct the sustainable economy's national accounts and its balance sheet, which in turn guides us to an understanding of what the sustainable level of consumption is, consistent with a sustainable growth path. It is remarkably different from what our current national income accounts report, and it shows just how misleading GDP is as a measure of both what we can spend and how the economy is growing. It transforms our understanding of macroeconomic policy and of the scope for tax cuts and extra current spending.

The assets approach is based upon *stocks* (assets); almost all modern macroeconomics, and especially Keynesianism, is focused on *flows*. The key difference between the sustainable economy's accounts on the one hand, and what the current national accounts and GDP really record on the other, is between an assets-based long-term perspective and a flows-based short-term account. They answer very different questions. GDP is the culmination of the vision of Keynes and Keynesians. Neither it, nor the Keynesian economic policies constructed upon it, answer the question of whether we are being good stewards of our natural, physical, human and social capitals, and hence whether we are fulfilling our obligations to the next generation.

Assets are about the longer-term sustainability of an economy. Keynes was never seriously interested in the long run. His concern was recessions and unemployment, and especially the Great Depression of the 1930s, and later how to pay for the Second World War. For the Keynesians who followed, the macroeconomic problems are about short-term effective demand, not supply, and, provided that the economy is using its capacity to the full, it can motor ahead, creating cumulative improvements from which the economics of the grandchildren, Keynes thought, would look very rosy.[13] The future is a set of overlapping short periods.

This is all very relevant to the (absence of) balance sheets and the neglect of assets. The national accounts which Keynes encouraged Richard Stone[14] and others to develop were all about the flows of income, expenditure and output, and GDP measured them in gross rather than net forms. Gross meant that no proper account was taken of capital maintenance. The economy is a vast circulating machine of flows, where income = expenditure = output.[15] The accounting task for them is to estimate output (and output gaps compared with full capacity utilisation) and then to manipulate consumption and investment (effective demand) to increase that output up to full employment. This was the answer to a very different question. It is one we shall tackle more extensively in developing the concept of sustainable consumption when we come to the macroeconomics of the sustainable economy.

The sustainable economy approach starts in a very different place and asks a different question about the accounts. The question is whether the assets, rather than the flows, are being maintained and enhanced, in order to work out the longer-term economic outlook and to calculate the sustainable level of consumption consistent with this.

[13] See J.M. Keynes (1931), 'Economic Possibilities for Our Grandchildren', reprinted in J.M. Keynes (2010), *Essays in Persuasion*, London: Palgrave Macmillan.
[14] L. Johansen (1985), 'Richard Stone's Contributions to Economics', *Scandinavian Journal of Economics*, 87(1), 4–32.
[15] See W. Beckerman (1968), *An Introduction to National Income Analysis*, London: Weidenfeld and Nicholson.

This does not rule out short-term stimuli and measures to better use existing capacity in the labour and capital markets. Idle workers are not good, full stop. But it does create a deep conflict between the view that consumption is too high to match the maintenance of the natural, physical, human and social capitals, and hence standards of living have to adjust downwards, and the Keynesian preoccupation with taking current wages as the baseline and then increasing consumption. Because the assets approach puts the emphasis on capital maintenance, remedial investment and asset enhancements, from the baseline that consumption is already too high, the 'output gap' should be measured against the long-run sustainable growth path and sustainable consumption path, not the GDP path.

The Assets Balance Sheet

Let's now consider the national accounts with the sustainable economy in mind. The starting point is the conventional balance sheet, that accounting framework familiar to most businesses and organisations (but not economists and economics textbooks). The balance sheet is a statement of assets and liabilities. The assets are listed and, where appropriate, valued. Liabilities are then similarly documented, comprising, in particular, debt. The balance sheet balances: an organisation where liabilities exceed assets is bust. The balance sheet is a modern version of William the Conqueror's Domesday Book.

Starting with the national assets, these should contain the main system network infrastructures for which the state is the guarantor, as well as incorporating natural capital. They should add in the ideas and technologies (World 3) and social capitals too. That is what a comprehensive asset side of the accounts would contain.

It is immediately obvious that national accounts do not do this, other than in specialist satellite accounts. Why? Partly because they include only publicly owned assets, and not private ones. When the great nationalised utilities were privatised, they moved from the public national to the private company accounts. There was no corresponding recording of the decline in the asset base for the state. The proceeds were treated as cash income, making the governments of the day look in better shape. This is classic GDP accounting at its worst.

There is no perfect hard-and-fast rule about what should be on the state's balance sheet and what should be in private company accounts. It depends upon which question the accounts are supposed to provide an answer to. The criterion currently used is that the state's accounts should include only those assets that depended on taxpayers for their remuneration and as a generator of their liabilities. They should be *taxpayer* accounts, just as William Gladstone had once promoted in the Victorian era.[16] When the utilities were privatised, provided they received no state support, the assets were taken onto the companies' balance sheets, and the interest and the dividends remunerating them were charged to customers' bills.

This all assumes that what matters is ownership and the neat distinction between consumers and taxpayers. Citizens are both, and what actually matters is those aspects of the economy that are determined by, and rely on guarantees from, the state. These include the great system infrastructures, with their long-term assets, a big gap between marginal and average costs, monopoly and public good excess capacity margins. Most of the owners of these have some sort of explicit (and sometimes implicit) guarantee from the state that their assets will not be expropriated and that they can finance their functions. No government can let them fail. If the question is about the sustainability of the economy, all the main infrastructures should be on the government's books. These are *citizens'* accounts, given the state's role is to ensure that these provide their services and meet the duties to the next generation. Only governments can guarantee this. Indeed, so essential are these functions that they should form a requirement of the sustainable economy's constitution.

One particularly interesting case relating to the physical infrastructure, relevant to the sustainable economy, is agriculture. In developed countries, agriculture is no longer the driving force in the economy, and in the UK's case produces only around 0.5 per cent of GDP. Much of this is made up of explicit subsidy, supplemented by a host of implicit subsidies.[17] This is repeated across much of the world, and notably in the US and EU. On the criterion of reliance on the state and the implicit guarantee, quite a lot of agriculture should be on the national balance

[16] H. Matthew (1979), 'Disraeli, Gladstone, and the Politics of Mid-Victorian Budgets', *Historical Journal*, 22(3), 615–43.
[17] In the UK, these include exemptions from business rates and inheritance tax, subsidised diesel and a host of payments for flood damage, livestock deaths and other events. Crucially, the agricultural industry does not pay for the considerable pollution it causes, including the carbon emissions, and water and air pollution.

sheet. This is true of most developed countries, with the exception probably of New Zealand, which abolished its subsidies, though, even here, it might be argued that land ultimately belongs to the citizens, and ownership is more leasehold than freehold from a generational perspective.

A further example is provided by energy, and in particular power generation. Almost all UK investments rely on a contract with the state (through, for example, contracts-for-differences, feed-in tariffs and capacity contracts), not customers. In the nationalised days, the assets of the Central Electricity Generating Board (CEGB) in the UK were those of the state. Today, they are treated as private. Arguably, they should all be back on the state's balance sheet now that the state is again the primary contractor and guarantor.[18] They are in this sense also *citizens'* assets. In the EU, there is a host of supports and guarantees, and the US is tiptoeing in this direction too. There would be a credit on the national current account for the income net of the subsidies, as there was in the nationalised industries.

Asset Valuation

The next problem is how these assets should be valued on the balance sheet. Here, there is a shortcut. Recall that these are mostly assets-in-perpetuity. Once built, they are not going to be depreciated and no debt should be set against them in the balance sheet because they should already have been paid for. In consequence, the overall asset value is not very interesting. Where valuation of the assets matters is for remedial investment and where enhancements take place. If assets have been allowed to deteriorate because they have not been properly maintained, the balance sheet needs an adjustment downwards for the value of the impaired or lost assets and their services. Where enhanced, there is a positive adjustment upwards. Both of these are crucial for the inter-generational accounts. But there is no need to try to value the plants and the animals and the ecosystems in which they abide and rely upon. These only require a qualitative list, an asset register. Nor do we need an empirical valuation of social capital or even current human capital.[19]

---

[18] When the assets were owned by the CEGB, and on the government's account, customers paid most of its costs.

[19] C. Mayer (2013), 'Unnatural Capital Accounting', Natural Capital Committee, https://assets.publishing.service.gov.uk/government/uploads/system/uploads/attachment_data/file/516947/ncc-discussion-paper-unnatural-capital-accounting.pdf.

This point is missed on many economists engaged in cost–benefit analysis. The conventional economic argument is that everything has a price, either explicitly or implicitly through its shadow value.[20] It leads to inane and silly arguments about the value of bats and birds and flowers. Renewable natural capital assets are not to be bought and sold (in discrete units), all with neat prices to insert into the competitive marketplace. Renewable natural capital is not just another sort of capital: it is a special type of capital because it is renewable and hence can go on delivering its benefits in perpetuity at little or no cost other than capital maintenance. Only in very exceptional cases would one want to get rid of it, and only then does the question of compensation arise. Similarly it is silly to try to say how much the equation $E = mc^2$ is worth, or to put a monetary value on trust.

It is here that the Keynesian approach to the accounts has a positive contribution. If the economy is about the circular flows, there is cash spending on consumption and investment by government, and this is all one aggregate flow. The way this was carried over to the great nationalised industries, and hence the systems we are most concerned about, was through the principle of *pay-as-you-go*. The current generation paid for the building of power stations out of current revenue, and each generation did the same. It was an intergenerational chain letter, biased to the benefit of future generations. The nationalised industries had virtually no debt. Provided that the government maintained the assets, there was no need for a balance sheet valuation. Pay-as-you-go solves the problem of intergenerational capital maintenance responsibilities. It did so too in education, including in universities. There were no tuition fees. There were of course costs to meeting the capital maintenance requirements, but these do not require valuation of the underlying assets. We do not need to value the London Underground or the London sewers. We just need to maintain them. Where underlying assets were sold in privatisations, the opening valuation was somewhat arbitrary and circular, in effect, capitalisation of the revenue stream from customers' bills which had evolved in the public sector to make pay-as-you-go add up in cash terms and by the arbitrary application of a rate of return.[21]

---

[20] A shadow price arises for goods not traded in markets. It is an estimate of what the price would have been had the goods been traded, reflecting both demand and costs.

[21] See I.C. Byatt (1986), 'Accounting for Economic Costs and Prices: A Report to HM Treasury by an Advisory Group' (the Byatt Report), 2 vols., HMSO. For detailed comment, see

A balance sheet is needed to show whether the assets are main-tained and the balancing of enhancement investment against debt finance. It is all the more important because the pay-as-you-go principle was widely abandoned in the 1980s, and it is now not only enhance-ments that are paid for by future generations through debt finance, but even current spending and capital maintenance and remedial spending are partly funded by borrowing too.[22] It was (and continues to be) a great betrayal of future generations, little noted at the time. All this should be reflected in a decline in the balance sheet, and a writing-up of the consequent liabilities. Properly accounted, it should shame the current generation.

As the debt piles up, but the assets do not, what stops the gov-ernment from going bankrupt is the assumption that all these liabilities will be guaranteed and honoured by the next generation. In contrast to the sustainable economy, the current approach relies on an increase in liabilities and a higher standard of living of the current generation that will be paid for by the next generation. In effect, the increase in liabilities is offset by a promise to pay on behalf of the next generation, assuming that they are going to honour this. The liabilities on future generations should be reported for all to see in the national accounts. They should be reported annually in finance ministers' budgets.

It remains to be seen whether future generations will in fact pay, or whether governments have to implicitly default through infla-tion, exchange rate depreciation and even allow outright explicit default. In the UK, inflation and the exchange rate declines have been the implicit preferred routes for defaulting for the last 100 years. No accountant would sign off these accounts for a private entity.

Incorporating Capital Maintenance into the Accounts

The remaining accounting point relates to how to handle the profit and loss account – current revenue, current expenditures and the current balance. For the state, this includes all of its educational, health and

---

G. Whittington (1988), 'The Byatt Report: A Review Essay', *British Accounting Review*, 20, 77–87. On applications to asset value, see D. Heald (1989), 'The Valuation of Power Stations by the Modern Equivalent Asset Method', *Fiscal Studies*, 10(2), 86–108.

[22] Transport for London is a recent addition to the list of public companies borrowing to cover current expenditures. See https://tfl.gov.uk/info-for/investors/borrowing-pro gramme.

social welfare provisions, the police, the army and much of the local government services. These are not relevant to the capital account, provided the capital maintenance (and remedial spending) is paid from current revenues, as it should be for our generational rule.

There should be an additional charge against this revenue line, so that the budget 'balance' on the current account (analogous to companies' profit and loss accounts) is net of the total of this capital maintenance and remedial spending. This means that the costs of maintaining the natural capital asset base intact, the costs of the decarbonisation and the costs of maintaining the great physical systems (and the costs of 'making good') would all be deducted *before* the finance ministry decides how to spend what is left. They are all pay-as-you-go.

There is little doubt that the net revenue left for spending after the deduction of capital maintenance would be significantly lower. If the government sought nevertheless to maintain the current spending level, and unless tax was raised, borrowing would be higher. The higher the borrowing to cover current spending, including capital maintenance, the greater the burden that is shifted from this generation to the next, and the greater the violation of the intergenerational equity first principle, for this is not enhancement investment to create new assets. This is one measure of how far we are living beyond our means, for which sustainable, asset-based national accounts should give an estimate.

It remains to sort out savings and the funding of investment for enhancements (but not remedial investments). If, as is currently the case in the UK (and the US), saving is very low,[23] then it is foreigners who do much of the lending. If, in addition, the current account of the balance of payments is consistently negative, then again it requires foreign inward financial flows. There has to be a capital inflow to balance the external current-account deficits, so that the balance of payments balances. This is one reason why so many of the UK's (and some US) assets, including much of its infrastructure systems, are now owned by foreign companies. Quite a lot of land, especially in the UK, is also in foreign hands. It is another consequence of living beyond our means: selling off our core assets to foreigners to pay for our lifestyles, by buying more imports than the exports we sell. It is the selling-off of capital

---

[23] The exception is saving during the pandemic.

to boost current spending, an exercise that the Labour government of the 1970s and then, on a greater scale, the Thatcher government that succeeded it in 1979 accelerated by selling off the nationalised industries (as well as council houses), and most European governments followed suit.[24] Everyone in the UK, US and the EU has been in the business of this creative accounting.

Changing the Questions

Macroeconomics, as it has developed over the twentieth century, has had almost nothing to say about the development and sustaining of the asset bases of economies and especially renewable natural capital. Yet this has not stopped a confluence emerging between those on the left who want a bigger state; those Keynesians who regard the current difficulties as the consequence of deficient effective demand; and environmental activists who want to reduce pollution, notably from carbon, but also generally to upgrade natural capital through large-scale borrowing.

　　None of these parties has shown much, if any, concern about the consequences of the debt this implies, and none has questioned the opening level of consumption and its relation to sustainability. For environmentalists, the benefits from a loss of demand during the lockdowns for aviation (and transport in general) and for a host of hospitality expenditures (in other words, a reduction in environmentally damaging consumption) should have been not only welcomed, but reinforced by a desire to limit any rebounding in consumption generally. What unites all these parties (the environmentalists and the political left and indeed even centre-right Conservatives) is their hostility to 'austerity', by which they mean measures to reduce fiscal deficits and hence to limit consumption. It is classic 'cake-ism': more consumption *and* a better environment. In the case of Covid, all wanted a return to the level of consumption and living standards that prevailed before the pandemic broke out.

　　The assets-based accounting rules set out here would reveal the true scale of the deceit that those Keynesian policies disguise. They would reveal that such deficits increase the gap between current and

---

[24] The Labour government at the end of the 1970s started selling off BP. Council houses were the biggest item in the first Thatcher government from 1979 to 1983.

sustainable capitalism. The debt which plugs this gap is a liability placed on the young and the next generation to support our unsustainable lifestyles now. It is a large-scale increase in liabilities on the balance sheet with the counterpart being future citizens as customers and taxpayers. It is a gross violation of the duty to leave the next generation with a set of assets at least as good as the current generation inherited. Proper accounts shine a bright light on this deceit, analogous to William the Conqueror's attempt through the Domesday Book to shine a light on what he had stolen.[25]

---

[25] The Napoleonic Wars (1803–15) kicked off income tax to cope with the national debt incurred to fund them. See M. Slater (2018), *The National Debt: A Short History*, London: C. Hurst & Co. Publishers Ltd. See also E. Chancellor (2022), *The Price of Time: The Real Story of Interest*, London: Penguin Books; and B.S. Bernanke (2022), *21st Century Monetary Policy: The Federal Reserve from the Great Inflation to COVID-19*, New York: W.W. Norton & Co.

6 POLLUTER PAYS

Sustainable consumption is defined net of the capital maintenance spending on the current national account. Together with remedial investments, this knocks back the current consumption level. That
leaves a further adjustment that needs to be made: adjusting the prices
to internalise pollution costs. Sustainable consumption is net both of
capital maintenance and of the costs of pollution.

Polluters should pay for the pollution they cause. This is a secondary principle of the sustainable economy, alongside the precautionary principle. Ultimately, it is you and me who buy the stuff, and hence
we are the ultimate polluters. Since we are currently not paying the full
costs of that pollution, it is another reason why we are living beyond
our environmental means, and hence implies one more notch down in
consumption.

This adjustment is likely to be large. In most economies, it is
the polluted who mostly pay, and worse some polluters are actually
subsidised, notably in agriculture. A world where polluters pay would
have widespread carbon taxes on domestic production and imports,
pesticide and fertiliser taxes, ammonia and air pollution taxes, higher
prices for water to reflect the damage of abstraction, higher prices for
sewage disposal, taxes on plastic, palm oil and cement, and so on.

All that stuff listed in your carbon diary and your wider environmental impacts diary would be more expensive, and those alternative
lower-polluting things would benefit from relatively lower prices. No

prices would go down absolutely, and the sum of all of those that go up would be a measure of the costs of the pollution you and I are causing. Trade would go down: all that polluting carbon-intensive stuff imported from China would be more expensive, as would the hardwood and beef from the cleared Amazon rainforest. Food prices would rise, as would many of the use-once clothes and anything wrapped in plastic.

In response, companies would try to minimise packaging, plastics and waste to bear down on costs. Entrepreneurs would seek new ways of reducing pollution to cut costs. Local organic food would be relatively cheaper, as would locally produced products. There would be significant re-shoring of major industries as importers were caught by the polluter-pays principle. As an example at the global scale, building the new road through the Amazon – the BR-319[1] – to enable loggers to get more hardwoods out to sell in international markets would not be so attractive, given that the full environmental costs of the destruction by the loggers would make the price of the timber incredibly high. The new set of corrected relative prices would change the structure of the world economy and each national economy in profound ways and change your shopping habits. This is what it means to put the environment at the heart of the economy.

Getting people to pay for their pollution, and to pay for the capital maintenance, is a tough ask. But it would be necessary to meet the requirements of the sustainable economy. It is a further requirement if we are to live within our means. The fact that we may (and almost certainly will) resist does not make the problems go away. As ever, what is not sustainable will not be sustained. The climate will get ever hotter, the rivers will continue to decline and biodiversity will continue to go down.

Pollution and Market Failure

In the 1920s and 1930s, when the great economic theories, both conventional and the Austrian, which shape the way we live now, were being developed, very little thought was given to the environment. It was largely an afterthought, as it would continue to be throughout the great industrialisations of the twentieth century. On the

[1] See P.M. Fearnside (2022), 'Amazon Environmental Services: Why Brazil's Highway BR-319 Is So Damaging', *Ambio*, 51, 1367–70.

macroeconomic front, Keynes did not appear to care much about it at all, being keen to increase output and reduce unemployment, not conserve nature. On the microeconomic front, the primary market failure considered was monopoly. Marx had predicted that capitalism would end up with monopoly, and hence monopoly capitalism, whilst the mainstream economists focused on the conditions for a perfectly competitive general equilibrium, with efficient prices that fully reflected costs, but had no monopoly mark-up.

The market failure paradigm persists today as the main way to analyse how markets measure up against this perfectly competitive equilibrium, how far prices deviate from their 'correct' level and how to identify cases for potential interventions. Back then, some had begun to recognise that pollution might be one of those market failures that needs addressing, though in the great summaries of the mainstream theoretical outlook, notably Hicks's *Value and Capital*, they are hardly prominent. It is not even in the book's index.

Arthur Pigou, in his *Economics of Welfare*,[2] is widely credited with being the first major economist to take environmental considerations seriously. The environmental problem as he saw it was that there were certain costs which were not internalised in market prices (externalities), and since all prices should fully incorporate all costs in an efficient economy, the way to address the environment was through the application of what become known as a Pigouvian tax to correct for these externalities and hence ensure a more efficient outcome. It is rarely recognised that if fully applied to all externalities, Pigou's taxes would have been much more radical than all and any of Keynes's ideas. The vector of prices, which is the solution to the economic allocation of resources, would be very different. Put another way, in every circumstance there is always pollution, and hence all market prices are wrong, distorting choices and outputs.

In the economics textbook, the marginal costs and marginal damages are adjusted to include the pollution costs, and hence the new equilibrium price is where the social marginal costs equal the social marginal damages. Putting aside the technical issues of what happens to income when the price is adjusted,[3] the neat theoretical comparison

[2] A.C. Pigou (1920), *The Economics of Welfare*, Basingstoke: Palgrave Macmillan.
[3] In comparing the two equilibria, there is an income and a substitution effect. Hence, in estimating the impacts, there is a technical issue about whether the new equilibrium should be income-compensating, as described for example in the general analysis of price changes

of the new equilibrium, inclusive of the externality costs, has three problems: that the marginal costs and marginal damages have to be estimated; that there are no additional market failure distortions like monopoly which might interfere with the corrections; and how the tax revenues are spent.

How would the economists know the social marginal costs and social marginal damages? There are no controlled experiments, so the experts have to rely on engineering, statistical and other tangential evidence. On many bits of these calculations, they face radical uncertainty, peering into the future, and cannot observe what would happen if these marginal costs and damages changed *marginally*. As we shall see later in this chapter, there is no obvious agreed way to estimate the social cost of carbon, and many of these exercises are conducted in the context of deep vested interests and lobbying.

Supposing for a moment the experts get the right answer. If the rest of the economy is distorted by market power, then correcting the particular prices for the externality will be a correction to a price which is already distorted for other reasons. A monopoly may be charging a price above costs already, so the externality tax is an additional price increase. Put together, these price increases will be excessive. This is called the problem of the second best,[4] and is very prevalent.

The theory of the second best suggests that making one market correction while ignoring other market imperfections in a *ceteris paribus* fashion can be counterproductive, since it can exacerbate the substitution effects between the corrected prices and all the others, widening the misallocation of resources. The perfect in particular circumstances can actually be the enemy of the general good. We could, for example, unilaterally decide to limit territorial carbon emissions in, say, the UK (we have), but having fixed our carbon markets and emissions accordingly, we could make global warming worse by the incentive thereby created to buy imports rather than produce at home. This is a classic example of the second best,[5] and it helps to explain

in J.R. Hicks (1939), *Value and Capital: An Inquiry into Some Fundamental Principles of Economic Theory*, Oxford: Clarendon Press.

[4] On the second best, see the classic paper: R.H. Lipsey and K. Lancaster (1956), 'The General Theory of Second Best', *Review of Economic Studies*, 24(1), 11–32.

[5] This is why unilateral carbon pricing requires a carbon border adjustment mechanism. See Helm, *Net Zero*, pp. 120–4; and D. Helm, C. Hepburn and G. Ruta (2012), 'Trade, Climate Change, and the Political Game Theory of Border Carbon Adjustments', *Oxford Review of Economic Policy*, 28(2), 368–94.

why, despite all the efforts in the UK (and the EU), raising the cost of unilateral territorial carbon emissions has not limited the growth of carbon concentration in the atmosphere. It may have even made emissions worse.

The final problem is what to do with the money. Pollution taxes raise revenue, and where the demand is inelastic (demand holds up even as prices rise), potentially the amounts can be large. That is why general taxation goes after fossil fuels and tobacco and alcohol (another second-best problem), and historically has gone after salt. There are two broad approaches: recycle back into general taxation, spending on capital maintenance, health, education, public goods and welfare; or targeted spending on creating substitutes for the non-polluting technologies, such as low-carbon energy. Both options raise the possibility of what is sometimes called the 'double-dividend' from pollution taxation. We will return to this point later on, notably in considering the inflows to the national fund and national dividend.

But before we do, there are a couple of other aspects of the Pigouvian tax approach to note. What the adjustments to include social costs and damages show is that it is only in very special cases that the optimal level of pollution is zero. To an economist, this is pretty obvious, but not to many environmentalists. Human economic activity changes the world from what it would be without humans. Almost everything we do has costs and benefits not only to ourselves but to all the rest of the natural world. Just the act of breathing inhales oxygen and expels carbon dioxide. Only where the impacts have really big detriments – say mercury discharged into a river – is the optimal level of pollution zero. But if it were generally zero, then the human times are pretty much over.

Pigou and his followers, armed with their techniques for estimating marginal social costs and damages, move on to intervening to correct the market failures, by adjusting the prices (though they could regulate these by adjusting the output).[6] Such corrections of market failures are worth doing only if the resultant expected 'government failures', caused by political incentives, corruption,

---

[6] In theory, they could change prices, outputs or regulate rates of return. See D.M. Newbery (1997), 'Rate-of-Return Regulation Versus Price Regulation for Public Utilities', Department of Applied Economics, Cambridge University, www.econ.cam.ac.uk/people-files/emeritus/dmgn/files/palgrave.pdf.

lobbying, imperfect information and capture, are expected to be less than the identified costs of the market failures. They usually are not. Hence, most market failures go unchecked for fear of making matters worse. In the case of externalities, this means that there is, by default, lots of pollution which continues despite being inefficient, on the grounds that government interventions would make things even worse.

The most that can be said for this mainstream market and government failure paradigm is that it is a classification that enables us to look at any market and at least diagnose some of its problems. It points us not only to externalities, but also public goods, monopoly and informational failures. It illustrates that almost all prices are wrong. What it is less good at is working out what to do when there is little prospect of getting the prices right. Intervening depends on whether governments know what they are doing, and that the government intervening is not swayed by lobbying from oil companies, farmers' unions, renewables advocates and indeed lobbyists for every interest affected by interventions. The costly failure of many climate change policies is best explained by climate lobbying. Looking at both market failures and government failures requires that experts do their homework properly. Not surprisingly, those on the left focus on market failures, and are optimistic about governments getting the right answers; those on the right worry more about the failures on the government's side.

A classic recent example can be seen in the cost estimates provided by the UK CCC for the trajectory to net zero in the UK. This is pitched at the (implausibly low) 1 per cent per annum of GDP.[7] How could it cost so little to switch from a carbon-intensive economy (around 80 per cent dependent on fossil fuels) to a low-carbon one in a matter of less than three decades? The answer is that the CCC (and then the Treasury) *assumes* that all the interventions necessary to decarbonise will be perfectly executed. There will be no government failures. Indeed, the Treasury's interim report of its 'Net Zero Review'

[7] Climate Change Committee (2020), 'The Sixth Carbon Budget', December, www.theccc .org.uk/wp-content/uploads/2020/12/The-Sixth-Carbon-Budget-The-UKs-path-to-Net-Zero.pdf; and (2020), 'Building Back Better – Raising the UK's Climate Ambitions for 2035 Will Put Net Zero Within Reach and Change the UK for the Better', 9 December, www.theccc.org.uk/2020/12/09/building-back-better-raising-the-uks-climate-ambitions-for-2035-will-put-net-zero-within-reach-and-change-the-uk-for-the-better/.

has a whole chapter on market failure, and an annex too, but fails to mention government failure *at all*.[8]

To the extent that there are remaining costs, a Keynesian macroeconomics perspective assumes that the spending will increase aggregate demand and hence spur economic growth. Investment, on this analysis, is not a cost, and there is no need to forgo consumption to provide the savings to finance it. None of this is remotely credible. That this is at best naive is demonstrated below in chapter 7 when we come to the macroeconomics framework.

The Alternative – Coase Bargaining

Pigou and the conventional market failure paradigm have not gone unchallenged. An alternative school of thought, associated with the Chicago successors to the Austrians, as staunch defenders of markets and opponents of intervention, offered an ingenious answer to the externality problem: to deny it existed. In a famous paper in 1960, 'The Problem of Social Cost', Chicago school economist Ronald Coase suggested that, if left to themselves, externalities would be internalised by bargaining between the affected parties.[9] If, for example, an upstream chemical plant polluted the river with its effluent, a downstream fish farm would find its output and profits damaged as it faced the costs of cleaning up the pollution. In Coase's bargaining model, the fish farm could bribe the chemical firm not to pollute so much if the chemical firm had the right to pollute, and if the right to clean water lay with the fish farm, it could sue for compensation. The outcome, in the absence of any transaction costs, would be to internalise the pollution between the two parties at the optimal level. It would be the outcome that would have resulted if the two firms had merged together to jointly profit-maximise.

Coase's remarkable paper triggered a focus on property rights, and on the law as the bastion for the guarantee and sacred protection of those rights. It aligned with Robert Nozick's *Anarchy, State, and Utopia*,[10] in which the economic borders of the state are confined to

---

[8] HM Treasury (2020), 'Net Zero Review 2020: Interim Report', December, https://assets.publishing.service.gov.uk/government/uploads/system/uploads/attachment_data/file/1004025/210615_NZR_interim_report_Master_v4.pdf. Its final report is slightly more nuanced.
[9] R. Coase (1960), 'The Problem of Social Cost', *Journal of Law and Economics*, 3, 1–44.
[10] R. Nozick (1974), *Anarchy, State, and Utopia*, Oxford: Basil Blackwell.

the minimum protective state, and it echoed Hayek's *The Constitution of Liberty*. The economic problem, including the environment, became a problem of the law, a matter of making sure that everything is owned by someone and property rights are enforced. In effect, the problem is solved if the environment is fully privatised.

The difficulties that Coase's approach faced mirrored the difficulties the conventional economists had with the theory of perfect competition. It is an argument largely based on assumption, and the assumptions required for Coase's result to hold are so restrictive as to render the outcome of bargaining reaching the optimal level of pollution a very special (utopian) case. Coase assumes zero transaction costs, so that the legal enforcement of the property rights would not need expensive lawyers and judges, just as Adam Smith needs his invisible hand (and the modern version of the general competitive equilibrium needs a costless auctioneer)[11] to make markets work, equating supply and demand. In all these cases, the game is over before it started. The results are in effect just the working out of the assumptions.

As for Pigou, knowledge of the extra environmental marginal costs and damages is often notable by its absence, and the estimates presented are often the result of lobbying and spending on 'expert evidence' by the incumbents. The uncertainty is multifaceted and has a serious time dimension too. Much pollution is diffuse, and the great pollution problems are about regional and global ecosystems, and beyond individual countries' legal systems. The impacts of the pollution tend to show little respect for legal institutional boundaries. Burning the Amazon rainforests might make sense to some Brazilians, and burning coal might appeal to some Chinese, but possibly not to most of the other 8 billion people on the planet as the earth's systems are undermined. The added difficulty of non-marginal environmental systems is that they are not disaggregated in neat, discrete legal property units. Addressing these multiple issues is about bargaining over the whole Amazon system, not specific trees or hectares.

That both Pigou's and Coase's approaches are hamstrung by their assumptions does not of itself render them of no value in

---

[11] An alternative is given in A. Chandler (1977), *The Visible Hand: The Managerial Revolution in American Business*, Cambridge, MA: Belknap Press.

considering how to tackle pollution. Coase makes us concentrate on the rights and duties of ownership, rather than on who owns them. Taken seriously, the environmental, social and governance (ESG) movement – the attempt by shareholders to influence the behaviours of corporates on environmental, social and governance issues – has realised that these rights and duties can be changed. Pigou makes us take pollution taxes seriously.

Coase's approach adds one more challenging implication. For Coase, the distinction between polluter and polluted is irrelevant. It is about who owns the rights. In the Amazon case, the polluted could pay the polluter not to pollute. That indeed is what the Brazilian government continually suggests,[12] demanding to be paid not to cut down more of its rainforest. Other developed countries could pay the Chinese not to burn coal. India argued at COP26 that developed countries should pay for its transition to net zero.

These are all examples where there is no agreed and binding legal framework or enforcement mechanism. It opens up the possible role of the state as proactively defining and newly assigning property rights over environmental assets.[13] For Coase, the crucial point is just that everything should be owned. Ownership is a necessary condition for addressing pollution. Hence, some economist-minded environmentalists have tried to extend ownership to the sea, building on the UN's 1982 Convention on the Law of the Sea, and to divide up and auction everything from fishing quotas to carbon permits and carbon offsets. The remedy for pollution is to privatise environmental assets as much as possible.

Pigouvian taxes also require property rights in a negative form – property obligations and liabilities. To own something is to be responsible for it and assigning responsibility is necessary to designate who should pay the tax to correct Pigou's externalities. Unowned commons cannot be taxed. If nobody owns the open oceans, no one can be held responsible for polluting and then overfishing. They are literally beyond the law.

---

[12] That indeed is what Brazil has proposed. See news reports including www.reuters.com/business/environment/brazil-demand-us-pay-upfront-stalls-deal-save-amazon-forest-2021-04-15/.

[13] See T.H. Tietenberg and L. Lewis (2018), *Environmental and Natural Resource Economics*, London: Routledge.

The Polluter-Pays Principle

For Coase, the reason why there is no distinction between whether it is the polluter or the polluted who should pay is that it is just a matter of who has the property rights at the outset. It is about economic efficiency, and considerations of fairness, responsibility or stewardship have no part to play. Coase does not advocate that the polluter should pay, but rather that property rights should be taken seriously.

Putting aside the ineffectiveness of the Coase approach against the scale of environmental damage and the systems nature of the atmosphere and biodiversity, why then might it be better, both in terms of efficiency but also on wider moral grounds, for the polluter to pay? Why should the polluter-pays principle be universally applied? How might it be effected in the case of Brazil?

There are two separate justifications for the polluter-pays principle: economic and political. The economic case starts with the observation that the price of polluted goods is too low, and hence output will be too high. We consume too much of the polluted goods, and thereby live beyond our environmental means. Add up all this excessive consumption of polluting goods and you get a measure of the aggregate excess consumption over the sustainable consumption growth path. The optimal pollution may not be zero, but if the polluter does not pay then it will be excessive.

If the polluter is paid not to pollute by the polluted then the polluter's income will not be reduced. It will be the same, if the payment equals the cost of reducing the pollution. Output will therefore remain higher than is consistent with the sustainable economy. In the Brazilian example, money will flow to the Brazilian government to offset the loss of income from not cutting down the rainforest. It can then be spent on other activities, many of which might be polluting and the aggregate level of consumption will remain above the sustainable level.

There is also an incentive implication. If the polluter pays a pollution price, this is translated into an incentive for the polluter to seek out less-polluting methods of production or just to lower output. A carbon tax encourages the polluter to switch to less-intensive carbon fuels (gas rather than coal, for example) and wind, solar and nuclear electricity generation, and the higher price reduces the general demand for fossil fuels. The oil company is worse off than it otherwise would have been. Over time, it will be encouraged to first switch away from and then, if the costs are high enough, to exit fossil fuels.

Now consider the Coase possibility of paying the oil company not to pollute. The (perverse) incentive might be to increase pollution to attract a higher price, and the output of oil and gas is unlikely to fall much. In Brazil's case the prospect of being paid not to cut down the rainforest might actually encourage it to increase the rate of destruction in advance. That arguably has been the case since 2014, and after COP26, with a fund being made available to pay polluters to stop chopping down rainforests by 2030.[14] Not surprisingly, since the prospect has been opened up of being paid to protect the Amazon, the rate of destruction recently accelerated. Farmers who similarly face the prospect of being paid not to strip out carbon from the soils, and even better being paid to put it back, might increase the destructive farming methods ex ante. Carbon offsets offset more carbon, the poorer the baseline is. It might pay to trash the soils in advance of being paid to put the carbon back again. There is here a policy asymmetry between polluter and polluted pays. The former avoids the perverse incentive problem; the latter positively encourages perversion.

If the prices are corrected to internalise the pollution, and hence the polluter pays, the competitive economy takes on the challenge of reducing pollution. Entrepreneurs look for new technologies and ways of capturing emissions, for example through carbon capture and storage (CCS) and natural carbon sequestration. That is what even oil companies, faced with carbon prices, are now trying to do, challenged by a plethora of new entrants with new business models. With carbon prices in the EU and the UK rising sharply towards €100 and £100 respectively at the end of 2021, and stabilising after Covid through 2023, these incentives are greatly increased. Ironically given the very different schools of thought, Pigouvian taxes might be the best way of improving the effectiveness of the Austrians' model.

The political case is one of fairness, and making those who harm others pay is a basic requisite of fairness that pervades most legal systems. Again, there is an irony here, given that the Austrians rely so heavily on the law. It turns out that their concept of the law differs markedly from the one that embeds fairness and justice. For Coase and

---

[14] https://ukcop26.org/glasgow-leaders-declaration-on-forests-and-land-use/.

Hayek (and Nozick too), the law is the enforcement of contracts and hence property rights. Fairness and justice demand much more. They do not take the property rights as given.

Fairness and justice are critical parts of social capital. We do not want to pay the criminal protection money in order not to steal or murder. We assign the duty not to harm others a central role in a civilised society. This general legal principle is supported by consideration of capabilities and the interests of the poor. Pollution tends to have its biggest impacts on those worst-off in society. Air pollution damages the lungs of the urban poor most, and hence physically stunts their ability to fully participate in society. Slum dwellers around the world live among the waste, rubbish and sewage of the rich. The Mafia's attitude to pollution and its cannibalisation of waste industries plays out most forcibly on the poor who cannot avoid living with the immediate consequences. The polluter-pays principle, as a reflection of the demands of justice, is therefore a candidate for constitutional protection.

The argument could be extended. The job of the state is to protect and enhance nature as the key system infrastructure, as a core capability for citizens, not only because it is efficient to do so, but also because of fairness and justice considerations. This is a key part of Sen's theory of justice we met in chapter 2. Clean air, clean water and access to nature are essential, and the state should prevent the pollution of air and water, and the destruction of biodiversity, because its prevention aligns with justice to all citizens. Making polluters pay is in consequence an essential function of the state, and one that is very recent, as the world's population has grown and the environment has deteriorated.

Making polluters pay is really radical and would result in radically different prices. This would, in both the conventional and Austrian worlds, transform the environment. Consider how land use might change. In many developed countries farmers are heavily subsidised, and some polluting agricultural methods benefit from these subsidies. Farmers argue that if we want them to reduce fertiliser and pesticide use, protect the carbon in the soils and generally protect nature, we have to pay them to do so. They own the land and hence claim the right to pollute. They demand a Coasian bargain from the taxpayers, and have built very powerful lobbying organisations to hammer this home.

Imagine if the carbon content of fertilisers is taxed, and the biodiversity loss caused by pesticides is charged to the chemical producers. The prices to farmers of fertilisers and pesticides would go up. Imagine, too, if the emissions through carbon loss from the soils and peatlands were taxed at the same rate as emissions from power stations, creating a common price of carbon. Costs would go up, farmers would switch to lower-input technologies, and their pollution of the atmosphere and the damage they inflict on biodiversity would fall too. Because food prices would rise, consumers would have a lower overall level of aggregate consumption.

The shock in both energy and grain prices caused by Russia's invasion of Ukraine and the blockade of the Black Sea ports is a proxy for such pollution taxes in raising energy and food prices, and explains why there need to be supporting policies to protect the poor, disproportionately hit. The increase in energy prices has in turn increased the costs of fertilisers and pesticides and caused a reduction in these inputs. Crops are less fertilised and less heavily sprayed. The increase in the underlying fuel costs is a rough proxy for a carbon tax.

Consider a UK example of how radical the impacts might be. Ceasing farming on some of its most productive land in the peat-rich Fenlands might follow from a carbon pollution price. Even at a low price of carbon, the peat lost, blowing off this land, is so great that when combined with a carbon tax on the fertilisers and the pesticides tax too, the carbon taxation might render some of the agriculture there uneconomic.[15] While almost all of the attention has been on emissions and overwhelmingly on electricity generation, largely to the exclusion of sequestration, a carbon tax would bring transport, heating, trees and soils into play.

Setting Pollution Taxes the Austrian Way

Taxes are just ways of adjusting prices, but the way the taxes are set differs between those, on the one hand, who assume they can

---

[15] See A.R. Graves and J. Morris (2013), 'Restoration of Fenland Peatland under Climate Change', Report to the Adaptation Sub-Committee of the Committee on Climate Change, Cranfield University, Bedford, www.theccc.org.uk/wp-content/uploads/2013/07/Report-for-ASC-project_FINAL-9-July.pdf; and P. Landshoff (2020), 'The State of the Fenland Peat: Why Peatland Loss Is a Serious Challenge and What We Can Do About It', 21 May, www.zero.cam.ac.uk/who-we-are/blog/state-fenland-peat-why-peatland-loss-serious-challenge-and-what-we-can-do-about-it.

calculate precisely what the pollution costs are, following Pigou, and those, on the other, who take uncertainty seriously, following the Austrians, respectively. Conventional economists, following Pigou, try to equate the social marginal costs of reducing emissions with the social marginal damages, coming up with an estimate of the 'right' Pigouvian price. The Austrians doubt that there is a right price because of the central role that uncertainty and lack of a defined future play in their mindset, as discussed in chapter 3. Instead of trying to get the 'right' answer straight away, they could go for an initial tax and see what happens (provided of course they are not seduced by Coase's argument). This is in effect *learning-by-taxing*, experimenting in a fog of uncertainty to learn from the market reaction. The wider the coverage of the tax, the more consistent the learning-by-taxing will be.

In the carbon tax case, the strategies are very different. The Pigouvians try to estimate the social cost of carbon by estimating the marginal damage of carbon emissions, as against the marginal costs of abatement. The Austrians could instead set an arbitrary carbon tax, and let the market then reveal these marginal costs and damages, and then iterate a better approximation that meets the targets.

A third option is to create new property rights in carbon, effectively making it a private good, and then the Coase process of bargaining might work as polluters bought and sold the permits. The advantage of the tax over the permits is that, as the consequences are observed, the tax can be adjusted, whereas adding or reducing the number of permits may prove more difficult.[16] Worse, the political attraction of manipulating the issue and circulation of permits is much less transparent than simply changing the taxes. The permit approach is much more prone to lobbying than taxes are. This difference can be seen in comparing the actual volatile prices in the EU emissions trading scheme (EU ETS) with the smoother price that a carbon tax would yield.[17]

---

[16] See on EU ETS https://ec.europa.eu/clima/eu-action/eu-emissions-trading-system-eu-ets_en; and A.D. Ellerman, V. Valero and A. Zaklan (2015), 'An Analysis of Allowance Banking in the EU ETS', Working Paper, EUI RSCAS, 2015/29, Florence School of Regulation, Climate, https://cadmus.eui.eu/handle/1814/35517.

[17] See graph on EU ETS since its inception: https://tradingeconomics.com/commodity/carbon.

Pollution and the Link to Living beyond Our Means

If, as seems a reasonable assumption, pollution across all major economies, indeed all economies, is excessive, and if this can be reduced by
imposing pollution taxes so that prices fully reflect the environmental
costs, then the aggregate consequence of pricing pollution will be to
reduce demand for pollution-ridden products, and this will add up to
a reduction in total demand. The standard of living will go down, so
that we live within our sustainable means.

The reason why consumption goes down is because we – the
citizens and the consumers – are the ultimate polluters. In the example
above, raising input prices for things like fertilisers, pesticides and fuel
to farmers raises their costs. The farmers are not polluting for their
own sakes, but in response to the incentives they face. They are polluting for us, the consumers. We pay less for the food produced by
the chemical applications, and the reason we pay less is that someone
else – other citizens – ultimately end up on the recipient end of the
pollution from the excess carbon and other emissions. It is easy to
blame the supermarkets for pressing farmers to lower prices, but supermarkets are competing for our business. We buy 2-for-1 bargains, the
cheapest intensively reared chickens and the cheaper imported meat.
Supermarkets can sell only as much organic, high-welfare and low-
environmental-impact meat as we are willing to pay for. The chickens
and the imported meat are cheap because they do not internalise the
pollution costs in their production.

The importance of this point cannot be overestimated. The
polluters are us, the principals, and the oil and gas companies and
the farmers are our agents. When people vote against increases in fuel
taxes and food prices, they are voting to protect their polluting habits
supported by the cheaper food and cheaper petrol and diesel. They are
voting to make other people pay, those immediately affected by the
pollution, and the next generation who will get the climate change.
Not to pay for the pollution we cause is selfish. The consequences of
that excess pollution which the absence of proper pollution prices
causes cannot be escaped. That is one of the main reasons our environment is in a mess.

Some argue that a lower standard of living is not the inevitable result of pollution pricing because there will be revenues from
the taxes and these can be recycled back to consumers, rather than to

governments, who can then spend the money on other things. Consumers will not necessarily be worse off. There can be a substitution effect without an income effect; we are not, on this argument, living beyond our means, but simply consuming the wrong things.

Whilst the spending of environmental taxes offers lots of opportunities, the 'no-worse-off' result is very unlikely for two reasons. The first is that there need to be comprehensive non-polluting substitutes available at an *equivalent* cost. But for much of our economic activities there are few if any substitutes. Consider carbon. It is true that electricity can be generated in low-carbon ways, but at higher costs compared with fossil fuels, despite the claims, primarily by interested parties, to the contrary.[18] Oil, in particular, is an incredibly useful high-energy-density fuel. Although the relative costs are disputed, and indeed may one day be lower,[19] the full costs of intermittent low-density wind and solar power, once all the costs of transmission, distribution, back-up and most importantly the minerals (cobalt, lithium, copper and nickel) are fully factored in (including all the pollution caused by their mining and refining), remain higher.[20] If the demand for electricity is inelastic, then the costs of the final outputs consumed will go up as a result of the pollution taxes. It is a similar case for transport. The carbon tax encourages investment in substitutes, but they take time. If and when substitutes are available *at no extra cost*, then few will pay the tax and the standard of living will hold up. In this nirvana, there are no climate change mitigation costs at all; it costs nothing to switch to net zero technologies, and all the subsidies, regulations and carbon taxes can simply be abolished.

The second reason why the no-worse-off result is unlikely is that the pollution taxes raise money needed to invest in the less-polluting technologies. Restructuring the economy takes time. It requires lots of investment and lots of new ideas and new technologies to bring forward low-carbon alternatives and to reduce their costs.

---

[18] See Helm, *Net Zero*.

[19] See Helm, *Burn Out*. The argument is that, as and when the world decarbonises, the demand for oil will fall, as will its price, as production is concentrated on low-cost resources, such as those in the Middle East. The marginal cost of oil from Saudi Arabia may be as low as $5 a barrel, creating the result that the more successful decarbonisation is, the more competitive the fossil fuels become.

[20] On equivalent firm power auctions, see D. Helm (2017), 'Cost of Energy Review', Independent Review for the Department of Business, Energy and Industrial Strategy, October.

This is what can *in the end* increase the sustainable level of consumption – but not yet. Thinking more generally, and including all the damage done to the biodiversity and other dimensions of nature on top of carbon and other air pollution, leads to the conclusion that the lack of full and proper pollution pricing is one of the main ways our consumption outruns the environmental capacity to cope with it.

In order to meet the conditions for sustainable economic growth, we would need to internalise all the main externalities. This is a primary function of the state, and a grossly neglected one. It adds pollution pricing to the capital maintenance and enhancements of natural capital, and the provision of the core system infrastructures. It further aids the protection and maintenance of the natural capital assets and the natural system infrastructures since it reduces the harm caused by current economic activities. There would be less need for capital maintenance of natural capital assets because there would be less damage. A market economy will be efficient if the assets are maintained and enhanced, if the system infrastructures are in place, and if all environmental externalities are internalised at what would be the right prices.

When environmentalists, like for example James Rebanks,[21] rail against economists and blame them for the environmental damage, driven as they see it by the pursuit of efficiency, they equate efficiency with cost cutting, and they thereby display a deep ignorance about the critical role efficiency plays in protecting and enhancing the environment. Economics is about the allocation of scarce resources. Doing this inefficiently is not good for the environment. It is in fact very bad for both the environment and the people who will have to pay the cost of the pollution.

Polluter Pays in the Absence of Global Enforcement

How can the polluter-pays principle work in the global context? Overcoming pollution between jurisdictions makes Coase bargaining even more difficult, since there is no agreed court to appeal to. Some very limited efforts have been made to shape international agreements, like the Law of the Sea, the UNFCCC and the Convention on Biological Diversity, but none is really enforceable. In the

[21] J. Rebanks (2020), *English Pastoral: An Inheritance*, London: Penguin Books.

Brazilian example, if other countries pay Brazil not to cut down more of the Amazon, how can they be sure that Brazil will stop, and, if it does not, what security for their payments do they have through courts?[22]

Since the two main environmental problems – climate change and biodiversity loss – have global dimensions (and in the case of carbon emissions the problem is completely independent of specific locations), global agreements and treaties depend on each country forgoing the obvious free-rider advantages. Pricing can, however, make an impression on the incentives. It is not possible to force a country to use an international pollution tax, but it can be applied to that part of domestic production that is exported and traded.[23] Suppose the UK and the EU unilaterally impose a carbon tax or an ETS on a territorial production basis but ignore imports. One way in which EU terrestrial emissions can be reduced is by ceasing domestic production and importing instead. That indeed is what has been going on with increased imports of carbon-intensive goods from, in particular, China. If the UK and EU impose a carbon tax or an ETS, and China does not, there is in effect an extra incentive to produce in China as its relative competitiveness will have been improved by the amount of the tax. It is a perverse tax when production and transport from China are more carbon-polluting than production in the EU. It is in effect a pollution subsidy to China in our example.

The answer in this case is to apply the pollution tax to *all goods consumed in the UK and the EU*, regardless of the location of their production, in recognition that it is consumption that is the cause of the pollution, regardless of where it is produced. There would be exemptions if China imposed a carbon tax similar to that in the UK and the EU, and China would be incentivised to do so because it would then keep the tax revenues rather than pay them to the UK Treasury or European Commission. It is an obvious way to extend the pollution tax beyond the borders of a specific country, and thereby engender some further cooperation, without resorting to the ineffective Coase bargaining. There might still be diplomatic pressure where there is multiple and mutual engagement between states, but the payoffs may

[22] See Dasgupta, 'Final Report – The Economics of Biodiversity'.
[23] It could also be made a requirement of a future revised World Trade Organization trade deal.

be sufficient to offset these in other areas. The EU has finally proposed a carbon border adjustment mechanism, making this a live policy option, rather just than a threatened idea.[24]

If fully implemented, citizens of the EU would genuinely no longer be causing climate change if and when they reach net zero. But otherwise, on a carbon territorial production basis, they will still be causing climate change, as they would be in the UK without a border tax. Whilst it is not true, in the words of John Gummer, chairman of the CCC, that 'by reducing emissions produced in the UK to net zero, we also end our contribution to rising global temperatures', it would be true if carbon taxes were applied on a consumption basis, including imports.[25]

Why not Regulate and Prohibit Polluting Activities?

The striking feature of the above discussion about making polluters pay by pricing our pollution is that so far it is not the main way in which public policy has gone. There are very few pollution taxes, and very few assignments of property rights. Instead, the overwhelmingly dominant approach is to use regulation: for the state to define how much pollution is to be allowed, and which things to ban. It reflects our preference not to be explicitly confronted by the costs of the pollution we cause by our consumption with in-your-face taxes.

It is easy to see the appeal of regulation. It provides a sense of certainty, especially when it comes to banning products. It allows experts (economists) to pick the 'right' answer, using cost–benefit analysis. Banning things has a reassuring certainty. The EU has had bans on GMOs, neonicotinoids and a host of chemicals. For others, it sets 'acceptable' limits. Drinking water must not contain more than x amount of a variety of chemicals, bathing beaches must meet a list of minimum conditions and car exhaust emissions must be below specified levels.

---

[24] See European Commission (2021), 'Proposal for a Regulation of the European Parliament and of the Council Establishing a Carbon Border Adjustment Mechanism', COM(2021) 564 final, 14 July; and for the more general argument for border taxes, see Helm, Hepburn and Ruta, 'Trade, Climate Change and the Political Game Theory of Border Carbon Adjustments'.

[25] Climate Change Committee (2019), 'Net Zero: The UK's Contribution to Stopping Climate Change', May, p. 8, www.theccc.org.uk/publication/net-zero-the-uks-contribution-to-stopping-global-warming/.

There are two general objections to this regulatory approach. The first is that it is open to capture by lobbyists and vested interests. The second is that the state is in an informationally very inferior position compared to the market.

The history of capture of regulatory standards is long and detailed. Take two current examples: the proposed ban on the use of peat in horticulture; and the treatment of biomass as a renewable energy. In the peat case, the damage is well known, comprising emissions, the loss of carbon sequestration, biodiversity losses and impacts on water retention and flooding and on water quality,[26] and yet it is widely used in the horticultural sector as a compost and potting material. As we keep repeatedly noticing, lobbying plays a big part: the industry says it is taking voluntary measures, and protests that there are not good substitutes readily available, and many gardeners carry on using it, or buying plants grown in it. Why, if regulation is the preferred route, is this not simply banned in both cases? Why rely on voluntary steps by the polluters? Belatedly, the UK government is going to ban the *domestic* use of peat.[27]

Biomass benefits from considerable subsidies, and there are deep vested interests bent on capturing these subsidies. Take the burning of wood pellets in power stations. The emissions are exempt from carbon taxes and permit requirements, and the burning itself is subsidised. Biomass has been making up over 50 per cent of all claimed renewables in the EU, and its status as being in the renewables class yields considerable economic rents.[28]

The uncertainty leads to decisions that have unintended and unanticipated consequences and reinforces capture by the lobbyists with specific superior information. For example, the regulation of biofuels in the EU has mandated that a proportion be included in fuels for vehicles. The fuel of choice has been made from palm oil, itself

[26] Peat has also been used extensively as a fuel in power generation in Ireland. See www.seai .ie/data-and-insights/seai-statistics/key-statistics/electricity/.

[27] The UK government has recently changed its position on peat. See www.gov.uk/ government/news/sale-of-horticultural-peat-to-be-banned-in-move-to-protect-eng lands-precious-peatlands; and www.wildlifetrusts.org/news/governments-set-low-bar-phase-out-gardeners-use-peat.

[28] The Drax power station in the UK is paid subsidies indexed in real terms through to 2027, for example, equating to just under £1 billion per annum. See graph of the growth of DRAX subsidies over time at https://ember-climate.org/insights/research/subsidies-for-drax-biomass/. Its emissions from burning the pellets are exempt from pollution charges, and these emissions do not count against the net zero target.

produced by clearing existing forests, notably in South East Asia, and sometimes grown on peat soils. The strong regulatory pressure towards diesel rather than petrol because of emissions regulation led to serious unintended public health damage through air pollution, notably in urban areas. Palm oil and diesel are dreadful examples of the perverse impacts of well-intentioned policies.

In the US and the EU, these regulatory rules and their formulation are the outcome of processes conducted by institutions that have an element of transparency, though in the US the environmental administration leads are appointed by each president and hence there is always a key political element. These blemishes pale into insignificance when compared to those in authoritarian regimes. The cases of Russia and China show what happens when regulation is overtly political in the absence of an independent legal system capable of enforcing the law and the constitution. It is no accident that Russia and China have such terrible environmental outcomes.

Better Prices

Prices are the key way in which information about costs is transmitted in an economy. They matter to firms in revealing the costs of inputs to producers, and to consumers in revealing the costs of production. The gap between the two is profit, and it is the possibility of excess profits that motivates entrepreneurs. All compete for prizes. The Austrians are right about this.

Prices are never perfectly right. Economies are riddled with imperfections. They can be improved upon, without trying to perfect them. The most glaring gap in prices is pollution, and if pollution costs are not reflected in prices, the economy will be an unsustainable one. Pricing pollution is a necessary condition for the sustainable economy. The polluter should be made to pay. In the case of renewable natural capital, the prices applied to the services provided by these assets should be set so as to stay well above the thresholds, and indeed above safe limits, to prevent the loss of the benefit, not just now, but in perpetuity. This applies to species, habitats, ecosystems and, of course, to carbon emissions and sequestrations. The gap between the economic efficient outcomes and our unsustainable pollution is consequentially immense.

7 PUBLIC GOODS AND ZERO MARGINAL COSTS

The polluter-pays principle applies because markets do a very poor job on their own in tackling pollution, but it is not sufficient, nor is it a strictly stand-alone problem. Pollution goes through systems. The car pollutes as it drives down the motorway, the coal pollutes as the electricity generated from it goes through the electricity system and the sewage goes through the rivers. All go through the natural systems, directly or indirectly.

These systems will not be well provided without public support. All have their own market failures. Most of them are in part or in whole public goods and natural monopolies. All of them have high fixed and sunk capital costs and low variable costs. For many, the variable costs (the marginal costs) are close to or at zero. There is little or no extra cost for producing an extra unit of output. This is the zero marginal cost problem and all systems need to be designed, supported, maintained and enhanced with this in mind.

Zero marginal cost is nothing new, but is becoming much more pervasive across the economy. It is at the heart of decarbonisation: nuclear and wind and solar are all near-zero marginal cost technologies. The wind and sunshine are free, and the costs of nuclear fuel are trivial compared with the capital costs of building a new nuclear power station. In all these cases, it is the high initial capital investment that dominates the economics, and once built the running costs are relatively small. More generally, digital technologies share this characteristic, and as more and more of the economy becomes digi-talised, with Big Data and AI and in due course probably quantum computing, zero marginal costs are going to become the norm. This is an economic revolution in the making.

Zero marginal cost will define the cost structures of the sustainable economy. There will still be some marginal costs of pollution which require pollution charges, but the maintenance of the systems and their enhancement will need to be funded and financed on the basis of their overwhelmingly fixed capital costs. That presents a whole series of new challenges.

Public Goods

Public goods mean something very precise in economics and it is distinct and different from the public interest. There are many things that are in the public interest but which are not public goods, whereas the provision of public goods is typically in the public interest. Conflating the two sometime suits lobbyists and vested interests. Farming lobbyists, for example, try to reinterpret the new agricultural policy of 'public money for public goods' as meriting subsidies for anything in the public interest, and then conflate the public interest with the interests of farmers. Again, lobbyists obstruct the path to the sustainable economy, in this case erroneously claiming that food, a private market good which is in the public interest to produce, is a public good. Definitions matter if lobbying and capture are to be resisted.

Recall the discussion of the Coase approach to pollution, and his focus on property rights. These are at the centre of the incentive problems in respect of public goods too. Technically, a public good is one which is *non-rival* and *non-excludable*, contrasted with a private good, which is *rival* and *excludable*, and contrasts with an externality, which is *rival* but *non-excludable*. Public goods (and externalities) are a problem of defective property rights. Non-rivalry means that if you consume a good, so can I and everyone else, and at no extra cost (i.e. zero marginal cost), both now and in the future. The classic example is broadcasting: if you watch a film, so can everyone else without harming the quality of your experience. The only way a private business would produce this is if it could exclude you, unless you pay, for example by claiming a copyright enforceable through the courts and controlling your access to a platform to watch it on. Subscription allows all the subscribers to watch or listen at the same time, so Netflix, Spotify and the BBC licence fee do not price each viewing and listening even though they do exclude the non-subscribers. Contrast this with food: it is excludable and rival. If you eat it, I can't; and you and I can be excluded.

The problem with even this broadcasting example of creating excludability to the general service is that it excludes. The optimal amount of the good to produce is that which satisfies *all* the demands, whether or not everyone can pay the subscription or licence fee. Some people will place a very high value on watching and listening. Others less so. But each gets a bit of benefit, and if the aggregate of all these benefits can be delivered without changing the costs of delivery, then price should be equal to zero, the zero marginal cost, for the optimal economic benefit, which happens to be the maximum economic benefit because it costs nothing to deliver to each extra person.[1] Put simply, for the system public goods with zero marginal cost, no one should be excluded and the price should be close to zero, as it is for example in a number of free-to-use services. Where these are primary assets as part of the requirements for the citizens' capabilities to participate in the economy and society, there is a coincidence between the economically efficient outcome and maximising the citizens' capabilities.

These circumstances of zero marginal costs for additional users of the system or service arise in industries with lots of capital fixed and sunk costs, and increasing returns to scale: the average costs per unit fall with each extra unit of output. It is for this reason that public goods tend to natural oligopolies or even pure natural monopolies. Competition can actually be bad: for if there are competing capital structures in place, the average cost goes up. One water and sewerage system, one electricity grid and one motorway system are much more efficient than two or more competing systems.[2] Think of the duplication costs of multiple overlapping fibre networks and electric car charging networks which are currently being encouraged in many countries, compared

---

[1] This is the Samuelson formulation. P.A. Samuelson (1947), *Foundations of Economic Analysis*, Cambridge, MA: Harvard University Press. Formally, Pareto optimality is achieved when the sum of the marginal benefits equals the marginal cost, which is zero, rather than where the marginal benefits equal the marginal cost.

[2] The case of multiple fibre networks turns on whether the cost of additional cable is so cheap as to render these duplication inefficiencies sufficiently small relative to the gains from competition.

with the costs of concentrating on a single integrated fibre and car charging network. For renewable natural capital, there is and can be only one ecosystem.

Modern examples include Amazon, Google and Apple. Putting more stuff, digital or physical, through these platforms does not cost extra, just as putting an extra parcel on a postal delivery van which is making the journey anyway does not add any extra marginal costs. Ideas and knowledge are the ultimate public goods, with open-ended increasing returns to scale in their diffusion and applications.[3] Trust, the key feature of social capital, tends to display similar character-istics. A generally trust-rich society benefits all, even those criminals who free-ride upon it. Man-made network systems, natural systems and human and social capital all have these non-rival characteristics.

Zero marginal cost does not however mean that the provision of these system public goods is without costs. Quite the contrary. It is just that they are fixed. Someone has to pay, and this is where the funding question becomes central to their provision. If customers are not charged for use, there has to be some other basis for recovering the costs. Average and marginal costs are not the same thing. Marginal costs are those costs that are incurred by adding an extra unit of out-put, *given* the system. Average costs are those that average out the total costs, and hence in the systems where fixed costs dominate, the average cost equals these fixed costs, divided by the number of units of output.

Where there are some elements of variable costs, these can be separated out. *Access to the system* or platform (at zero marginal cost) should be priced at zero, but some *uses of the system* have positive costs, and these might be priced accordingly. For example, in electric-ity, this could be divided into a use of system charge (the fixed element, sometimes called the 'standing charge') and a use charge for energy transmitted through the system networks which will have marginal costs if it is generated from, for example, gas, but not if it is gener-ated from nuclear, solar or wind, which are all technologies with near-zero marginal costs. As, if and when nuclear, solar and wind, all with

---

[3] Romer argues that it is these increasing returns to scale that lead to economic growth, and offset the Marxian view that the rate of profit must fall as scale economies from physi-cal capital are exhausted. See P.M. Romer (1987), 'Growth Based on Increasing Returns to Specialization', *American Economic Review*, 77(2), 56–62. See also C.I. Jones (2019), 'Paul Romer: Ideas, Nonrivalry, and Endogenous Growth', *Scandinavian Journal of Eco-nomics*, 121(3), 859–83.

near-zero marginal costs, increasingly dominate the generation of electricity, so both generation and networks together drive the marginal price to zero, the electricity industry morphs into a capacity system, rather than a commodity market.[4] Since you either are or are not a customer of the system as a whole, you cannot switch. The result is a de facto monopoly, with the important consequence that who pays what contribution to the fixed costs can take account of social justice considerations because no one can escape paying. It is switching between suppliers that inhibits cross-subsidies to poorer customers.

Viewing public goods through the zero marginal cost lens is very different from the perspective of the public interest. It is also distinct from arguing that there are social and other benefits. It may be in the public interest to provide the social benefits of a free healthcare system to all, free of charge, but many areas of healthcare have considerable marginal costs, not least because of the labour involved in operations, treatments and consultations. Each hospital patient adds extra individual costs. These may be provided free of charge because it is widely agreed that, as a matter of social justice, access to these services should depend upon need, not ability to pay. Making the price zero when the marginal cost is not creates problems of excess demand: if healthcare is free at the point of demand, but not zero marginal cost, some form of rationing will typically be required. Queues are the way this is manifest in the UK.

It is important to sort out those bits of the sustainable economy that do and those that don't have zero marginal costs. Some aspects of healthcare do also have public goods characteristics. Examples include vaccination and immunisation, where if the population is fully vaccinated, then herd immunity is created, and all benefit from the reduced risk of infection. It is true that there is the (marginal) cost of each vaccination, but the benefits accrue to all for free, including the unvaccinated.

The ultimate public good is renewable natural capital. Nature provides at zero marginal cost its great bounty. It is not only non-rival and non-excludable now, but potentially forever. Privatisation of nature creates barriers to access for citizens, and private interests should never be allowed to determine the future of natural assets and in particular their ability to reproduce and stay renewable. Campaigns

---

4 See Helm, 'Cost of Energy Review'.

for access to the countryside reflect its public good, and controls over the use (or abuse) of peatlands, moorland and the seas are necessary to prevent harm. Protected areas should be just that: open to citizens now and in the future. What all this tells us is that a purely private market economy cannot meet the requirements of the sustainable economy.

Digitalisation and More Zero Marginal Costs

This gap between private and public will get bigger. Over time, there is likely to be a significant further erosion of marginal costs across the twentieth-century economy we have inherited and which was designed around marginal costs for a range of activities, for two reasons: first, as in the wind, solar and nuclear examples, high marginal cost production may be replaced by low marginal cost production; and, second, because digitalisation is a zero marginal cost driver, changing the very nature of production.

The electricity case illustrates a wider point. The twentieth-century great economic and population expansions were driven by fossil fuels, primarily coal and oil and then nuclear and gas. These all display variable costs, making spot wholesale energy markets impact on the whole economy. It is why, for example, despite an increasing amount of electricity coming from near-zero marginal cost renewables, the price of electricity followed the gas price shock in 2021 through to 2022 and beyond. This is because the gas power stations are the ones we rely upon at the margin to ensure there is enough supply to meet total electricity demand. Gas is the marginal fuel, with marginal costs. But all the rest (nuclear, wind and solar) have no marginal costs, and hence make a windfall profit at citizens' expense when the price of gas shoots up.

As more and more of the economy is digitalised, two overlapping things happen: labour is replaced by capital; and information technologies push and broaden technologies towards zero marginal costs. Consider a couple of examples. Online shopping is an automated process. A virtual shop sets up an IT system, supporting apps and websites. Algorithms do the ordering and accounting, not only fulfilling orders at close to zero marginal cost, but increasingly matching goods and services to people through advertising based on Big Data scraped from multiple past individual decisions and choices. A physical shop has heating, lighting and insurance, and it has shop assistants to deal with individual customers and their payments. The virtual shops and service providers have some remaining positive marginal costs primarily in the messy business of dealing with customers, and it is not surprising that major efforts have gone into replacing the option to call and speak to a human with AI and related chatbot services. It is all about driving out the residual marginal costs. Many customers of multiple products, including those of energy, water and transport utilities, have, as a result, been dealing with chatbots, not people.

A further example is provided by agriculture. Traditionally, farmers worked the land, and gradually farm workers have been replaced by machines. In the UK, cheaper EU labour has been deployed at scale to pick the crops and do other more menial tasks in abattoirs, particularly since the expansion of the EU to include Eastern European countries from 2004 onwards. The shock of BREXIT and the anti-European immigration policies have driven up the cost of labour. (There is always a wage that someone will accept for these tasks; it is just that it turns out to be a lot higher for UK workers than that paid to Eastern Europeans.) The result has been to speed up the digitalisation of farm work, increase the use of robots and add these to the gathering of data-rich mapping and granular digital detail of soils, crops and so on. Farming has always been a fixed-cost business: land is the key factor input. Digitalisation changes the ratio of fixed to variable costs further, with the marginal costs edging down. Even the fertilisers may tend towards lower marginal costs if they are made using zero marginal cost sources of electricity. The marginal costs – the farm workers – are squeezed out.

What these examples illustrate is a major change in the underlying technologies and, in turn, a significant change in the importance of public goods in the sustainable economy. As the new digital technologies proliferate, as everything is gradually digitalised, as the key assets become data, manipulated by AI, as fossil fuels are replaced with near-zero marginal cost nuclear, wind and solar, so the balance of the economy changes, and with this comes a radical shift in production and production costs, and hence in the fundamentals of markets, market design and the role of prices. These two examples give an insight into what is to come. Digitalisation will transform almost all economic activity. The coming of Big Data and AI on the back of the internet will make every sector of the economy have closer to zero marginal costs. The very nature of work changes, as it, too, becomes the application of fixed human capital to an ever-greater sphere of activities. Manual labour, the essence of marginal cost activity, will retreat further. In a fully digital world, it is reduced to a rump of personal services. Even here, it is surprising how much can be done by robots.

The scale of these changes will be made all the greater by new technologies to handle the mass of data. Quantum computing goes beyond digitalisation, utilising the space between the 0 and 1 of conventional computing. It is several orders of magnitude faster and capable of handling vastly more data.[5] The information technology revolution may have only just started.

What this means is that public goods in the sustainable economy of the next generation will move from a series of important cases to the mainstream, and the focus of the economy will be on their provision and the problems of incentivising their creation, investment and maintenance when the optimal (marginal) price is close to zero. This changes the game from just the simple correction of variable pollution charges discussed in the last chapter, to one where the provision of public goods is ever more important, and necessary for the limitation of pollution. Carbon has a marginal cost (howbeit small). The energy systems increasingly will not.

Why Markets Fail to Deliver

This big structural change towards more and more zero marginal cost production of goods and services raises the importance of the incentives, or rather the lack of incentives, for private businesses to produce them. It is here that the monopoly dimension comes in.

If digital technologies tend towards continuingly greater and greater returns to scale, and if the marginal costs are always as a consequence below the falling average costs, marginal cost pricing will result in losses. Where the marginal cost is zero, marginal cost pricing yields no revenue at all. Why, then, would businesses produce these sorts of public goods? How could they possibly recover their costs and make profits?

One answer notable in the broadcasting case, and the digital platforms, is to sell something else. Big Tech and broadcasters take

---

[5] On the potential of quantum computing, see www.imf.org/en/Publications/fandd/issues/2021/09/quantum-computings-possibilitiesand-perils-deodoro.

your data, a by-product of your use of the service. The data is a positive externality you produce; it has a value for other companies who want to exploit the data about your choices to sell you and others something else.[6] Advertising-funded services are rife across the media. You produce your data free of charge to them, at zero marginal cost, and the Big Tech and media companies commoditise it and sell it on at a positive price. The bigger the audience of users, the more valuable the data is in aggregate, and hence scale not only shapes the costs of the platforms themselves, but also the value of the data.

This model tells us that there is an alternative. You could own your data and sell it, thereby capturing the profits from doing so. Behind the quite separate arguments about privacy lies a serious economic issue. To ensure you cannot do this (own your own data and sell it), you are asked to 'consent' to cookies and the site visited can then use your data, free of charge. In return, you get the public good, the network, for free, howbeit the one that produces the greatest by-product value to the provider.

Suppose one day governments legislate to make you the proud owner of your data, and thereby give you the property rights. What could Big Tech do? There are several answers, most of which are common to the other mainstream networks. Big Tech could create a monopoly and impose a user charge. If you want to use the service, even though you are zero marginal cost to the platforms, you have to pay. The monopoly could be protected by all sorts of barriers to entry to prevent others entering the market and bidding down the price towards the marginal cost. It becomes a market in capacity, in the systems and assets, not the marginal use of the system.

When new technologies come along with these network and system properties, there is typically a 'land grab'. Businesses scramble to gain as much market share as possible, hoping to end up with enough market power to impose high enough capacity charges to recover their costs. The great railway boom in the late 1840s is the classic example, and now there is the great land grab in rolling out fibre and car charging networks. Once they can charge you a user charge, the public good becomes a club good. You can be excluded from what is still a non-rival service, and interoperability barriers limit your ability to switch.

---

[6] When nature provides you with the sight of a kingfisher, you capture the image with a camera, and then the photo can be shared and even commoditised.

Winning market power is the prize, but the temptation to exploit a monopoly once created is typically so great as to lead inevitably to government intervention. The systems of the sustainable economy cannot be left in the hands of unregulated private monopolies. With no competitors to check pricing, the incumbent has an incentive to both ramp up the prices and enjoy what Hicks called 'the quiet life'.[7] Profits are maximised by higher prices and lower outputs. Why bother with capital maintenance, why invest in updating systems, when there is nowhere else for their customers to go? Why bother to innovate? Indeed, why not squeeze out potential entrants and rivals to protect existing assets and prevent new technologies rendering them stranded? Even if the profits are very high, any competitor entrant knows that the incumbent could retaliate by lowering its price and since it has a large market share, this is a very credible threat.

The result is suboptimal and there are lots of historical examples where it becomes seriously suboptimal. Why? Because the marginal cost is zero and hence demand that could be satisfied at no extra cost is not being met as the price is pushed up by the monopolist; and because the impact of lower-quality networks and less intervention is felt throughout the economy.

It is not just that there will be an economic loss from the poorer quality itself, but also that the resulting service failures from a poor network are asymmetric in their impacts. If the electricity networks are of excess capacity and hence have greater resilience to shocks, someone has to absorb the extra costs of the extra capacity margin; and it can be spread over the whole population of users. But if these are of poor quality, poorly maintained and underinvested, resultant power cuts have much larger impacts on all. In a context of uncertainty, it pays not only to have too much rather than too little capacity, but higher quality too. This asymmetry is felt on motorways with the costs of traffic jams, and it can be a huge factor in water. A failure of water systems stops much economic activity, whether it comes from failures to provide sufficient capacity in flood defences or failure to over-size water treatment works and water storage facilities.

When it comes to renewable natural capital, it is much better to be comfortably above the thresholds from which the assets can

---

[7] J.R. Hicks (1935), 'Annual Survey of Economic Theory: The Theory of Monopoly', *Econometrica*, 3, 1–20.

reproduce and sustain their populations, than just below. The safe limits give resilience and avoid the risks of the renewables natural capital becoming non-renewable. From the perspective of the sustainable economy, the precautionary principle points to the need to regulate the quality and quantity of the core systems, to have excess rather than deficient supply.

An example that will most likely come to dominate these considerations in the physical networks supporting sustainable economy is the resilience of cyber networks, and in turn their reliance on resilient electricity supplies. The systems are now intimately intertwined. No electricity means no internet and no internet provision can mean no electricity. The costs of a major communications network failure are asymmetrically so much larger than the costs of over-provision. Just a short-term interruption in the payments systems can cause panic and bring much activity to a halt. That is why a cyber-attack is central to any offensive hostile military action. Taking down the electricity system is such a serious threat that in consequence many more businesses are investing in their own stand-alone electricity generation, even if the costs are much higher than reliance on the nationwide system.

The desirability of the resilience that having excess supplies of public goods brings further disincentivises businesses from providing them. Excess supply capacity is an additional pure public good, separable from the public good itself. It is designed to deliver resilience in the face of possible future shocks. If these shocks are not amenable to probabilistic calculation, then in the sustainable economy the level of this provision is a matter for the state. At the level of the planet, it makes little sense to consider these margins for the climate and biodiversity as a matter of cost–benefit analysis. Resilience is, as noted, particularly relevant to the safe limits above the thresholds for renewable natural capital.

In theory, a business could invest in these sorts of excess supply services, but they are unlikely to be sufficient, because the business can capture only some of the costs unless regulation forces someone to pay the full additional costs. If the benefits from over-capacity in fibre, electricity, water and transport are all at zero marginal costs, the classic public goods problem remains.

At the national level, whichever way you look at it, the monopoly route looks the most attractive for the private sector. It represents

the best bet to get the fixed and sunk costs back. It is perhaps no accident that as the digital technologies develop, so too has the concentration of markets, helped by the digitalisation of the financial markets
that in turn assist in the processes of mergers and acquisitions which
help to create and reinforce these monopolies.[8]

The monopoly question arises in both the private and the public sector. Recall that it is generally less efficient to have competing
providers of public goods. Monopoly may throw up problems, but
competition could raise costs. There are essentially two solutions to
the monopoly problem: designate monopolies and regulate them; or
nationalise them.

In theory, the nationalised model shortcuts the choice of output, investment and cost-recovery mechanisms. The state can choose
the output and prices without having to engage in the regulatory games
that the private monopolists might play, and without the asymmetries
of information that come from separating principals (the state) from
agents (the private monopolies). But in practice, there are countervail-
ing inefficiencies on the public sector side. Investment may be constrained by public finances, there may be political lobbying over the
location of investments, and the principal–agent problems do not go
away. The public sector can choose the balance between customer
charges and tax funding, and has the option of providing the services
free of charge, but it does then have to consider the impacts on the
overall national budgets.[9] Either way, the monopolies will need regulating, a task we will return to.

The Coordination Problem in Systems and Infrastructures

The public goods elements considered so far comprise the production
of the good or the service and their regulation, and the excess capacity margins to create and sustain resilience. The sustainable economy
needs both. To these, there is a third element: coordination of the systems and infrastructures.

---

[8] The evidence of recent increasing concentration and associated market power is to be
found in T. Phillipon (2019), *The Great Reversal: How America Gave Up on Free Markets*,
Cambridge, MA: Harvard University Press.

[9] The Labour Party proposal to make broadband free of charge is an interesting case-study.
See Labour Party (2019), 'It's Time for Real Change, Labour Party Manifesto 2019', www
.labour.org.

Coordination is something markets are supposed to be good at. Through prices and markets, supply and demand are brought into equilibrium and goods and services are allocated accordingly. But when it comes to the main system networks, the coordination requires that the prices are right *in each system*, so that they mesh together into the sustainable economy. The electricity networks need to be built in tune with the development of digitalisation, and all the networks need to take account of the common data and communications infrastructure that increasingly supports, and is gradually dominating, all the other networks.

A moment's reflection on the zero marginal cost and the monopoly issues discussed above tells us that network coordination is unlikely to be optimally provided by private markets. Imagine a new business called 'National Coordination plc'. How would it go about its tasks? Who would pay and how would the free-rider incentives be overcome? It is most likely that coordination would be underprovided and ad hoc in its provision, as is witnessed in most countries.

A better way of thinking about coordination is to ask what the objectives are and what the aspects of each system that depend upon the others are. The UK's National Infrastructure Strategy makes a big play of the importance of resilience (as do the parallel plans in the EU and the US), but does not define how much of what sort of resilience is required, who is to decide how much and how it is to be paid for.[10] Resilience gets discussed in the silos of each system, with each system's regulator. Who simulates the impact on all the systems of a series of shocks that might happen? Suppose there is a cyber-attack on the electricity grid? How is this taken into account by the water sector and the water regulator? Suppose there is a heatwave or a drought? Or a pandemic? Suppose critical upstream natural capital is damaged by land clearance? How are the resulting flooding risks to be taken into account?

These examples illustrate a central point: the sustainable state needs a systems plan, and this is a role for the state not the private monopolies. The plan needs to be supported by an institutional structure. Someone has to be in charge. It can't be simply left to Austrian

---

[10] HM Treasury (2020), 'National Infrastructure Strategy: Fairer, Faster, Greener', November, https://assets.publishing.service.gov.uk/government/uploads/system/uploads/attach ment_data/file/938539/NIS_Report_Web_Accessible.pdf.

economics-style competition. In chapter 9, it is proposed that this is a role for a system operator with a system plan on the basis of system regulation.

A plan has to prioritise and focus on the primary public goods. Some public goods are more important than others, and the sustainable economy will be one that ensures that the main ones are delivered before worrying about the minor ones. Which ones really matter?

The answer is framed in terms of the assets that are required for citizens and businesses to flourish, and the ones through which much of the economy flows. We can try to work out some core principles to distinguish between them, but a more pragmatic approach starts with those that are definitely inside the boundary, before moving to the outer rings. To achieve the provision of just these, and their capital maintenance, would be a major first step.

They include the primary or core assets identified in the capabilities and citizens' approach set out in chapter 2, supporting the capitals identified in chapter 4. For citizens to flourish, they need energy, water, transport and communications, and they need renewable natural capital. They need human capital and social capital. They also need health and education assets, though not all of these are public goods. These are the primary assets. No citizen and no business can thrive without them.

That is the easy bit. The next question is harder: how much of each public good is required? We could resort to principles and sophisticated technical arguments, but as we have already seen cost–benefit analysis will not sort this out (because they are systems rather than discrete projects) and there are no *practical* economic tools for working out optimal public goods and optimal systems that provide them, other than saying that they should be large enough to incorporate all the demands and be resilient against shocks, subject to the overall resources available.

A pragmatic approach is the best place to start. On energy, it is a system capable of providing each citizen with the capacity that makes system access possible and a resilience that limits the chances of an interruption. It would have been helpful to have built in some resilience to Russia choking off gas supplies to Europe. The affordability crisis in 2022 demonstrated just how big the asymmetry between a resilient energy system and an inadequate one is. Many of the citizens will not be able to pay, and hence funding will have to be a mix of customer and taxpayer charges. On communications, a broadband network with system access is needed so that all citizens can access the basic services in the economy, including banking and education for children.[11] Resilience in the event of a Chinese invasion of Taiwan to interruption in the supply of chips would be a good idea, as well as to the supply of critical minerals from China. On water, clean drinking water and a sewerage system that prevents river water quality falling below a set of minimum standards and addresses storm overflows are essential. Resilience to droughts, flood and storms in the face of climate change is needed. On transport, a road system which facilitates the charging of electric cars and has a low probability of serious congestion, and a rail system which facilitates at least city access (instead of cars) and a supporting bus network are also essential.

In order to provide these systems, there needs to be coordination between them. All of them require a set of assets, and since these core services are likely to be needed for the rest of the century at least, they should be treated as assets-in-perpetuity, as described in chapters 4 and 5. All of them will need capital maintenance to ensure that the services they provide do not deteriorate, and as the bundle of system public goods changes with technological progress, they will need enhancements. All should go into the national balance sheet. All should use the same accounting basis.[12]

The most difficult part of defining the primary public goods and the assets required to deliver them is renewable natural capital, what nature gives us for free at zero marginal cost and which it can carry on delivering for free at zero marginal cost forever. What climate would be best? How much biodiversity is optimal?

Tempting though it might be to try to answer these questions, it is neither theoretically nor practically possible to do so. Nor is it necessary. With the renewable natural capital, we are where we are. As noted, it is not feasible to try to work out whether the concentration of carbon in the atmosphere prior to the Industrial Revolution was optimal. Those who lived through the very cold conditions of the

[11] During the Covid-19 pandemic lockdowns, when children were taught online, it turned out that many were excluded for lack of broadband access.
[12] An example of what happens when different accounting rules are used between gas and electricity networks. Electricity was historical cost; gas used current costs and this affected the location of new gas power stations. See D. Helm (2003), *Energy, the State and the Market: British Energy Policy since 1979*, Oxford: Oxford University Press.

seventeenth century would probably have taken a very different view. Similarly, we noted that, given that we do not even have a good and practical definition of biodiversity, it is impractical to try to work out even the optimal number of species. The reason is obvious: the natural assets all depend on their supporting systems, and defining optimal rainforests or optimal soils is not amenable to analysis unless first the optimal condition of all the other ecosystems is determined. The numerous economics articles and books on optimal public goods are of limited practical relevance.[13]

Given how radically the provision of these public goods would be compared with the status quo, the scale of the challenges to make the economy sustainable is obviously considerable. Public goods are not in a good place now. The provision of these systems of core assets requires a step change from what is currently happening. The renewable natural capital is not being maintained (it is going backwards), the electricity system and the transport charging systems lag the net zero requirements and the mobile, broadband and future networks for the digital economy are only now being created. Drinking water quality is mostly holding up, but the rivers and the sewerage side is grossly inadequate, and water supplies are jeopardised by housebuilding, high consumption and climate change. The global gap between what is needed just to hold the line and what is happening is huge. The academic question of what the optimal public goods systems would look like is just that – academic.

Paying for Public Goods

Given the scale of the challenge, how should public goods be paid for? In theory, if the marginal cost is zero, the price should be zero at the point of use. This means that the revenues required to remunerate the core assets and to pay for the capital maintenance must come as a system charge from some combination of current customers and current taxpayers and future customers and future taxpayers. Pay-as-you-go places the costs of these systems on the current generation. Pay-when-delivered pushes the enhancement costs onto future users.

The public goods problem is, at heart, a problem of the lack of property rights, the non-rivalry and the non-excludability we met

---

[13] C. Jones (2005), 'The Optimal Provision of Goods', chapter 10 in C. Jones (ed.), *Applied Welfare Economics*, Oxford: Oxford University Press.

earlier. We can either try to rectify the failures in the property rights, or the state can step in. In both cases, someone has to pay, and the only option which allows all and anyone to use the systems is one in which there is no *access* charge, and hence no access barriers, and no *user* charges. This is a neat approach: it is economically efficient and it separates out the provision from the revenue-raising. The revenue to cover system costs becomes in the very general sense a taxation question. The non-marginal costs can be a tax on all users on an ability-to-pay basis; a local tax in the case of municipalities and the application of this taxation classification to water and sewerage; or from direct taxation. Having social tariffs for poorer citizens allows for everyone to have access to these systems, and hence provide the capabilities to choose how to live their lives.

Yet this solution of zero access and use charges, and a general capacity charge, is almost never applied. The mainstream approach is to create a property right, and demand that users purchase some sort of licence to access the good or service. There are explicit or implicit licences for road users, for broadcasting, and there are even requirements for access to all but the basic health services in most countries. You pay a licence or subscription fee – a fixed charge – to access broadband. Even planning and other services from local government often come with a fee. Almost all licences collect money. Indeed, that is their primary purpose.

The obvious question is why charge for licences. If the free provision of these services is economically efficient, why do we not pay more tax and then have more public services free of charge? The answer goes to the heart of the sustainable economy. Voters demand more public goods, but also lower taxes. They want to free-ride, and where governments resort to borrowing, pass the costs on to the next generation. It is a well-known incentives problem, to which all sorts of technical solutions have been proposed, all essentially trying to confront us with the cost implications of the public goods we demand. Since we are not prepared to vote for the taxes to pay for these public goods, the second best is to introduce user charges and create licences as property rights. Privatisation is part of this second-best approach, and it has accelerated this shift to user charges. The likely alternative is to have limited or even non-existent public goods. In this regard, it is noticeable that European countries tend to have more and better public goods provision and higher taxes, whereas the US has the opposite.

Rethinking the Provision of Public Goods

Piecemeal charging to meet the systems maintenance and investment requirements has become endemic as the nationalised industries have been disaggregated, dismantled and privatised across many countries since the 1980s. Piecemeal charging is often a consequence of the way competition has been introduced to undermine monopolies, unbundling has taken place, and the emphasis on customer choice has confused the distinction between choosing the services that go through the systems and the impossibility of aggregating individual choices to define 'optimal' systems. Statutory monopolies focused on the delivery of systems have been replaced by the gradual unpeeling of the monopoly activities.

Ironically, as this agenda has unfolded, the state has repeatedly had to step back into a monopoly role, nowhere so obviously as in the case of electricity generation, where, in the UK, it has come full circle back to a CEGB-style central planning role, and across Europe the concept of a central buyer (implicitly or explicitly the state) has re-emerged. The state is the contracting party again, and not the customers of electricity. In water, disconnection ceases to be a legal option if customers do not pay, and large-scale state subsidies of the railways and buses have come back to displace the ambition to make these services rely entirely on user charges. Museum charges have had to be abolished. The great experiment of privatisation, unbundling, liberalisation and user charges has not lived up to the expectations of its proponents, and it is in retreat almost everywhere, and most notably in the UK.

For natural capital, this privatisation agenda has not been a positive one, though much deterioration took place before Margaret Thatcher and Ronald Reagan came along. Natural capital public goods are almost everywhere neglected. That is, after all, why we have environmental crises. There is no evidence that privatisation is improving them.

If the taxpayers are to pay for more of the provision of public goods in the sustainable economy, then it matters which taxpayers make what contributions. If users are to pay fixed charges, then it matters which users make what contributions, given that most of the costs are for fixed capital. The issue of social justice cannot be disentangled from the question of citizens' access to these public goods. That is the subject of chapter 8.

8 SUSTAINABLE CONSUMPTION, DEFICITS AND DEBT

How much can we sustainably spend? How much can we borrow and for what? What does living within our means actually mean? How far are we adrift, over-spending at the expense of the next generation?

The balance sheet approach to national accounts shapes the answers. The rules are that debt should be incurred only where it enhances the assets, and that otherwise the sustainable economy should be on a pay-as-you-go basis after the application of the polluter-pays principle. We can spend the surplus from taxation after paying for the capital maintenance of the core system assets. That way we can look the next generation in the eye and ensure that their capabilities will not be impaired by our excessive consumption.

To some, these may seem like very old-fashioned Victorian ideas and they are anathema to conventional modern economics, and to Keynesian macroeconomics in particular. The concept of sustainable consumption faces a formidable mainstream challenge. Keynesians do not follow a capital maintenance rule because there is no account for capital maintenance. To Keynesians it is all just spending, and part of aggregate demand. Far from curtailing spending to the sustainable path, Keynesians' aim is to maximise aggregate demand up to the full capacity of the economy, and indeed Keynesians expect higher demand to cause more capacity to come on stream. Spending is generally a 'good thing', and the worry for Keynesian economists comes when the news headlines are all about falling retail sales. When this happens, the policy response is to find new ways of boosting back that spending, for example by increasing government spending. Cut taxes, increase spending, cut interest rates, all to get growth going again. This should give all those environmentalists who see this as the way to lots of environmental spending and borrowing, resulting in extra 'green growth', pause for thought. Many Keynesians now exacerbate our problems: they encourage debt to fund current consumption, encouraging consumption beyond our sustainable means. Environmental concern and Keynesian economic policies don't generally mix.

There are deep philosophical undercurrents to what is presented as the technical economic argument, as science rather than political economy. Keynes's focus on consumption was always more than a piece of economic theory. It had much deeper roots, and it has become entrenched in the paradigm of a consumer-led economy. The idea that consumption has to be limited, that it can sometimes even be bad, and that in particular it can exceed the capacity of the environment to cope, were not concerns for Keynes. He was a prisoner of his times, as we all are. His economics was part of the rebellion against all things Victorian. Keynes, Lytton Strachey and the Cambridge Apostles rejected the moral strictures, and especially the moral constraints, of their parents' generation.[1] Keynesian economics is best viewed through the lens of the Bloomsbury Group and the rejection of the broader Victorian outlook.[2] Its validity ultimately depends upon the assumption that the Victorians were generally wrong about the virtues of thrift and savings, the fear of debt and the constraints they tried to live within.

We live in a Keynesian world, one that is incompatible with the sustainable economy. Keynesians have achieved this mainstream status for two reasons: first, they have a theory, taught in all the main universities, dressed up as science, which dominates economics; and second, it gives the politicians we elect a free pass to pander to our preference for more spending and less taxes, even if this means borrowing from

[1] See R. Skidelsky (2010), *Keynes: The Return of the Master*, vol. 1, chapters 1–3, London: Penguin Books.
[2] For a general review, see L. Edel (1979), *Bloomsbury: A House of Lions*, London: The Hogarth Press. The classic anti-Victorian statement is L. Strachey (1918), *Eminent Victorians*, London: Chatto & Windus. See also P. Levy (1975), 'The Bloomsbury Group', chapter 8 in M. Keynes (ed.), *Essays on John Maynard Keynes*, Cambridge: Cambridge University Press.

the next generation. Boris Johnson expressed it succinctly: 'My policy on cake is pro having it and pro eating it.'[3]

The consequences have been far from happy. The last twenty-five years of this Keynesianism have produced asset bubbles, including housing and land price bubbles, a global financial crisis and a Covid-induced expansion of debt, an increase of another 40ppm in the carbon concentration in the atmosphere, and an acceleration in the destruction of major ecosystems and the biodiversity they had been home to. The environment cannot stand more of the same.

Like most paradigms that become conventional wisdoms, the origins of today's Keynesians lay with very different problems, and it has morphed from being a solution to unemployment in the 1930s to being the answer to boosting economic growth. The context was that wages failed to adjust to the weakened economic circumstances in the post-First World War period that the British economy found itself in, and there was a slump followed by the Great Depression.

In order to puncture the current enthusiasms for Keynesian policies, let me take you back to what may seem a very academic debate about sticky wages and inflexible labour markets. Bear with me, as it turns out to have a major consequence for the sustainable economy and creates a very special difficulty about the transition to the sustainable economy and how to avoid a deep economic recession and unemployment if consumption is reduced back onto the sustainable path. We need to work out how consumption can fall back to the sustainable level without triggering a major recession.

Bear in mind too that sticky wages are just another way of saying that we resist any attempts to make us live within our means if it makes us worse off. We always want more income and resist the pressure to make us pay for the costs of great shocks like the Covid pandemic and the costs of addressing climate change and biodiversity loss. This includes not just workers, but pensioners too. At issue are the very different theories about how the labour market works, with profound consequences for designing social justice into the sustainable economy, and the role of investment and savings, and how much the current generation should set aside spending for savings to repair and enhance the primary assets.

---

[3] L. Barber, 'No More Mr Nice Guy', interview with Boris Johnson in *The Guardian*, 19 October 2008, www.theguardian.com/culture/2008/oct/19/boris-london.

The Victorians and the 'Classical' Theory

Analogous to how the sustainable economy is developed as a reaction to the Keynesian models that it challenges, and as the major environmental problems of our age replace those that Keynes focused on, Keynesian theory was developed in reaction to and rejection of what went before, the so-called classical theory and conventional wisdoms of the Victorians underlying it.

Classical economics had very much a supply-side approach to the economy and it built upon the central idea of Adam Smith, that a decentralised economy, left to its own devices, with each of us self-interestedly pursuing our own utility, could be the best way to organise an economy. This fitted with Smith's deep scepticism about the corruption of government and the drag of its spending on the economy. It was at the time, and still is, a very radical idea – that the best way to organise an economy and a society is for each to pursue their own interests, rather than cooperate. Self-interest becomes a virtue, not a vice, as long as it is tempered by competition. Given this, the policies the Victorians subsequently trumpeted – the nightwatchman minimalist state, and free trade – would be amongst the best ways to organise an economy.

There is no role for proactive macroeconomics. Money has no real function over and above its role as a means of exchange and a store of value, and could be treated as one of many goods, with a supply, a demand and a price (the interest rate). It has no significant general effects on the economy, as all markets clear all the time. Money, credit and banking are bit-part players, facilitating not shaping the real economy. They are useful servants, but nothing more.

In this perfect theoretical world, refined and developed by economists in the nineteenth and early twentieth centuries around utility and marginal analysis, involuntary unemployment does not exist; wages equal the marginal product of labour, so that the labour market clears. If wages are too high, or just sticky, the unemployment that results is voluntary; if workers want a job, they have the option of accepting lower wages. Unemployment is a supply-side problem, caused by market failure, and in particular by attempts by trades unions to raise wages above their marginal products. Striking railway staff destroy railway jobs. Zero-hours contracts create employment. Minimum and living wages are the way to destroy jobs.

The rules of the game of this older classical economics tradition were: savings equal investment, and Say's Law, which states that supply creates its own demand.[4] The classical economists like Smith, Marx and Mill viewed the economy as a supply-side exercise in combining the fixed factor of production – land – with the variable factor – labour (treating capital as embodied labour). This is how they got to the labour theory of value. More labour meant more economic output. More land, for example the discovery of North America and the gradual development of colonies, temporarily relieved the constraint of the fixed factor. But ultimately no one is making more land and, following Thomas Malthus, more labour would be checked by limits on food supplies. For Malthus, population increased geometrically, whilst food production increased arithmetically. It would all end up in a stationary state, whether Marx's communist utopia or Malthus's hell on earth as reflected in the Irish potato famine in the mid-nineteenth century.[5] The bit missed by the classical economists, and surprisingly by Adam Smith, whose *Wealth of Nations* was published in 1776 just as the Industrial Revolution was getting going, was the impact of technical progress, opening up the prospects for growth in both food supplies and industrial output rather than a stationary state of affairs.[6]

What could possibly go wrong? The answer for many Victorians of Adam Smith's persuasion came when the state interfered too much with the normal operation of markets, straying beyond its nightwatchman's role. Worse, organised labour, with socialism as its motivating political theory, would, by driving up wages and reducing hours, drive a wedge between the costs of labour and its productivity.

The macroeconomic theory challenge, to the extent that there was one, was to explain the trade cycles that bedevilled the nineteenth-century economy, and how investment could first run ahead and then be too little to maintain a steady growth path. There might be irrational exuberance, later highlighted by Joseph Schumpeter and the

---

[4] J.B. Say (1803), *A Treatise on Political Economy*. See also T. Sowell (1972), *Say's Law: An Historical Analysis*, Princeton: Princeton University Press; and D.P. O'Brien (1975), *The Classical Economists*, Oxford: Clarendon Press, especially pp. 159–62.

[5] K. Marx and F. Engels (1848), 'The Communist Manifesto', in K. Marx (1969), *Karl Marx and Fredrick Engels: Selected Works*, vol. 1, Moscow: Progress Publishers, pp. 98–137; T.R. Malthus (1798), *An Essay on the Principle of Population as It Affects the Future Improvement of Society, With Remarks on the Speculations of Mr. Godwin, M. Condorcet and Other Writers*, London: J. Johnson.

[6] Smith, *An Inquiry into the Nature and Causes of the Wealth of Nations*.

Austrian economists, and there might be an excessive expansion in credit-fuelled booms. Both irrational exuberance and credit needed to be carefully constrained, and the stability of the currency and the Gold Standard disciplined the market players and especially speculators. Get credit right, if necessary by manipulating the bank rate (the interest rate), and that was about as far as the state should interfere. (For most of the nineteenth century, there was no inflation, arguably because of the Gold Standard.) A good dose of the Victorian values might insulate those exposed to the cycle since they would have saved for such rainy days.

Growth itself was explained by increases in population and fluctuations in agricultural output at the mercy of weather, itself some thought was partly explained by sunspots, which were believed to influence agriculture output, and later, by changes in technology.[7] Classical economists opposed trade restrictions, and were vehemently opposed to mercantile protection, particularly from Smith onwards, persuaded by David Ricardo's theory of comparative advantage. Abolishing the Corn Laws had centre stage in their ambitions.

As the realities of the unemployment in the 1920s and 1930s sunk in, it would be a mistake to think this classical theory was dead and buried. Keynes moved on from his concerns in the 1920s about the Gold Standard (which he had supported, albeit at a lower exchange rate) and manipulating the bank rate, and looked for further levers to tackle mass unemployment. In doing so, he naturally focused on the labour market (unemployment was the problem) and considered how to tackle the stickiness of wages. He defined himself in opposition to those who thought the solution lay in cutting wages, which, his opponents claimed, would have recognised that the costs of the First World War had made the country worse off (a bit like Covid now) and improved its competitiveness in the context of a fixed exchange rate.

---

[7] William Jevons investigated the link between sunspots and agricultural output, and hence the business cycle. See S. Peart (1991), 'Sunspots and Expectations: W. S. Jevons's Theory of Economic Fluctuations', *Journal of the History of Economic Thought*, 13(2), 243–65. Robert Solow famously said: 'You can see the computer age everywhere but in the productivity statistics.' This became known as 'the Solow Paradox'. R.M. Solow (1987), 'We'd Better Watch Out', book review, *New York Times*, 12 July, p. 36. For a sceptical view about the prospects for technology-led growth, see R.J. Gordon (2016), *The Rise and Fall of American Growth: The U.S. Standard of Living since the Civil War*, Princeton: Princeton University Press.

Keynesian Policies

Keynes's general theory was less general and less revolutionary than he and his followers claimed. It was more an evolution on fast-moving theoretical and practical grounds.[8] But it was a revolution in economic *policy*. What Keynes eventually did was to shift the lens through which the economy was viewed. He switched from the supply side of the classics and the Victorians to the demand side. He made aggregate demand the key variable and the central focus of policy. Demand created its own supply, not Say's supply creating its own demand. This was new, radical and different.

Keynes took the world as he found it as largely given and that included much of the supply side. He had limited interest in industry (despite the various commissions he sat on). On the cotton industry and his involvement with the famous Liberal 'Yellow Book', and with Lloyd George's various policy initiatives, Keynes saw large industries as essentially corporatist and more like extensions of the state. He viewed management as needing to move towards a wider public interest perspective. With an academic's distain for commerce, he thought that most of the captains of industry were at best average, if not often stupid. Keynes saw no prospect of lowering wages: they were sticky and they would remain sticky, whether they were sustainable or not. Workers were not willing to reduce their consumption, as they are unwilling to do so now, and if wages were cut, he saw a vicious circle of falling demand and hence even higher unemployment. Consumption had a floor, regardless of whether it was sustainable. Breaking through that floor risked causing a depression.

There were two main interpretations of Keynes's 'general' theory that emerged following its publication, both focused on sticky wages. The first was the attempt, pursued ever since, to give Keynes's theory conventional, mainstream legs, less a revolution in economic theory as Keynes had claimed. Don Patinkin's famous restatement in

---

[8] The classical theory Keynes had in mind was all about money, interest, credit, savings and investment, and he had the banking system and the setting of interest rates very much to the fore. Many 'classics' like Knut Wicksell did too. See K. Wicksell (1907), 'The Influence of the Rate of Interest on Prices', *Economic Journal*, 17(66), 213–20. Keynes's theory turned out to be much more of an evolution from theirs, not the theoretical revolution he and his followers claimed. His *Treatise on Money* preceded the *General Theory*, and carried on a long tradition. J.M. Keynes (1930), *A Treatise on Money*, London: Macmillan. Keynes was as much a prisoner of defunct economists of the past as his interlocutors.

Money, Interest, and Prices,[9] as well as Paul Samuelson's exposition in his *Foundations*,[10] took the guts out of Keynes's theory, rendering it a special case of the general equilibrium construction. That special case was to add wage rigidity into the labour market model, and show how this could lead to unemployment. Essentially, the special case was the market failure of wage adjustment, caused by either money illusion (confusing real and nominal wages) or union monopoly power. This approach of trying to provide microeconomic foundations carries on today. The 'consensus' new Keynesian models are of this variety, as was the new classical synthesis of the 1980s.[11]

A less-noticed interpretation, and one very relevant to our concern with the sustainable economy, was provided by Hicks (which went beyond the IS–LM model for which he is famous). With hindsight in 1955, he wrote that 'it is hardly an exaggeration to say that instead of being on a Gold Standard, we are on a Labour Standard'.[12] In effect, the economy, and money and credit in particular, had to adjust to the *given* wages. We might today rewrite this as the claim that environmental policy needs to adjust to given consumption, with the environment a luxury good, affordable in good times, but not for example when the cost of living and energy prices are rising, as in 2021 and 2022.

This idea can be generalised. If workers decide what their wages are going to be, and hence demand a particular standard of living, this can be accommodated in two ways. There could be redistribution from the rich to the workers and from capital to labour. Labour could get more of the national income at the expense of profits.[13] The alternative is that this ex ante *nominal* Labour Standard is adjusted in real terms by inflation and devaluation, so that real wages are not given. In other words, something else has to give to deliver full employment, and the answer is indirect, but really a version of the old theory that wages are

---

[9] D. Patinkin (1965), *Money, Interest, and Prices: An Integration of Monetary and Value Theory*, New York: Harper & Row.

[10] Samuelson, *Foundations of Economic Analysis*.

[11] See T.J. Sargent and N. Wallace (1975), '"Rational" Expectations, the Optimal Monetary Instrument, and the Optimal Money Supply Rule', *Journal of Political Economy*, 83(2), 241–54.

[12] J.R. Hicks (1955), 'Economic Foundations of Wage Policy', *Economic Journal*, 65(259), 389–404; and in (1982), *Money, Interest and Wages: Collective Essays on Economic Theory*, vol. III, Oxford: Blackwell, pp. 193–209.

[13] D. Bergholt, F. Furlanetto and N. Maffei-Faccioli (2022), 'The Decline of the Labor Share: New Empirical Evidence', *American Economic Journal: Macroeconomics*, 14(3), 163–98.

driven to their marginal products by competitive forces. On this view, the Labour Standard is an illusion, a money illusion.

It is not hard to see both of these factors at play since the 1920s and 1930s: the UK has been devaluing for 100 years since then, to continually recalibrate the current account of the balance of payments given a declining relative competitiveness, and there have been periods of inflation, notably in the 1970s, the early 1990s and from 2020 onwards. Both force consumers and workers to live within their means. The breakdown of the Bretton Woods architecture in the early 1970s was in response to inflation, and that inflation had the labour troubles of the 1960s behind it, before the Organization of the Petroleum Exporting Countries (OPEC) oil shocks.

In the period after 1990, and particularly after 2000, the coming of zero-hours contracts, cheaper migrant labour and cheaper Chinese goods has been a notable example of enforcing competitive (low) wages, and employment has been high. Having gained wage bargaining power in the 1960s and 1970s, workers lost that power from 1980 onwards, and thereafter capital gained at the expense of labour in national income, with technology encouraging further substitution away from traditional types of work. As minimum wages and living wages are imposed, the inflation option opened up again in the post-coronavirus world and in the face of high private and public debts. QE is just one example of monetising the debts. The inability, post-BREXIT, to hire British butchers, lorry drivers and seasonal agricultural labour reflects an ex ante desire to live beyond the UK's means.

From the Labour Standard to the Consumption Standard

The Labour Standard has a broader context. It could be argued that a democratic voting system will always seek to protect standards of living, and politicians will find it necessary to promise ever-higher consumption. The generalisation of the Labour Standard is what I call the *Consumption Standard*. In the aftermath of the 2000 stock market crash, the subprime crash in 2007/8 and the lockdown crash in 2020, governments strove to underpin consumption by increasing debt and lowering the cost of public, corporate and private borrowing. This was true even in the context of 'austerity'. The government strived to protect voters from the consequences of the shocks that would (and should) otherwise have made them worse off. Voters insisted upon this. It morphed into its modern version, 'cake-ism',[14] with debt underpinning the Consumption Standard.

Of course, the consumers and workers were, and are, in reality worse off, as they will be because of climate change and biodiversity loss, and the consequences of the financial excesses and asset price adjustments that follow. The political trick is to treat consumption as the target, and then to use the macroeconomic instruments to meet it in money (rather than in real) terms. This eventually involves devaluation, inflation and monetarising the debt. The real value of consumption cannot be shielded permanently, unless the debt burden falls on the next generation, breaking the first principle of the sustainable economy. It is not sustainable and hence will not be sustained. Eventually, living beyond our means has to stop, unless the next generation pays for it, and it is limited by environmental damage and inflation. There is no free lunch as the cake-ists claim.

Investment

Concentration on aggregate demand does not automatically lead to higher consumption. Demand equals consumption plus investment for the domestic economy. Keynes (though not modern Keynesians) was at pains to put investment rather than consumption at the heart of his *General Theory* (but not so much his policies), even though (extraordinarily) he had no credible theory of what actually determined investment, and thought that this was about 'animal spirits' and the mindsets of those generally rather stupid businessmen. This is the controversial, some say notorious, chapter 12 of the *General Theory*.[15] It offended mainstream economists because animal spirits did not have a microeconomic utility-maximising underpinning, pointed to a very different (and Austrian) theory of human nature, as discussed in chapter 3, and

---

[14] 'But this strategy shows how we can build back greener, without so much as a hair shirt in sight.' See HM Government (2021), 'Net Zero Strategy: Build Back Greener', October, p. 9.

[15] Keynes wrote: 'Even apart from the instability due to speculation, there is the instability due to the characteristic of human nature that a large proportion of our positive activities depend on spontaneous optimism rather than on a mathematical expectation, whether moral or hedonistic or economic. Most, probably, of our decisions to do something positive, the full consequences of which will be drawn out over many days to come, can only be taken as a result of animal spirits – of a spontaneous urge to action rather than inaction, and not as the outcome of a weighted average of quantitative benefits multiplied by quantitative probabilities.'

sat separately and out of place with the rest of his book. Keynes's continuous engagement with Hayek (his principal theoretical adversary in the great debates of the 1930s) will have informed his views on entrepreneurs and he expressed a lot of sympathy with Hayek on matters of wider political economy.[16] If animal spirits were the ultimate driver of investment, it is hard to see how his theory could drive them forward, or what economic policies could make people more animal-spirited.

Whatever the causes of investment, it is the problem of investment that helps Keynes theoretically explain why the economy once in recession can get stuck in an unemployment equilibrium. This is where his liquidity trap comes in. For Keynes, investment drives (or should drive) savings, not the other way around, as he ascribed to the views of the 'classicals'. The Victorians, in Keynes's caricature, thought savings accumulated to facilitate investment. Whereas the Victorians had triumphed thrift as a moral virtue, Keynes thought that thrift could be the problem. What mattered was how savings translated into investment, and here the issue was the prospect of profits from enterprise and all those animal spirits that profits were supposed to excite. Investment was the pull factor; there was no supply-side push. The interest rate was secondary, but the economy would get stuck in unemployment because businesses lost confidence, and held cash balances rather than investing in new enterprises. Once stuck in this liquidity trap, the interest rate would not help much. And wages would not adjust.

The Victorians start with thrift and ethics and then show how virtuous this personal set of values is for the economy. Indeed they went further, with a deep fear of debt, a form of guilt (in German *Schuld* means both debt and guilt – the two are conflated). The prudent Victorians save, and then invest their savings in the family business, government bonds, the new utility bonds and in the emerging joint stock companies. For the Victorians, retained earnings played a key financial role. This money underpinned the great industrial boom, built the railways and facilitated the emerging municipal utilities. It is what built the sewers.

[16] Keynes wrote after reading Hayek's *Road to Serfdom*: 'The voyage has given me the chance to read your book properly', 'In my opinion it is a grand book. We all have the greatest reason to be grateful to you for saying so well what needs so much to be said. You will not expect me to accept quite all the economic dicta in it. But morally and philosophically I find myself in agreement with virtually the whole of it; and not only in agreement with it, but in a deeply moved agreement.' See further N. Wapshott (2011), *Keynes Hayek: The Clash that Defined Modern Economics*, New York: W.W. Norton.

This thrift is forgone consumption. At the heart of this nineteenth-century model is a focus on the long term, as it is for the sustainable economy. It is a model close to that pursued by China since 1980 until the global financial crisis in 2007/8, and Japan until the late 1980s. In these and other great economic transformations (including Germany after the Second World War), the core feature was very high savings. In both China and Japan, this exceeded 30 per cent of GDP for significantly long periods. Consumption was suppressed both by a risk-averse population and the deliberate hand of the governments. The Germans, Japanese and Chinese had good historical reasons for being very personally risk-averse. They were all very thrifty.

In all these cases, the important success factors were first the savings themselves, and then how these savings were channelled into investment. In the case of Germany and Japan, the notionally private banking system played this role; in China, it was the state and state-run financial institutions that did this job. In all three cases, like Victorian Britain, it worked. When it began to fail, Japan and China tried to boost consumption and used Keynesian deficit spending to do so. In Japan's case, this has been a thirty-year failure; in China, the results of trying to boost domestic consumption are just beginning to play out, as its great property bubble collapses. In both cases, declining fertility and eventually declining populations might further undermine the Keynesian policy measures. Fewer workers relative to pensioners is not consistent with maintaining living standards.

Keynes might claim that Victorian success was because there were lots of very profitable investments to make in the Victorian economy, and the savings were the consequence, not the cause of, a virtuous circle encouraging enterprise. Investment begat profits which begat more savings. Yet, if it is enterprise that is the driving force, then the question Keynes might have asked is why the profitable opportunities were so absent in the 1920s and 1930s in Britain. This would have driven him to take seriously the supply side and productivity growth. The opportunities that the new technologies provided were considerable. It was a great age of technical progress. It was not low wages that suppressed demand, but rather the want of enterprise itself and a lack of competitiveness that sticky wages reinforced.[17]

---

[17] This plays into Martin Wiener's theory of decline, and its deep cultural roots. See Wiener, *English Culture and the Decline of the Industrial Spirit, 1850–1980.*

In the late 2010s, increasing the minimum wage and generally rising wages were argued to be a positive contribution to raising productivity, though there was scant evidence to suggest they did much to shift the poor performance. The Uber economy, whilst it lasted, pointed to a more mainstream pre-Keynesian response, as did the flow of migrant labour from Eastern Europe. Both provided cheaper labour. The remarkable fact is that, following the financial crisis in 2007/8, productivity growth stopped, and has remained close to zero ever since, despite the opportunities provided by the current great burst of technical progress.

If Keynes had delved further into the primacy of enterprise,[18] he might have engaged more with the fact that the Victorian model was remarkably successful, helping a very small island and a very small population dominate the global economy and make sterling the global currency. Quite why it was so successful is not a question that Keynes spent much time on, sharing the Bloomsbury general prejudices against all things Victorian.

The UK economy only exceeded the Victorian economic growth performance in the period 1945–70, and arguably for non-Keynesian reasons. In retrospect, the period looks more like a weaker, catch-up version of the German, Japanese, Korean and now Chinese models, not a period when demand management was the key determinant, indeed if at all.

The turn to boosting consumption is a counsel of despair, a dose of short-termism and a belief that it is better that people do something in employment rather than waste their potential on the dole. There is after all so much to be done, and with idle people on tap, there is an essential common-sense argument that the tasks and the people ought to be applied to each other.

An obvious question to ask is: if wages do not fall to clear the labour market and utilise those idle hands, why should government borrowing funding and financing increased government spending work

---

[18] He would probably have fallen back on Sigmund Freud, who was fashionable at the time among Keynes's circle. This is also part of what lies behind the psychological chapter 12 and its 'animal spirits' in the *General Theory*. But if it is an exogenous psychology, or perhaps national culture emerging out of history, and, in Britain's case, the searing experience of the First World War, then it is not clear how society might snap out of doom-and-gloom, other than to go for a bit of hedonism and stop being Victorian. It fits with the general revolt against the perceived strong big stick of Victorian morality.

any better? Keynes's answer (or rather Richard Kahn's answer[19]) was the famous multiplier, a bit of magic that made borrowing and spending now pay for themselves and more. It looked too good to be true. The government could borrow, increase public works, and the resulting spin-offs in increased demand in terms of the spending of wages would lead to secondary and tertiary, and indeed effectively infinite, rounds of demand increases through the economy. Kahn much later remarked there is no obvious reason 'why the multiplier is not infinite'.[20] The resulting higher tax yields would make the stimulus self-financing or better, the purest form of cake-ism.

It was a nirvana that Keynesians returned to after the 2007/8 financial crisis, and again after the Covid-19 lockdowns, and it lurks behind the 'green deals' in the UK, EU and US. Deficits do not matter because debt does not matter, because spending funded by debt would more than pay for itself. It is a magic debt tree. It would all work up to the point where full employment was achieved. But since many Keynesians believed that there is a general underconsumption tendency in modern economies, this mattered less.

Keynes had private investment as the vehicle, but he and the Keynesians slipped to advocating increasing investment in public works, the sort that the Victorian municipalities went for with sewers, water supplies, railways and so on, and in principle compatible with the asset enhancement of the sustainable economy. But as this also took time (not much is genuinely shovel-ready), Keynesians slipped back further to just increasing spending to increase aggregate demand.[21] More consumption had the political merit of improving standards of living now, whereas investment was more long term and hence likely to reap its benefits to voters later. In contrast, Franklin D. Roosevelt's New Deal in the US did have more investment, notably in dams and infrastructures. Later China's great expansion gave preference to investment over consumption, at least initially. After the Second World War, Britain

[19] R. Kahn (1931), 'The Relation of Home Investment to Unemployment', *Economic Journal*, 41(162), 173–98.
[20] R. Kahn (1984), *The Making of the Keynes' General Theory*, Cambridge: Cambridge University Press, pp. 101–2, quoted in R. Skidelsky (1992), *John Maynard Keynes: The Economist as Saviour, 1920–1937*, vol. II, London: Macmillan.
[21] Keynes was a member of the Executive Committee of the Liberal Industrial Inquiry, and its report has become known as the 'Yellow Book'. Keynes was largely responsible for 'Book II: The Organisation of Business'. Liberal Industrial Inquiry (1928), *Britain's Industrial Future, Being the Report of the Liberal Industrial Inquiry of 1928* (the 'Yellow Book'), London: Ernest Benn; second impression, with a foreword by David Steel, 1977.

and Europe suppressed consumption with high taxes to boost the great post-war reconstruction. Keynes himself promoted just such a policy of suppressed, or at least delayed, consumption in his 1940 proposals in *How to Pay for the War* – high tax to fund high war investments, funded by a capital levy after the war ended.[22] All very Chinese.

A further line that Keynes took was on the problem of where the savings went, and in particular into investment outside Britain, as a counterbalance to the then current-account trade surpluses.[23] He wanted these savings to be spent at home, not abroad. Despite his earlier support for free trade, he came to favour home over abroad, another break with the classical economists who were united in their opposition to protectionism. This pool of funds should, he argued, be added to the potential fire power for tackling home unemployment. To the extent that he thought through this dimension of dealing with unemployment, he also favoured population control to limit the work-force,[24] but presumably exporting surplus labour might have done the trick, as it had during the eighteenth and nineteenth centuries, with the Scottish and Irish rural poor, and, in Scotland's case, the Clearances.

It did not take long for the magic of the multiplier to come under attack. One line of attack was expectations, where Keynes escaped one of the biggest holes in his multiplier by focusing only on the short term. He greatly neglected what would much later be called the neo-Ricardian effect and the neo-Ricardian equivalent theory, developed by Robert Barro.[25] If the government borrowed now, might not people expect taxes to be higher tomorrow to pay it back? And if so, might they not reduce their spending now, expecting to be poorer tomorrow to pay the interest and the debt back? Fiscal policy could thereby be rendered impotent. Indeed, it could be worse. Not only would there be unintended consequences of government spending, but the incentives facing government, and its vulnerability to capture by vested interests, would mean that its spending would be inherently less

[22] J.M. Keynes (1940), *How to Pay for the War: A Radical Plan for the Chancellor of the Exchequer*, London: Macmillan.

[23] A current-account deficit reflects a desire to buy more imports than can be paid for by exports, and hence requires foreigners to lend us the money to pay for the excess of imports.

[24] He also thought that the quality of the labour force was a matter of concern, hence his flirtation with and support for euthanasia.

[25] R.J. Barro (1974), 'Are Government Bonds Net Wealth?', *Journal of Political Economy*, 82(6), 1095–117.

efficient than that of the private sector. The public sector would 'crowd out' the private sector, an idea that Smith had made one of the themes of his *Wealth of Nations*.

The public choice literature, and the theory of institutional sclerosis caused by vested interests and the bête noire of the sustainable economy, the lobbyists, set out by Mancur Olson,[26] showed how a less-than-zero-sum game could be created. Just as the multiplier painted a picture of the ripples of more spending increasing output and employment and producing the money to pay for the initial outlay, so expectations contracted the benefits, including expectations of the inefficiency of government spending. There would be even more to pay back in due course. People are rational and they cannot be fooled all the time. They learn and react in a dynamic way. Economic growth would not be cumulatively built on the initial fiscal expansion, and hence the future would not pay for the current spending stimulus. On the contrary, such fiscal deficit funding could make matters worse. 'Going for growth' based on fiscal deficits would actually have the opposite effect and might add to inflation too.

Although there is little evidence that people measure up to the stringent rationality of Barro's theory, especially when it is the next generation who will have to pay back the debt, there developed an empirical analysis of the impacts of fiscal policy which encouraged a deep scepticism. While it became fashionable to argue that the great golden age of economic growth and its associated full employment in the period 1945–70 was the result of applying Keynes's *General Theory*, the facts hardly bear this out. It is not hard to see a general post-war tide lifting all boats, built on sustained investment, underpinned by the profitable opportunities of reconstruction and new technologies. Furthermore, that investment had very important supply-side dimensions: it was centred on rebuilding and expanding the energy industries, roads and housing – all key systems infrastructure assets and all key parts of the sustainable economy. Only later would the UK great white elephants, like Concorde and the AGRs (advanced gas-cooled reactors), start to deliver negative-value public investments. (Most countries have their terrible examples too.)

As noted, and contrary to the Keynesian reinterpretations of history, the post-war path in the UK (and in major European countries

[26] M. Olson (1982), *The Rise and Decline of Nations*, New Haven: Yale University Press.

and the US) was characterised by very high taxation, and the state directing the surplus from consumers garnered by these taxes through to physical infrastructure investment. As electricity demand increased at around 7 per cent for each year of 3 per cent economic growth, the power stations were built on a pay-as-you-go basis going beyond capital maintenance to include enhancements for future benefits, paid for out of current consumption and current tax revenue. There was not much on the consumer side until well into the 1950s and 1960s; people were forced to be savers. Rationing carried on well after the war into the mid-1950s. To claim that this post-war economic growth was achieved by manipulating aggregate demand through government surpluses and deficits has little foundation. It is true that there was a stop–go cycle, and an electoral cycle, but for the UK the ever-present threat to sterling after the devaluation of 1948 repeatedly put the brakes on.

What drove the final nail into the coffin of simple post-Second World War Keynesian remedies was the experience of the 1970s. The UK suffered two years of near 25 per cent inflation, followed by three years of near 10 per cent inflation. It was in effect a massive default on the debt. The very Keynesian fiscal medicine administered by the Edward Heath government in 1972, aiming at 10 per cent GDP growth over three years onwards, fuelled the inflation that followed, as did Arthur Burns's policy of not raising US interest rates as US inflation took off, further exacerbated by the OPEC oil price shocks. By 1976, even the UK's Labour leadership recognised that 'you can't spend your way out of a recession'.[27] It is echoed in the great post-2007/8 financial crisis and pandemic spending of 2020–2.

When the economic crises struck in 2000, 2007/8 and 2020–3, the UK (and eventually the EU) gradually gave up on any semblance of fiscal rectitude. With inflation suppressed in part by Chinese export competition, the shift of emphasis came back to managing the business cycle, just as American economist, Robert Lucas, famously declared that economists had solved the problem of managing cycles (and Gordon Brown famously stated that there would be no more 'boom-and-bust'). By the time that the coronavirus pandemic hit in 2020, it was clear that trying to head off recession with ever-greater fiscal and monetary policy would not usher in higher economic growth or raise the productivity growth much above zero, even if it bought time, and

[27] J. Callaghan (1976), Prime Minister, speech to Labour Party Conference.

up until 2020 it looked like the labour market reforms of the 1980s and 1990s had indeed made the labour market flexible, creating what became known as 'The Great Moderation'. As mentioned, zero-hours contracts were a reflection of labour being priced into employment, and in the UK case large numbers of European immigrants were both absorbed into the labour market and thereby a lid was kept on wages. This was the opposite of Keynes's population control: the UK population started to rise sharply. Labour supply went up, and so did employment. It looked surprisingly as if a greater supply of labour was leading to higher demand for it.

The post-2000 period has also been a period of unprecedented monetary laxity. Negative real interest rates for two decades had never been witnessed in economic history. By mid-2022, the real interest rate in both the UK and the US was around *minus* 6–8 per cent. Negative real interest rates encouraged both a spending boom and a series of asset bubbles, little investment but lots of financial engineering. Had Keynes been around, this would no doubt have attracted his criticism. It was a case of animal spirits in financial markets, rather than the sort of investment he had in mind. That the financial engineering was caused by the monetary policy would not have been wasted on him, and the coming of QE would have reinforced the criticism.

Modern Monetary Theory and the Magic Money Tree

The extreme point of Keynesian (but not Keynes's) policies is reflected in the 'Modern Monetary Theory' (MMT),[28] an approach designed to bolster the case for QE and unlimited fiscal expansion, up to a point of inflation. It is perhaps the greatest general economic policy threat to the sustainable economy, despite its advocates advancing this as a way to pay for decarbonisation. The advocates of MMT share with many Keynesians the assumption that the economy is almost always prone to under-utilisation of capacity, and hence they argued that this inflation point is far off, and more of theoretical than practical concern. It did not take long for this complacency on inflation to prove dangerously wrong.[29]

[28] N.G. Maniw (2020), 'A Skeptic's Guide to Modern Monetary Theory', *AEA Papers and Proceedings*, 110, 141–4.
[29] For a popular version of MMT, see S. Kelton (2021), *The Deficit Myth: How to Build a Better Economy*, London: John Murray.

The idea is simple and one that has beguiled many cash-strapped rulers in the past. It is that it is possible to print an unlimited amount of money in a country's own currency. This is indeed strictly true: there is no limit to QE, whereby the Bank of England and the Federal Reserve and the European Central Bank (ECB) print money to 'buy up' debt issued by the Treasuries (and once the Treasuries stop issuing, buy up private debt as well). The Treasuries keep issuing, and the central banks keeps buying, and the Treasuries then spend the proceeds. By early 2021, the Bank of England had, for example, bought around half of all UK government debt.

MMT goes further: there should be no interest paid on this debt, because it is riskless. This is only true in the sense that central banks 'buy' the debt at a price they choose. Were they to subsequently sell the debt to the market, unless the private financial institutions are compelled to buy it (which MMT advocates might force them to do – exchange controls might do the job), the market will price the risk, and almost certainty at more than zero interest. Indeed it already has.

In earlier times, this would have been called monetarising the debt, or even debasing the currency. It was attractive to the medieval King John and a number of successors, and it has been tried in many countries, including Zimbabwe. The 2020 episode of QE by the Bank of England, the US Federal Reserve and the ECB arguably follows MMT fairly closely. MMT advocates would quarrel only about the amount, and argue that it should be an order of magnitude greater. It is seductive politics too: it breaks free from the usual question about who will pay it back and when, and therefore the consequential eventual tax rises and expenditure cuts. A recent example is the argument for paying for net zero policies with debt, itself financed by QE. It is another example of pure cake-ism.

MMT comes as close as it is possible to get to the idea that debt does not matter, notably when it is held within a country and hence directly challenges our approach to debt in the sustainable economy, as only appropriate to finance asset enhancements. In the MMT world, the debt is owed to the citizens who are themselves the recipients of the spending and the taxpayers who avoid higher taxes. Only overseas lenders need to be repaid. If the real interest rate is zero then there is no net cost. At one leap, governments can spend as much as they like on social care, healthcare, infrastructure projects and indeed widespread industrial subsidies. They can spend an unlimited amount of money on 'green' stuff too. Taxes can be reduced since they are not needed to continue to pay for services because new debt can be issued to pay for them instead at zero cost. At the limit, taxes are not needed.[30] Capital maintenance and capital enhancements to meet our obligations to the next generation can all be easily and costlessly met by printing money. It is the antithesis of our balance sheet rules and the requirements of the sustainable economy. Worse, it helps dig an even deeper environmental hole.

This is a nirvana for those in favour of big government and many environmentalists on the political left, and on the right those like Donald Trump and Liz Truss who want unfunded tax cuts. But, like miracles, it is too good to be true: an economy has to live within its means and the resources it can command. There is a good reason why monetarising debt tends to result in inflation, and using QE to finance government spending and then even to finance the interest on the debt ends in implicit or explicit default. For a relatively small open economy like the UK, if the money markets expect the government to monetarise the debt, the incentive is to switch out of sterling. Where there is also a current-account deficit that needs to be financed, a crisis can quickly develop, with capital inflows falling sharply, as they did in the 1960s and 1970s. The balance of payments can then balance only at a sharply reduced exchange rate, and that in turn means a lower standard of living and imported inflation. Whereas the UK has been gradually devaluing for a century, MMT could induce a full currency crisis. Inflation and devaluation are the likely results. What staved this off in 2020 and 2021 was that all other major countries were doing the same thing. But none of these countries has staved off inflation. The US, EU and UK all experienced rising inflation rates by the end of 2021, and by the second half of 2022 inflation rose to 10 per cent. As with the 1970s, the inflation started and then (in the 1970s) oil prices pushed it up sharply and (in 2022) Russia's invasion of Ukraine kicked up inflation further as oil and gas prices rose.

The External Position

For both conventional Keynesians and MMT theorists, the focus is the nation state considered largely in isolation from the world economy. Keynes accepted that UK industry was sclerotic, in need

---

[30] See Kelton, *The Deficit Myth*, pp. 31–7.

of rationalisation and fundamentally uncompetitive. He just thought there was not much that could be done about this, an attitude some take to the zero productivity growth now. The MMT theorists start (and end) with sovereign currencies. As already noted, by 1930 Keynes was beginning to favour protectionism. The MMT theorists largely neglect the link between the currency and domestic prices and policies.[31] The calls for protectionism are again growing, including amongst environmentalists.

This is just not credible for a small open economy like the UK, which relies on services and on imported manufactured goods, and increasingly on imports of non-renewable natural capital. The trade position matters. With 8 billion people, the world economy is to all intents and purposes a source of unlimited effective demand for goods and services. There is no lack of potential demand, and if there are Keynesian aggregate demand problems, these can be solved by increasing exports and outcompeting imports, as Germany, Japan, Korea and China had done. The central problem for the UK is that home production is not competitive: wages are relatively high, capital equipment dated, the infrastructure is often poor and productivity is stagnant. UK workers want to live beyond their competitive means, as well as beyond their environmental means. UK pensioners want to carry on spending, forcing the young to pay for them. Whereas the US, as a very large economy that trades much less of its GDP, can take a more relaxed view about its trade deficits, and is protected by the global dominance of the dollar, the UK has no such luxury.

It would be better for Keynesians to argue that a *world* slump is a special world situation warranting special short-term world demand-side measures, and admit that the medium-term problem is sorting out productivity, competitiveness and the environment. For the MMT theorists, unlimited monetary easing through the sovereign printing press is a backdoor route to devaluation, unless everyone else is doing it too (again a special circumstance as in the 1930s' protectionism). A falling currency means a lower standard of living and rising prices. It is an enforced return towards a more sustainable consumption path. MMT is not a free lunch. It is a dangerous delusion.

The retreat to protectionism in its various forms is an admission of domestic failure, a temporary bail-out which continues to

---

[31] See again Maniw, 'A Skeptic's Guide to Modern Monetary Theory'.

reinforce that failure. The difference between the Thatcherite position in the 1980s and that of the Keynesians now is in essence that the former attempted to improve productivity as a route to improving competitiveness through supply-side measures. That the Thatcherites failed, despite relaxing exchange controls and positively opening up the UK economy to the shock of foreign competition, reducing the trades union power they inherited and lowering tax rates, is a measure of the scale of the challenge, and it may be that the UK is more content to allow the gradual decline since the British empire in the nineteenth century to continue through a series of punctuated devaluations and bouts of inflation. Not even the temporary boost of North Sea oil and gas could bridge the gap. The seductive argument that BREXIT frees the UK up to engage in proactive industrial policies (meaning subsidies) is itself an admission of competitive failure. In any case, matching the US subsidies in the Inflation Reduction Act (2022), the CHIPS and Science Act (2022) and the Infrastructure Investment and Jobs Act (2021) is not a sensible option for the UK.

Moving on from the Keynesians

The Consumption Standard reflects a desire to maintain living standards whatever the external circumstances, and especially in the context of recessions, external shocks like Covid and inflation. Keynesian economic policies aim to do just this, because maintaining consumption is either thought to be a good thing per se, or because it holds up demand and leads via the multiplier to GDP economic growth.

The Consumption Standard stands in contradiction to the sustainable consumption path, the level of consumption which is consistent with passing on the assets to the next generation in at least as good a state as we inherited them, the first principle. The sustainable consumption path is the path of spending, which is consistent with living within our means, and especially our environmental means.

In criticising the Keynes theory and the Keynesian policies, two glaring problems remain for the sustainable economy: how to ensure full employment; and how to do this in a context that requires an adjustment down from the current Consumption Standard to the sustainable consumption path. This requires social justice, and in the next chapter the key steps are set out: the provision of a USO for the core primary assets to participate in the economy; a return to the flexible labour market, but protected by an element of universal basic income; and a stake in the national dividend. These measures turn out to be even more important as the economy moves towards digitalisation and more zero marginal costs, and capital increasingly replaces labour. The Keynesians have been broadly wrong in their policy recommendations for the twentieth and early twenty-first centuries, except in very short-term responses to very sudden shocks. They have brought us the legacies of debt and inflation, and much environmental damage too. This is true not only in the UK, from which the examples discussed in this chapter are largely drawn, but for most developed and fast-developing countries too. These policies will be even more inappropriate in the twenty-first-century world of digitalisation and the advances in ideas and technologies that will marginalise manual labour even more.

9 SOCIAL JUSTICE

In the transition to the sustainable economy, citizens will have to adjust to a lower level of sustainable consumption from which to build out sustainable economic growth. The level of consumption will go down before it can gradually rise again, to pay for the capital maintenance, the costs of pollution and to save enough to fund the investments. The poor will be particularly hard hit, and the clear implication is that such a transition can be made only in the context of a radical rethink of social justice. If some citizens already find it hard to have the capabilities to fully participate in society and the economy, the transition to the sustainable economy presents a whole new challenge. There can be no sustainable economy without social justice.

That challenge is compounded by the macroeconomics, and the incompatibility of much of the current Keynesian policies with the sustainable economy. If consumption is net of capital maintenance and if debt is only for enhancements to natural and the other capitals, then deficit funding of current spending, negative real interest rates and QE have no place in the sustainable economy. That means getting off the Labour Standard and returning to flexible wages and rethinking minimum and living wages, while at the same time achieving social justice. Social justice must handle flexible wages if we are to get away from the Keynesian policy framework which has done so much harm to the environment.

How to get from here to the sustainable economy, with its hits on consumption, and have flexible wages? The answers are: citizens should have access to the primary assets, through USOs backed up by social tariffs; and citizens should be entitled to an element of universal basic income, tied to the national balance sheet and an annual dividend. With both pillars in place, the sustainable economy sustains both the environment and its citizens.

The Universal Service Obligations

All primary assets carry USOs: access to them has to be provided to each citizen *regardless of that citizen's ability to pay*. It is their right. This does not mean that citizens should not contribute to the costs. This is their obligation. Recall that the four core physical systems and renewable natural capital all have low to zero marginal costs. Recall that if price equals marginal cost, then for many and probably most poorer users, the marginal cost is very close to zero, so charging them zero would be consistent with the marginal cost pricing principle.

The obvious problem we have already encountered is that since marginal cost is below average cost and often zero, there will not be enough total revenue to remunerate the assets. Hence, there either needs to be some people paying more than their marginal costs or the taxpayer makes up the shortfall. Loss-making nationalised industries are an example of this mixed model. The introduction of a fixed capacity charge for system access allows for this element to be raised across the entire customer base.

There is little chance of getting the pricing precisely right, but from the USO perspective the important point is that the poorest are not excluded. With a new system like broadband, where the marginal cost is zero, the challenge is to put in place sufficient capacity to ensure that the system is never congested. Since the overall cost of over-capacity is typically very small, and the costs of deficient networks are substantial, the cost of the excess is not a great burden and can also be made up of a mix of user charges for those who can afford to pay and taxpayer contributions for those who cannot. Like the roads, bridges and railways, once the system is in place, it can last, subject to capital maintenance, for a very long time.

The provision of health and educational USOs is common to most developed countries. The systems of healthcare vary, and user contributions vary too. Even in the UK National Health Service (NHS), users often pay for food and other facilities and conveniences, and the health service benefits from some demand going elsewhere to the private sector as it does in education.[1]

Although, in the case of the internet, energy, water and transport, it is pretty clear what the service comprises, and hence it is not hard to define the USO, it is not so clear-cut in health and education. Some health treatments are excluded from free provision, and some services are rationed. In education, class sizes can often be quite large, and additional support limited. The level of provision in both cases is an important consideration and will vary over time. For example, pupil access to laptops and tablets was not necessary ten years ago, but now these enable a higher level of provision without necessarily deploying as many resources. Such resources proved crucial during the coronavirus lockdowns.

It is no accident that these basic primary assets feature strongly in the design of the broader welfare states constructed after the Second World War across Europe. Even the US, notably with Lyndon B. Johnson's reforms of the 1960s, provides a welfare safety net. To the municipal utilities of the first half of the twentieth century, the post-war added the NHS and free education in the UK in the 1940s, and it nationalised the core infrastructure systems. Electricity and rail were fully nationalised, joining the Post Office, with communications incorporated within it. Although the details varied, the nationalised model was pervasive across Europe until the 1990s, whilst in the US, rate of return regulation of private utilities had somewhat similar consequences. In exchange for monopoly, the USO had to be met.

A critical feature of post-war nationalisation is that not only was ownership transferred from the private sector to the public, but competition was banned. These were statutory monopolies. Users could not shop around and go elsewhere, leaving the nationalised industries to decide how and from whom to recover their costs. The recovery of the average costs was in effect made into a taxation problem. The USO could be applied and there could be widespread cross-subsidies. It made social justice much easier.

For example, the electrification programme was more expensive as the rural and peripheral areas were brought into the system

---

[1] In the UK, 7 per cent of pupils attend private schools, and yet their parents pay taxes that contribute to the funding of state schools. Students widely contribute to university costs.

coverage. It obviously costs more to provide electricity to the tip of Cornwall than to the major cities. In a statutory monopoly, these peripheral areas could be cross-subsidised from the densely populated areas. It is a consideration now with the roll-out of fibre, and it was a key consideration as natural gas replaced town gas.

The rationale comes back to the concept of citizens rather than consumers. Each citizen has a right to participate in the society and to have the chance to reach their potential. Access to these systems needs to be common, even though the costs vary, and prices cannot reflect the full network costs of peripheral connections without many being unable to pay. The extreme example of this is the postal service, where a postage stamp costs the same for the delivery of letters and parcels to the Outer Hebrides, off the west coast of mainland Scotland, as to central London from any location. It needs a monopoly to prevent cherry-picking competitors.[2]

Privatisation had the potential to break down cross-subsidies, especially since the ambition was to combine private ownership with competition, allowing customers to switch supplier. Private suppliers have less interest in poorer and peripheral customers. These customers are more likely to have bad debt records, and, for the supplier, servicing a customer with a smaller value of consumption has the same fixed costs as dealing with bigger customers, and hence reduces the profit margin. Not only did privatisation move from pay-as-you-go to pay-when-delivered, hence shifting the cost of investment onto the next generation, but it also potentially threatened the delivery of the USOs to current customers.

Regulators, challenged on the distributional consequences, suggested that the government should use welfare payments to top up the incomes of the poor, rather than requiring incumbent companies to cross-subsidise.[3] Prices should equal costs in an efficient market. Distributional issues are a matter for government and the welfare system. Furthermore, citizens' inclusivity should be achieved by money rather than goods, and all goods and services should be treated alike. There would then be no special assets or goods; none would be primary. In a liberal and rationalist manner, giving the poor money would leave

---

[2] Debates about 'levelling up' and whether to introduce differentiated pay in the civil service on a regional basis are about common entitlements of citizens within a country.

[3] An early example was the E factor, which the then head of Ofgem, Clare Spottiswoode, argued should be transferred to the taxpayers.

them free to choose, with the implicit assumption that they would behave in the same manner as the educated elite who supported such ideas. They would not spend their limited money on 'booze and fags', fast food and lottery tickets.[4]

Competition is not a problem without solutions, and public ownership is not necessary for the delivery of USOs. But some element of monopoly is. Recall that the core networks remain natural monopolies, and hence their charges can reflect the USOs. They do not need to differentiate by geography, for example.[5] Once the UK government became a central buyer for electricity in the 2010s, by contracting for almost all new generation, these charges became in effect cost pass-throughs from which there is no escape for customers. The central buyer is a monopoly, as well as the networks.

All these central buyer costs, plus those of the network natural monopolies and the growing series of other levies and obligations, have eroded those already limited elements between which customers can switch suppliers and hence competition can drive these sectors. The direction of travel after privatisation has ironically been away from broadening the domain of customer choices and competition, towards a greater role for monopoly charges and cost pass-throughs. Expansion of the competitive domain has been more about competition to provide these monopoly and government-contracted investments and services, and less about retail competition. Where retail competition has been tried, notably in electricity supply, the results have often been bad, and in some cases disastrous. In electricity, UK retail competition ran into serious problems in 2022, with half the suppliers going bust, and with switching grinding to a halt. Domestic retail competition never got off the ground in water, and failed in railways. For all the rhetoric about competition and customer choice, most of the core system utility networks are still monopolies. In broadband and fibre, competition and switching are already very limited.

Even where there is duplication of networks, it is perfectly possible to impose an overall user charge, just as it is possible to apply a tax like value-added tax (VAT). For example, each business customer has

---

[4] George Orwell's *Down and Out in Paris and London* (1933) and *The Road to Wigan Pier* (1937) were attempts to explain to the elites just what being poor was all about.

[5] Economists regularly propose zonal and locational network charging, without taking account of how poverty and access to USOs are geographically distributed. There is a good social reason why network charges often have postage-stamp characteristics.

paid climate levies, and domestic customers share the costs of energy efficiency measures like smart meters. The issue is not the ability to recover these costs, but rather the precise mechanism and in particular the use of system charges. As we shall see later on, by designating system regulators and the system operators, and locating the USO duties with them, cross-subsidies to ensure that the USOs are met can sit in harmony with the otherwise competitive supply of the services that flow through these core system networks.

Other assets that are essential to citizens' capabilities, such as housing and food, have USO characteristics. Local authorities are required to house the homeless. The costs come from local taxation, and local government budgets are topped up by central government. The extent and quality of this housing is one of those boundary issues around the USOs. There is no right answer, but we know what wrong answers look like. A civilised society which treats its citizens fairly will not allow homeless people to live on the street. But when it comes to food, what constitutes the food itself is open to debate. Here, governments have typically opted to provide money rather than goods, although food banks now offer widespread direct provision and could become a USO, and there is much debate about both the level and the content of school meals. Obesity is more prevalent amongst the poor, for both children and adults. Some types of food are more primary than others.[6]

Social Tariffs and Cross-Subsidies

Recovering the costs of the systems under monopoly is a matter of choosing the balance between taxpayers and customers, and between different sorts of customers. What makes the development of social tariffs possible, differentiating between customers, and ensuring social justice for the USOs, is defining some costs as non-switchable.

Amongst the myriad of possible social tariffs, there are fundamental choices to be made. There are two broad types of social

---

[6] The Dimbleby 'National Food Strategy' starts to distinguish 'bad food' and proposes that the state guides choice by taxing sugar. It is not clear whether the rationale is to protect individuals from the consequences to themselves of too much sugar, salt and meat, or to reflect the externality costs to society of the health consequences, in terms of health and productivity. See H. Dimbleby (2021), 'The National Food Strategy: The Plan – An Independent Review for Government', 15 July, www.nationalfoodstrategy.org/.

tariff: charging less to the poorer customers; and providing an initial block of supplies at lower cost to all customers. Most current social tariffs are based upon targeted assistance to particular groups of customers designated as 'poor'. The help to these customers can be provided by lower charges contributing to the network costs, or for specific help in reducing consumption, such as energy and water efficiency. Groups of customers can be exempted altogether (for example, provided with free rail and bus travel), or given discounts (for example to students, elderly and welfare-dependent categories). These costs are recovered from the rest of the customers or taxpayers.

The problems with targeted assistance are multiple. Identifying who is poor requires that poverty is accurately measured, and that those entitled to the extra help actually claim the benefits to which they are entitled. In practice, the identification problem is anything but straightforward. Is it income? What about those with no income but with wealth? Is it age-related? Does the household count or just the individual? Are the number and ages of children relevant as dependants? Is poverty relative or absolute?

All these questions need answers, before we come to the problems that means-related benefits cause to incentives for people to work and accept wages appropriate to their productivity, and who has what access to the data, and how regularly the data is updated. There is also the politicisation of the targeted benefits. Given that in some developed countries (and in China too) the population is ageing, a growing number of voters are either pensioners or soon to become pensioners. Protecting pensions can then trump all the other deserving poor, as older people hog the benefits budgets through both state pensions and aged-related social tariffs.

The universalisation principle that underpins the idea that all citizens are treated equally points to an alternative approach to social tariffs. Instead of trying to identify and target the poor, all citizens could be provided with an initial block of services at a common lower price. This could be managed where the citizens' bills are calculated on the volume of the service they use – how much water and electricity they use, and how many rail and bus journeys they take. The zero marginal cost pricing principle for access would be violated, but, provided the initial block is very low cost, there is a trade-off advantage. If the tariff is fully volume-related then it can be graduated to rise with volume, but the access problem can then get exacerbated.

After the initial block of the USO on a social tariff, the tariff can rise in blocks, and these subsequent blocks can recover not only the rest of the network and monopoly costs, but also the implicit cross-subsidy in the initial social tariff block.

There are other advantages of taking this second route. It is massively simpler to administer, it does not require detailed information on the circumstances of each customer, and there are fewer data protection issues. It leaves incentives largely in place, since the social tariff block is independent of wages and income. In putting citizens rather than consumers in the driving seat, this route keeps faith with the capabilities approach. There will of course be special cases and special needs which will add more complexity back into the charging, but these can be very targeted cases, and leave the bulk of the problem met through the social tariff initial block.

The initial block could be free if the state paid this contribution to the total system network monopoly costs. This would get closer to zero marginal costs access and hence be even better from a capabilities perspective. In effect, the initial block of costs would come from the taxation regime and the better-off would be contributing more even if the tax system was flat rate, as discussed below. From an overall accounting perspective, whether taxpayers or customers pay for this initial block of system costs makes no difference to the economy as a whole. The costs have to be paid. It is just a question of who pays what.

Universal Basic Income

With energy, water, transport and communications, and with natural capital, citizens should have primary assets to draw upon, both now and in the future. The various social tariffs are one method of achieving this. But there is more to a decent life than access to these primary assets. Food, clothes and the ability to access nature and to engage in social life all require money. Although many of these requirements can be mediated through assets, including a sustainable agriculture, sustainable clothing production and materials, and social capital, in practice all developed economies provide for cash payments over and above access to the basic assets. In the presence of both pervasive uncertainty and government failures, there will be lots of incompleteness in mapping the capabilities onto social justice.

The mainstream approach to insufficient money coming in is to direct payments to those in poverty. Some in the liberal tradition regard this as an insurance problem, handling the risk of bad things that might randomly happen to people. This is the route taken by William Beveridge in his famous wartime report, 'Social Insurance and Allied Services',[7] and much earlier in the Bismarck scheme in Germany in the late nineteenth century. Pensions and health insurance schemes are the prime examples.

Beveridge's assumption was that the target was *absolute* poverty, and back in the 1940s he calculated that this would, with reasonable economic growth and his scheme fully implemented, be effectively abolished in a couple of decades. Thereafter, the costs would wither with the problem: people would have enough to eat and the public services would provide the other reliefs to the causes of poverty as economic growth increased incomes. He also had full employment in mind.

Poverty, however, turned out to be not purely absolute in an abstracted way from society, but to have a *relative* element to add to these absolute measures.[8] What counts as being poor depends on what others have, and how the capabilities shift over time. Not having a fridge or even electricity supply in 1900 would not count as evidence of poverty, but it would now.

Whereas for the capability approach it is poverty that counts, for socialists the aim is to reduce inequality. This is a purely relative concept and it could be achieved at any level of absolute poverty. We could all be equally starving. Eliminating inequality blunts the incentives that drive a market economy, and indeed that is the point for those who wish to replace capitalism and the profit motive with socialism and the focus on public duty and service, with the state deciding who gets what and all dependent upon the state. Why would anyone go to work except if instructed by the state?

This incentive issue lay at the heart of the debates between capitalists and socialists in the 1930s and in the Austrian economics we met earlier. The backdrop was the great experiment in Soviet Russia.

---

[7] W. Beveridge (1942), 'Social Insurance and Allied Services', Cmd. 6404. See also J. Harris (1997), *William Beveridge: A Biography*, revised edn, Oxford: Clarendon Press.
[8] A.K. Sen (1983), 'Poor, Relatively Speaking', *Oxford Economic Papers*, 35(2), 153–69; and 'Equality of What?'.

Hayek and the Austrians on one side of the debate, and Oscar Lange[9] and socialist economists on the other, argued out the relative merits of markets versus planning. Hayek was much more concerned with this debate than he was with Keynes and the Keynesians, and his great contribution was his theoretical critique of the Soviet system. This was on two fronts: one about human nature and what motivated people to come up with new ideas and be entrepreneurial; and the other radical uncertainty of the sort discussed in chapter 3. For Hayek, the market had two supreme advantages: it provided incentives for people by opening up the prospect of profits, and it was more informationally efficient than planning. For him, the market enabled freedom, and needed a constitution of liberty to protect it, and it would be more efficient than state planning.

This ruled out socialism (it was bound to fail), but it did not remove the poverty problem and it did not deliver social justice. The Soviet Communist model offered in the post-First World War context an alternative to that of the US, and one with much greater equality. As George Orwell pointed out in his review of Hayek's *Road to Serfdom*,[10] the trouble with competition is that someone wins and someone loses.[11] Hayek and the Austrian school were rather less sympathetic about concerns for the losers. One reason for the lack of sympathy was the link to unemployment and the extent to which state support would undermine the flexibility of wages.[12]

As with the social tariffs, this problem will never go away as long as poverty relief is targeted and explicitly or implicitly means-tested. Why work for a wage below the value of state benefits? It was the reason why so many economists have traditionally opposed a

---

[9] O. Lange (1938), *On the Economic Theory of Socialism*, Minneapolis: University of Minnesota Press.

[10] Orwell, 'George Orwell's Review of Hayek's The Road to Serfdom'.

[11] G. Orwell (1968), *The Collected Essays, Journalism and Letters of George Orwell*, vol. 1, London: Secker and Warburg.

[12] Indeed, one of the reasons Keynes took money wages as fixed was because of unemployment pay. See R. Skidelsky (1983), *John Maynard Keynes: Hopes Betrayed, 1883–1920*, London: Macmillan; R. Skidelsky (1992), *John Maynard Keynes: The Economist as Saviour, 1920–1937*; and R. Skidelsky (2000), *John Maynard Keynes: Fighting for Freedom, 1937–1946*, London: Macmillan. It was a point taken up by Lionel Robbins in the Council of Economic Advisers to Ramsay MacDonald's government in 1930. See S. Howson and D. Winch (1977), *The Economic Advisory Council, 1930–39: A Study in Economic Advice during Depression and Recovery*, Cambridge: Cambridge University Press; and L. Robbins (1934), *The Great Depression*, London: Macmillan.

minimum wage, because it effectively legislates for sticky wages at the bottom of the income distribution, and hence the Labour Standard.

Is there any way to both eliminate poverty *and* avoid blunting the incentives to work and thereby entertain flexible wages whilst generating social justice? One answer is universal basic income, the payment of money *independent* of income to *all* citizens. Basic income is a USO: everyone is entitled to get it, irrespective of other income or wealth.[13] It provides one route to the completion of the provision of basic capabilities to all citizens, providing money rather than goods for those things not already covered by the system infrastructures, healthcare and education.[14] Basic income plus USO access to natural capital and the other core systems provide social justice.

There is of course a snag: the jam is spread across the entire working population, and hence it is very expensive (older people can be covered by state pensions, and children by child benefit).[15] Furthermore, it is also wasteful, in that the billionaires do not need the basic income payment, whereas the poor do. These high costs would be partially offset by the more efficient functioning of the labour market, and in particular the effective abolition of involuntary unemployment, since everyone could choose a job if the wage was low enough to meet their marginal product of labour if they wanted to. All unemployment would be voluntary. Basic income is net of the abolition of all means-tested unemployment benefits. Tax revenues would be higher as a result of employment gains. Wages would be fully flexible. There would be no need for the manipulation of aggregate demand, à la Keynesians, for employment reasons.

Yet, the results would still be expensive, which raises the question of whether there is a modified version of the basic income that might meet these objectives of eliminating poverty whilst maintaining incentives to work.

It is not hard to think of ways to modify basic income, for example by cutting off the top half of the distribution, and therefore

---

[13] The concept has a long history, from Thomas More's *Utopia*, Bertrand Russell, through to a Swiss referendum in 2016. See T. More (1516), *Utopia*. For a more recent exposition, see P. van Parijs and Y. Vanderborght (2017), *Basic Income: A Radical Proposal for a Free Society and a Sane Economy*, Cambridge, MA: Harvard University Press.
[14] Biden's $1,400 helicopter money comes close to this on a one-off basis in 2021.
[15] The furlough support schemes during the Covid-19 pandemic lockdowns gave some taste of what broad employment protection schemes look like.

those for whom the minimum wage would not have been an obstacle to employment. Provided that the basic income is paid to a big enough number to very comfortably clear what would otherwise be the minimum (or living) wage, it would address the work incentive difficulties of the minimum wage and hence make sure that no one had insufficient income in society. Like the social tariffs discussed above, it provides for all citizens to have sufficient to be able to participate in the economy and society. Whilst critics argue that limiting the entitlements to basic income is a move in the direction of means-tested benefits, it remains very different for the bit of the distribution that matters – the poor. And it still radically alters their incentives.

Inequality and the Problem of the Ultra-Rich

If poverty could be abolished though basic income plus USO access to natural and other capitals, and healthcare and education, would there be any reason to worry about inequality? Consider the consequences of not worrying about the difference between an annual income of, say, £50,000, £100,000 and £500,000. If it is poverty and not equality that is the concern, these different annual incomes should not matter.

Consider one radical option to raise the money for the systems access and the modified basic income: a flat single rate for both income and capital gains, set at whatever level reaches the total current spending requirements including capital maintenance. All exemptions and special tax treatments could be abolished, on the grounds that the state is pretty bad at ranking what is more deserving of special treatment, in part because it is so easily captured by tax lobbying. A crude and simple tax system would radically reduce the costs of tax collection and of minimising taxation deadweight costs incurred to accountants and financial advisers. Similarly, the costs of welfare provision under the present means-tested and complex rules of entitlement would be replaced by the single basic income. The cost of administrating welfare payment systems is a significant part of their total budgets, and the cost of tax collection represents a significant percentage of total receipts once the private costs of accountants are also included. The interaction of the two adds yet another layer of costs.[16]

[16] National Audit Office (2017), 'A Short Guide to Department for Work and Pensions', NAO, London; (2017), 'HM Revenue & Customs 2016-17 Accounts', NAO, London.

Under the modified basic income and a flat-rate tax, the very large social security and tax bureaucracies could be radically slimmed down. They would no longer be significant industries in their own right probably in total employing over 1 million people, and hence on a par with the NHS in the UK.[17] Together, this would be an enormous saving which could be diverted to a more generous basic income. The incentives in the economy would be preserved, as the possibility of higher rewards would not be blunted by increasing marginal rates as incomes rise. Modified basic income and radical tax simplification go hand in hand.

Some may argue that the ultra-rich would remain a problem, and that allowing some individuals to own more than the GDP of some small countries is divisive and tends to break social unity. They tend to be ultra-polluters[18] and their detachment from society can undermine social institutions and hence be detrimental to social capital. If these arguments are taken seriously, there are various ways of addressing them while keeping to the broad outline of a flat-rate tax system. There could be a special second rate of higher tax applied to incomes and capital gains over a given threshold. This could, for example, be £500,000. It could be higher, and the higher it is set, the smaller the number of individuals involved. Above £1 million per annum, in the UK there are only a few thousand individuals to consider, out of a population of over 65 million. Similarly, there is a relatively small number of very high-wealth individuals.

There are several options beyond higher marginal tax rates on incomes. One is to address the causes of these high incomes and wealth directly, and in particular executive pay, and set a maximum ratio between the top and bottom paid in an organisation. This might appeal to concepts of fairness and worth, but would inevitably be complex in

[17] The total direct employment comprises 100,000 for the UK Department of Work and Pensions and around 70,000 for HM Revenue and Customs. The total number of accountants in the UK is 380,000. See Financial Reporting Council (2021), 'Key Facts and Trends in the UK Accounting Profession', www.frc.org.uk/getattachment/e976ff38-3597-4779-b192-1be7da79d175/FRC-Key-Facts-Trends-2021.pdf.

[18] For estimates of billionaires' carbon footprints, see R. Wilk and B. Barros (2021), 'Private Planes, Mansions and Superyachts: What Gives Billionaires like Musk and Abramovich such a Massive Carbon Footprint', *The Conversation*, 16 February, https://theconversation.com/private-planes-mansions-and-superyachts-what-gives-billionaires-like-musk-and-abramovich-such-a-massive-carbon-footprint-152514. See also O. Lai (2021), 'Billionaires' Single Space Flight Produces a Lifetime's Worth of Carbon Footprint: Report', 15 December, https://earth.org/billionaires-single-space-flight-produces-a-lifetimes-worth-of-carbon-footprint-report/.

the application and open to widespread evasion. If it is wealth that is the problem above a defined threshold, then a wealth tax is the obvious path to take, supported by a serious inheritance tax. The key point here is that modified basic income, and tax simplification, are not barriers to addressing what might be called *gross* inequality. If the ultra-rich are a threat to social capital, the answer is to address this group head on. A flat-rate tax plus a wealth tax can be very different in social justice terms from just a flat-rate tax.

From the 1980s onwards, several countries experimented with radical simplification, and steps towards the flat-rate approach.[19] The difficulties came both for the obvious political reasons and also because none was radical enough, failing to fully integrate all the various other dimensions of the tax system, notably capital gains tax, and to address the problems of poverty discussed above. Ever since, layer upon layer of complexity have been added back.

Even in the more radical version described above – a basic income for those below a threshold and a flat-rate tax – some further complexity is inevitable in practice. As with social tariffs, there are people with specific individual needs who will require extra support. There are special tax categories for people who live overseas. But the important point is that basic income *starts simple* and allows some *limited* complexities, whereas the existing social security system and the tax regimes *start very complicated*, and tend to get increasingly complex.[20] All of these extra complexities to the flat-rate approach already exist in current tax regimes, so the modified basic income proposal does not make matters worse. Few argue that the complexity that has been added to tax regimes in the last three decades has resulted in a much more equal distribution and poverty has not gone away. The evidence is unambiguously to the contrary. Complex tax regimes have become ever more complicated, and the overall scale of inequality has risen very sharply.

Even with the above modifications, questions remain about the level of the basic income. How high should it be in order to

[19] In the 1980s, Chancellor Nigel Lawson developed a two-rate system for UK income tax, at 20 per cent and 40 per cent with thresholds for each. The Czech Republic introduced a flat-rate 15 per cent on gross income in 2008, but by 2013 a higher rate was added.

[20] There are good political economy reasons for assuming that complexity grows once established in public policy because of rent-seeking, lobbying and capture. See Helm, 'Regulatory Reform, Capture, and the Regulatory Burden'. See also D. Ulph (2014), 'UK Tax System Complexity: Causes and Consequences', *Tax Journal*, 17 December.

abolish poverty (net of the system assets USOs)? How does it relate to the capacity of the economy to pay and hence to a stable sustainable economy?

Basic Income and National Dividends

A basic income is a special type of USO entitlement. It is a claim by citizens on the sustainable economy and its transition to a sustainable consumption path.

The capacity of an economy to support some or all of its citizens depends on how well the economy is doing, and on consumption not being allowed to outstrip that underlying performance. Borrowing from the next generation to support current spending is ruled out. The ultimate constraint is the maximum sustainable level of consumption consistent with the requirement to ensure that systems are passed down to the next generation in a properly maintained form. Given we are living beyond our sustainable means, once pollution charges are added, public goods are provided and assets properly maintained, and the transition via decarbonisation is paid for, the impacts on the poor are going to be considerable. There is no escaping the consequences of living within our sustainable means. The events in energy and food markets in 2022 and the associated 'affordability crisis' gave a taster of how painful this could be.

In the debates of the 1930s, Lionel Robbins argued that unemployment was high because workers demanded wages that failed to reflect the destruction of capital in the First World War. They had, in effect, not come to terms with the diminished circumstances caused by the war, and the need to pay off the debts incurred. UK industry was, in the 1920s and 1930s, uncompetitive; the UK could not pay its way in the world, and the Gold Standard simply made this explicit, rather than being the cause of the underlying problems.

What if this is true now? What if the UK is uncompetitive with Chinese industry, German factories and US tech giants? What if the things that the UK remains good at, like finance and professional services, are a function of hysteresis, a legacy from the past that makes switching elsewhere sticky? Now add in BREXIT, and the placing of the UK's service industries outside the EU and its single market, indeed outside all the major trading blocs around the world. As the major economies move away from open global trading (and especially the US and China, and the EU and China), where exactly will the 'sovereign' UK end up?

And what if the buying-off of recession across the UK, EU member states, the US and China in 2000, 2007/8 and in 2020 through monetary and fiscal stimuli has been an exercise in keeping the standard of living artificially high globally, at the expense of the next generation not just in the UK, but in all these countries? What if the coronavirus pandemic and the lockdowns had real costs which have made us all worse off? All may want a world-class and well-funded health service, a major upgrade of education and the new social care systems, all free of charge at the point of demand, but can we afford them with a balanced budget on the current account after paying for capital maintenance? Is not Robbins's point again highly relevant?

It is not in the immediate interests of the current major beneficiaries of the social security payments to argue for restraint, nor would the poor want to limit basic income payments, since these are a proportionately higher part of their total income. The poor currently have no direct stake in the overall performance of the economy. An obvious remedy is to give them a stake, in the form of a share in the national dividend.[21] This would be more like equity and come with the broader equity incentives. It would be directly tied up with the national balance sheet, and the delivery of the intergenerational requirements, net of capital maintenance.

It could work as follows. The national balance sheet is established as described in chapter 5. It has the assets on one side and the liabilities on the other. The publicly owned assets, which make up most of the national balance sheet, belong ultimately to citizens, as ultimately do the system assets in the regulated utilities. But so too does all the debt. The assets yield a return on the capital employed. The debt interest is subtracted, to give a net return, and this could then be distributed to all the citizens.

To make it simple, let's assume that all the systems are in state hands. The cost of capital would be passed through to the required rate of return, which would reflect equity risk and therefore be above the cost of government bonds.[22] Recall that when some of these assets

---

[21] For an early discussion on this, see 'The National Dividend', chapter 3 in Pigou, *The Economics of Welfare*.

[22] For the nationalised industries, this was last formally described in the 1978 White Paper. HM Treasury (1978), 'The Nationalised Industries', Cmnd. 7131, HM Treasury.

were privatised, they were sold in return for a cash payment. To leave citizens no worse off, this cash payment should have been added to the balance sheet, most likely to pay down debt, and hence reduce the liabilities side to balance the reduction on the assets side. Since the government of the day argued that privatised utilities would be more efficient than nationalised ones, there should have been a premium paid.

If this dividend on the portfolio of assets on the balance sheet is paid to all citizens, then this basic dividend takes up some of the role of the modified basic income payments, and it is asset-related. Any gap would be made up from tax revenues. The dividend might go up and down according to how well the economy is doing net of capital maintenance and in particular how well the assets are performing. It would be as if citizens had a portfolio of shares in all the utilities, public or privately owned, the intellectual capital (Popper's World 3 we met earlier) and the natural environment. The dividend is the level of payment, net of the requirement to maintain the assets intact.

The incentives on the system network utilities would be rather different. Instead of the massive financial engineering (and massive is the right word), gearing up the private balance sheets, the citizens' dividend would be net of the debt servicing costs on the national balance sheet.

It might be countered that these are mostly now purely private businesses paid for by customer bills, not taxpayers. The response is that this is a fiction: the assets, as represented by the regulatory asset bases (RABs), are guaranteed by the regulator and hence ultimately the state. The private utilities are running state-guaranteed assets. For this reason, the RABs should be added back onto the national balance sheet, thereby expanding the national dividend to include the cost of capital of the RAB. The sustainable economy could be even more radical, and add back the electricity generation backed by state contracts in its single-buyer model, which have RAB-like characteristics.[23]

Giving citizens equity in the core infrastructure systems could go further, to include land, given agriculture is everywhere heavily subsidised, and in effect farmers are in receipt of implicit state guarantees. The land has multiple uses, and citizens have a stake in this because they pay not only for the subsidies, but also for the use values. The UK planning system encourages land value uplift for developments, which could go to a land development tax, for example. Land

---

[23] New nuclear and now CCS projects are to have explicit RABs.

is much more than a cultivated field: it is a vital national asset and a natural capital one too. The national balance sheet might incorporate not only the state's directly owned land, of which there is lots, including that belonging to the Ministry of Defence, but also rights over notionally private land, including development rights. Interestingly, it was land that provided the main item in William the Conqueror's Domesday Book.

Citizens' Equity

The discussions of macroeconomics are in the main about debt, money, credit and interest rates. They are rarely about equity, and yet the concept of equity goes to the heart of the citizens' model and the sustainable economy. Equity is a stake in the assets and therefore in the outcomes. It carries risks. It can go wrong. When governments pick losers and pursue vanity projects, fail to properly conduct procurement and waste resources, this is a loss not to 'them', but to all of us. Much of the money spent in the pandemic on personal protective equipment and track-and-trace was, for example, wasted, yet few seem to care much about the consequences.

If citizens have a direct stake, they should care more, and when it comes to elections, citizens as voters might be more willing to demand that politicians and governments explain their stewardship of the citizens' assets. Citizens should be provided with evidence of that stewardship, audited by institutions like the UK National Audit Office, with an annual report on the national balance sheet and the management's performance. National accounts, on a sustainable basis, would really matter; they would help to determine how much money was paid out as the modified basic income. Government failures would reduce the basic income. That would sharpen up political debate and accountability, especially if debt was not an option to cover up the mistakes.

The stewardship concept goes deeper. The government is a steward because the balance sheet is open-ended. These are mainly assets-in-perpetuity, in the current generation's custody for all future generations. The national accounts are a report on how well current politicians are doing in meeting their duty to ensure that these assets are maintained, and that the next generation is on course to inherit a set of assets at least as good as the current one, and hence meet the first principle of the sustainable economy.

Equity further breaks the link between social security and wages. It is a return on capital separate from the return on labour, and becomes ever more relevant as digitalisation cuts into labour. There will still need to be top-ups to basic income to relieve poverty, taken directly from taxation revenues. The return on capital assets is the citizen's stake in the economy; the return on labour is the income from individual effort. Basic income is calculated as the return on citizens' equity plus a tax-derived top-up.

This equity approach would have a big impact on corporate governance, noticeably on the systems that have been privatised. The board of a water company would report to citizens as well as private shareholders and debt-owners. There would be less scope for paying themselves supernormal salaries. The citizens are unlikely to see the merit of paying an annual remuneration of £3 million to a chief executive officer, especially where there are manifest management failures. This could be further reinforced if, in these privatised utilities, citizens had a right to sack the managers and impose more reasonable executive pay.[24] In effect, utilities would return to being more like public corporations.

Citizens' Debt and Liabilities

The concept of citizens having a direct stake in the national balance sheet has one implication that might make for a reluctance to go down this path. Having a stake in the assets and a return on them provides for a positive payment. But having a stake in the debt imposes the opposite. It is a liability, and hence a responsibility, of current citizens and not just a debt passed on to the next generation when the debt is incurred to prop up current spending, not asset enhancements and investments. The liabilities side of the balance sheet is piling up, without corresponding assets on the other.

In a business, borrowing to cover current costs would point towards bankruptcy. The accountant would ask for a guarantee from the business owners that they can and will meet the debts. It would have to be an equity injection. In the stewardship model where citizens

---

[24] This is not the same as proposals to widen the duties of directors, as per some stakeholder capitalism models, as proposed, for example, by Professor Colin Mayer (see C. Mayer (2019), *Prosperity: Better Business Makes the Greater Good*, Oxford: Oxford University Press). It is a reporting function to the ultimate shareholders, the citizens.

have a direct stake, the accounting call is for them to make good on these debts being incurred for current consumption. It would be analogous to Keynes's proposal for a capital levy after the Second World War to pay for some of the war costs incurred.[25]

What is now in fact by default going on is that the guarantee is being provided by the future citizens. The implication is that, once intergenerational accounting is brought into play and the constraint on the national balance sheet is applied, the next generation will inherit a set of assets at least as good as those the current generation inherited. The debt finance of current spending would be replaced by a pay-as-you-go mechanism. Current citizens would have to pay for the increased current spending. That part of the debt which represents genuine enhancements, after capital maintenance and remedial investment, would be the only debt assigned as a liability to future citizens.

Debt for current spending, including capital maintenance, is, in effect, a negative USO. This debt is a liability shared by all citizens. It lowers their expected future income stream, and/or those of the next generation, and hence their standard of living. The national balance sheet lays bare what is really going on, and the extent to which the current generation is living beyond its means, at least in respect of the state's assets and liabilities. Balancing the books becomes a binding constraint if the economy is to be sustained, and if it is not, there will be a day of reckoning as and when it is not sustained. In the context of the very large deficit spending during the pandemic, this liability has shot up. We are worse off: the citizens' equity concept makes this explicit. We are back to the Robbins point above.

What, then, about the case for unbalanced books, made in particular by Keynesians we met earlier? This does not apply to good investments: they add assets on one side of the balance sheet against the cost of financing them on the other. No problem here as long as they really are good investments and as long as there are sufficient savings for the investments. The issue comes when Keynesians advocate increased *current* spending backed by debt (and, as recently, the debt backed by QE). Recall the Keynesian argument is that the spending will pay for itself since the unemployed will be employed, and the multiplier will work its magic. The extra current expenditure will boost effective demand, leading to cumulative growth and will therefore be self-financing.

[25] Keynes, *How to Pay for the War.*

But recall too that the rationale for the Keynesian medicine to restore full employment is that there are inflexible labour markets, and money wages are given. In the basic income/citizens equity model, the wages can be flexible and all unemployment is voluntary. The separation of the relief of poverty from the determination of wages should solve the problem. The reason why it might not is market power in the labour market, and the actions of trades unions. But it is also possible that monopoly market power may be applied on the producer side, keeping output below the competitive level. It may be that the prices in the market economy do not reflect all the costs. The citizens' USOs plus modified basic income can solve poverty, but the economy may not necessarily be efficient. For this, the prices have to be 'right', which in turn involves the state setting the rules – the market constitution – to ensure that market failures do not distort the outcomes. Citizens' USOs, the national dividend and basic income need an institutional scaffolding. This has two parts: in the regulation of the systems and in the constitution.

10 DELIVERING THE SYSTEM PLANS

The core system infrastructures of the economy have to provide the USOs. As natural monopolies, in whole or in part, and with low to zero marginal costs, they cannot be left for themselves to decide how best to meet the objective of leaving the next generation with a set of assets at least as good as it inherited. The state needs to regulate them. Regulating the systems of the sustainable economy requires not only ensuring that the systems are properly maintained and efficiently run, but also that they are resilient to shocks, particularly environmental ones. There is also the public decision as to how to allocate their costs. The boards of private companies cannot decide what is in the public interest or who should pay what.

Post-Second World War regulation was straightforward. It was internalised inside government across Europe and the UK. The state owned the infrastructures and told them what to do. The boards answered to ministers. Though much was achieved in providing the assets to underpin the great era of post-war growth, the trouble with this model is that the nationalised industries became tools for the achievement of particular short-term political objectives, and these were focused on the general election cycles. They ended up being less than perfect in pursuing the public interest.

The job of politicians is to win elections; it is not solely to achieve the overall objective of maintaining and enhancing assets. This has a particular twist, biasing decisions to the short run: utility prices impact on voters, and specific investments take place in key political constituencies. Unsurprisingly, the overall short-term spending took priority over capital maintenance and longer-term investments.

That for the most part the nationalised industries did build the power stations, motorways and the national gas system, keeping up with and supplying the golden age of economic growth, should not however be forgotten, and did so on a pay-as-you-go basis and hence closer to the sustainable economy rules. Whilst it remains fashionable to decry the nationalised industry model, it is not clear that it was actually worse than what followed.[1]

In the 1980s, as privatisation unfolded and the nationalised approach was largely abandoned, regulation came to mean the regulation of the now private monopolies, and the promotion of competition. The new mantra was: 'Competition where possible, regulation where necessary.' Investment, operating costs and strategy moved to the control of managers of the companies, directed by their private owners, subject to the rules about the outputs and the delivery of required services. The question was no longer (if it had ever been) how to be good stewards of the assets, but rather how to limit the abuse of market power, by price caps and by competition. The role of the state became overwhelmingly negative, leaving the private sector to decide what to build, and how to maintain assets. There was an explicit abandonment of system planning.[2] The questions became focused on incentives for maximum cost efficiency.

The results have not lived up to the ambitions of privatisation. Profit-maximising private utilities have, unsurprisingly, not prioritised asset maintenance and enhancements. The consequence is apparent across many developed countries. The transport, communications, energy and water systems are generally not fit-for-purpose. This matters at any time as part of the intergenerational bargain, but it matters more so now as climate change and biodiversity loss alter the constraints on these systems.[3]

---

[1] The US also achieved these outcomes, using rate of return regulation of predominantly private companies. In all cases, natural capital took second place and suffered accordingly.

[2] See N. Lawson MP (1982), 'The Market for Energy', speech to the British Institute of Energy Economics, Cambridge, June, reproduced in D. Helm, J. Kay and D. Thompson (eds.), (1989), *The Market for Energy*, Oxford: Clarendon Press.

[3] On water, see D. Helm (2020), 'Thirty Years after Water Privatization – Is the English Model the Envy of the World', *Oxford Review of Economic Policy*, 36(1), 69–85.

If the objective is to provide citizens now and in the next generation with the assets so that they are free to choose how to live their lives, and if this includes limiting climate change and biodiversity loss, and is best seen through the lens of the core systems that provide the capabilities, then the practical question that regulation has to answer is how best to make sure the maintenance and enhancement of the underlying assets, whether privately or publicly owned, are carried out. Regulation becomes positive and proactive, ensuring system plans are delivered, so that the intergenerational objective of the sustainable economy's first principle is met.

The System Regulation Model

The systems approach points to system regulation, to provide an overarching coherence within and between the infrastructures. It is a very much more integrated, and longer term, approach, very different from the atomised competition model, and the unbundling and disaggregating of the networks.

For all the main systems, there needs to be a 'plan' as to how to meet the first principle of the sustainable economy and a prime role of regulation is to make it happen. Turning a monopoly into a competitive market will not deliver the required results because these are natural monopolies with long lifespans, significant externalities and elements of public goods. The citizen has rights to the USOs, and is not just a consumer with a budget constraint responding to prices set in competitive markets.

The plan has to take account of multiple outputs and multiple periods, bearing in mind the secondary principles of polluter pays and precaution. It needs to be a plan for the short run, the medium run and the long run. The short run is about matching demand and supply at each instance, ensuring resilience with enough spare capacity.[4] It is about operating efficiency, not investment (which in the short run is fixed), and it has been the focus of the fixed-price, fixed-period regulation in the UK pursued by Ofwat, Ofgem and the other offices for sectoral regulation over the last three decades. Ironically, this replicates the short terms of the political cycles in the nationalised industries noted above.[5]

---

[4] It is Alfred Marshall's short run, when the capital stock is fixed.
[5] It is an unhappy feature of water regulation in the UK, for example, that the periodic reviews happen to coincide with the build-up to general elections, adding a further short-term bias.

The medium term is about the decade-long outlook, and largely about investment *within* the existing structures of the systems. It is about upgrading sewerage works, about new platforms at train stations, and about roundabouts and road extensions and accommodating electric car charging networks. It is about augmenting, improving and decarbonising the *existing* systems. Technology is largely given, subject to incremental improvements, so it is capital maintenance and remedial investments for the sustainable economy.

The long run is about the choice of system and it is the most important for the sustainable economy. In energy, it is about a partially decentralised largely net zero system, based on digitalisation, Big Data and AI, new generation, storage and demand-side technologies, and about the integration of transport, heating and agriculture into the energy sector, as they electrify. It is about technological change. In real time, this may be a matter of a few decades or indeed even within a decade. The long run is now forcing itself into the medium- and short-run time horizons, given both the speed of technical change and the urgency of net zero and the protection of biodiversity.

The system plan needs to have all these dimensions, all taking natural capital fully into account, and not just the short term that the current price cap regulation is mainly focused on. Five-year price caps tend to neglect the medium and longer terms. To make sure all three time dimensions are put together consistently, some general accounting rules need to be applied. These are the rules which ensure that the overall objective of the sustainable economy is met. These accounts, which we met earlier in chapter 4, have two key elements, capital maintenance and capital enhancements, and both need to be reflected in each of the system balance sheets, and then aggregated into the national accounts and the national balance sheet. These are not the same as the company accounts of the existing utility businesses, many of which were based on historical cost and depreciation, and which often cover only the parts of the systems the specific companies are responsible for. They are also not the same as regulatory accounts which the utilities are required to produce. They are the system accounts, incorporating *all* the system assets, regardless of who owns them.

Knowing What You Have Got

In order to know whether capital maintenance has been sufficient and to measure the impact of enhancements, there needs to be a baseline, showing what system assets there are and what state they are in. It is a massive advantage to this system regulation model that new digital technologies make this task much easier to carry out, and to repeat ad infinitum.

The starting point is natural capital and its ecosystems. This can be set at the national (and even global) level as the overall baseline.[6] Renewable natural capital as a whole has to be prevented from declining as the most basic necessary condition to ensure that the overall objective of the first principle is met. The baseline is a measure of assets, not flows, although flows can be helpful indicators. If the pollution load in a river goes up, it tells us that something is fundamentally wrong with the assets, the rivers through which the pollution flows.

A natural capital baseline reads off from satellite data and, where appropriate, drone and on-the-ground information, mapping the assets and identifying what condition they are in. It measures the trees and the soils, the peat and the rivers and water bodies, and the recreational assets; it creates layered natural capital maps which can be re-run at regular intervals to see how well the underlying assets are doing.

Similar exercises can be undertaken for the physical assets, assessing the condition of the bridges, ports, railway tracks and the electricity pylons, and so on. For the less tangible assets, the state of human capital in each sector can be surveyed, looking at the quality of the workforces. Baselining social capital is much harder, though there are proxies for measuring trust, and lots of data on crime.

We can now know a great deal more about all the critical systems, all the time, and as the data is continually augmented and updated, our detailed knowledge gets better and better. This is a massive advantage in designing, maintaining and enhancing the sustainable economy. It is remarkable that baselining and, in particular, the use of new technologies to map utility networks and assess the conditions, is so far largely a foreign land to regulators. It is a remarkable fact that none of the existing utility regulators in the UK does almost any of this, and the UK Environment Agency lacks proper digital mapping. Even more remarkable is how little system digital mapping is done by the utilities themselves. Some UK water companies do not have even the most primitive data about their pipes and sewers, and hence do not understand leakages and raw sewage discharges.

---

[6] This is the obvious starting point for the twenty-five-year environment plan.

A sophistication of the plan is to check resilience: how well the systems can cope with shocks. It is possible to remotely identify risks to resilience, like trees overhanging power lines, and to spot damaged train rails and road potholes by continual remote sensing.[7] Resilience scenarios test whether, if there is a prolonged heatwave, there will be enough water, and whether the rails will buckle. These can all be simulated as scenarios against the baselines, in multiple stress tests, continually repeated and updated in real time. Yet another remarkable fact is that, in the context of the 2022 failure of nearly half the electricity supply companies in the UK, not even proper financial stress-testing had been carried out.[8]

The System Regulators

The plans need to be developed and updated, and someone has to do this. Under price cap regulation, this is typically subsumed into the short-term (five-year) business plans. The privatised companies have licences which dictate the very general outputs they have to deliver, such as clean water, security of electricity supply, and so on. It is left to the companies to decide how best to achieve them, and to put together business plans for the next five years which their directors believe will fulfil their licence conditions. The regulator then comes in and challenges the companies, mainly on their efficiency assumptions and the cost of capital.[9]

In the system regulation model,[10] the licence conditions for outputs are transferred from the private companies to the system regulator. The latter then has the duty to ensure that the assets are maintained, to work out from the plan the enhancements required and

---

[7] This would no doubt have identified the impending disaster that Storm Arwen in November 2021 would cause to the electricity distribution networks in Scotland and the north of England, where the trees that should have been trimmed back fell on the power lines.

[8] Ofgem commissioned its own inquiry into its failures, and unsurprisingly it was somewhat bland, www.ofgem.gov.uk/publications/ofgem-publishes-report-its-regulation-energy-market.

[9] Indeed, it is revealing that the National Infrastructure Strategy introduced in November 2020 devoted a whole chapter to resilience – implicitly recognising that this area had been neglected. HM Treasury, 'National Infrastructure Strategy: Fairer, Faster, Greener'. Also, Ofwat, in its 2019 price review, stressed financial rather than physical and environmental resilience. See Ofwat (2017), 'Ofwat's Price Review: Delivering More of What Matters. Our Final Methodology for the 2019 Price Review – Executive Summary'; (2017), 'UK Government Priorities and Our 2019 Price Review Final Methodology'; (2017) 'Welsh Government Priorities and Our 2019 Price Review Final Methodology', 13 December.

[10] See D. Helm (2019), 'The Systems Regulation Model', 12 February, www.dieterhelm.co .uk/regulation/regulation/the-systems-regulation-model/.

ensure that these are delivered. The privatised companies are one way of getting this done. They become the contractors to achieve the system outcomes that the plan sets out, all consistent with the overarching objective of the first principle.[11]

The domains of systems are not the same as the current licence coverage of the privatised utilities. They cover *all* the main activities within the system, not just some. In water, for example, the current approach separates out flood defence and land use through agriculture from the water and sewerage companies, and from the surface drainage parties like the highways.

The overall duty of the system regulator in the water case is focused on the river catchment *as a whole*, within which the parts are set, rather than distinct and separately regulated silos, as at present. In England and Wales, Ofwat regulates the water companies, the Department for Environment, Food and Rural Affairs (Defra) and the Treasury oversee the Environment Agency, and a series of institutions covers farm subsidies. The Office for Environmental Protection holds Defra, the Environment Agency, Natural England and indirectly the water companies to account against statutory environmental targets. In the UK, in electricity and gas there is one regulator for the economic activities, Ofgem, and separate regulators for air quality and emissions trading, separate nuclear regulation, as well as a system operator for transmission, now to be separated out. Hydrogen, offshore and onshore upstream oil, gas and coal all come under different (and sometimes overlapping) regulatory bodies. Whilst pragmatism dictates how these system-wide plans are implemented, the wider system domains remain a central organising concept and focus for the sustainable economy. This would be a radical departure from the current institutional arrangements. It would dramatically simplify regulation and cut back administrative costs.

The system regulators have to be in the public and not private sectors. They are assigned the public duties, and these have to be delivered independently and impartially. The companies themselves have vested interests, and there are different ways of cutting up their own business plans to best maximise their profits. This matters because otherwise there is a large principal–agent problem between the state and

---

[11] This model is already applied to electricity generation, where bidders compete for contracts.

the private sector. It is not just that the objectives differ (public versus private interests), but there is also a sharp informational asymmetry if the private sector in effect decides on the plan. Capture is an ever-present damage to avoid through institutional design.

It has been suggested that one way around this within the existing regulatory structures is to try to make the boards of the private utilities incorporate wider 'stakeholders' representing other interests beyond narrow profits. Why not appoint an environmentalist, or have an advocate for the environment on the board, someone whose priority is the sustainable economy? Why not add a former regulator, who will take a broader view, or a consumer champion who will look to the customers' interests?[12]

This is the sort of structure that 'stakeholder capitalism' advocates promote. It is very popular with environmentalists and finds its most recent incarnation in the financial markets' fashion for ESG. If we get all the interests round the table then the boards of the private companies will choose outcomes consistent with the public interest.

This is a dangerous illusion, and for lots of reasons. The overall objective of maintaining and enhancing the assets is not the result of a summation of the wishes of the various interests. It is a hard, largely empirical exercise, requiring expertise. The stakeholders themselves will have their own interests. We are yet again back to lobbying and the risks of regulatory capture, and with the switches from gamekeeper to poacher, from regulators to the regulated, and sometimes the other way around.[13]

There is a democratic question here too: stakeholders are not elected, and they are not accountable to ministers, parliament or the electorate. Their interests are not equivalent to those of citizens. They are accountable to the companies and the company boards on which they sit and, particularly where they are non-executive, their futures can depend on the chair and chief executive officers. The chair may have particular pet projects, the chief executive officer may want a specific legacy, and the board is often shaped with this in mind, rather than

---

[12] In the case of ex-regulators, this is the 'revolving door' problem.

[13] Examples of careers in respect of senior positions at Ofwat include Jonson Cox, chair of Ofwat, who was previously Chief Executive Officer of Anglian Water; Cathryn Ross joined BT and then Thames Water after being Chief Executive of Ofwat; and Rachel Fletcher joined Octopus Energy after being a Senior Partner at Ofgem and Chief Executive of Ofwat.

the board leading and the company executives following. The state of our rivers, energy systems and the roll-out of fibre networks should not be decided by these unelected individuals. The companies are there to deliver the outcomes, not decide what they should be. None of this suggests that the various interested parties should not *contribute* to the system plans; it is just that they should not *decide* their contents. They should be consultees, not decision-makers.

The system regulators are public bodies, with public duties, many of which are currently in the private companies' licences. Their primary interest should be to ensure the system plans are delivered and that polluters pay and public goods are provided. In the sustainable economy, it is the responsibility of the system regulators to ensure this, not the responsibility of unaccountable 'stakeholders'.

The Delivery of the Plan

System regulators have the duty to develop and implement a system plan for the short, medium and long term. The way the plan is assembled and revised should be transparent. A website open to all citizens is an obvious part of this process. The development of the plan and its evolution can start with guidance from the government of the day, the guidance itself subject to parliamentary scrutiny and approval. This should all be within a constitutional context which protects the interests of future generations, set out in the next chapter.

In some cases, this is straightforward. For example in the UK, all sectors need to have regard to the Climate Change Act 2008 and the 2019 net zero amendment. The statutory targets under the Environment Act 2021 will also be requirements, not options. Other components require judgements about the ways in which the first principle can be met, in the context of the capital maintenance requirements and the overall opportunities for enhancements. This could be made a legal requirement in a new Systems Regulation Act, as part of the legislation needed to set up the system regulators.

With the plan uploaded to the website, with continuing opportunities for contributions and amendments and with perhaps also an advisory group of relevant parties with technical expertise, each system regulator can start to break down the system requirements into manageable chunks. A good way to start is to list on the website all the capital maintenance and enhancement requirements consistent with the sustainable economy and to invite initial expressions of interest for the delivery of any and all of them. This is an information-gathering exercise, and it is inclusive. There may be many businesses and organisations, including trusts and charities, that may be able to contribute to delivery. It is the right forum for the stakeholders, rather than through the boards of companies. It helps to build social capital by its inclusivity.

From the initial responses, the system regulators will learn a lot about who might bid, which bits are most attractive to whom, which bits will elicit lots of competitive bids and which bits might get little or no interest at all. This helps in designing the next stage: the rolling system auctions for those bits that are amenable to competitive bidding. This introduces an Austrian flavour to the system regulation: entrepreneurs can bring new ideas and new technologies to the virtual auction rooms. Some areas are obvious candidates for competition. Auctioned contracts for renewable electricity generation and auctioned capacity contracts in electricity have resulted in dramatic reductions in costs. Where they are possible, the great advantage of auctions is that they cut through lobbying and incumbent vested interests. They all have to make their bids. They enhance competition.[14]

Pragmatism is the order of the day. The system regulators will have different time dimensions and some contracts can be let for very short periods, and others for the medium and longer term. There will be a mix of contracts, and contracting will be a continuous process. This is actually much more like a competitive market: there are few, if any, examples where bundling everything in a single fixed-price, five-year period is efficient. In fact, it is very un-Austrian. Prices and contracts vary all the time in markets.[15]

Residual Monopoly and Contract Regulation

Where possible, auctions provide a good way of both widening the number of possible providers while at the same time minimising costs. By focusing on outcomes, they take us away from socialist planning.

---

[14] But not always; auctioning large franchises in railways has not proved so successful.
[15] It is ironic that Michael Beesley and Stephen Littlechild, in proposing the RPI-X approach, thought that making final prices rigid in the five-year straitjackets was a good way of mimicking an Austrian market. M. Beesley and S. Littlechild (1989), 'The Regulation of Privatized Monopolies in the United Kingdom', *RAND Journal of Economics*, 20(3), 454–72.

But not all activities within a system will be amenable to competitive supply, and there will inevitably be residual monopoly elements. Some of these areas, such as the coordination of the particular bits of the system and the building of major new assets, could even be undertaken by competing potential suppliers. This is reflected in the fact that existing incumbent utilities subcontract many of their own projects.

The day-to-day system operation, as opposed to the system planning and auctions, can often be devolved to a single supplier. Take the operation of regional or national electricity systems. These require real-time matching of supplies with demand, and the ability to react immediately to problems in networks and power stations.[16] In the face of Russian interruption of gas supplies to Europe, operators have to game-plan possible emergency measures. This is not a job for a regulator, but for a specific operational company. It could be let as a limited-term franchise contract or more permanently remain with the network owner. The economic border of the state stops at system design and coordination; the private companies and other organisations can do the work.[17]

Similar considerations apply to natural capital and ecosystems, where design and coordination are critical. What is required is distinct from who provides it. The environmental objectives are not, for example, set by farmers and landowners. They get subsidies – contracts – to carry out environmental measures, but they should not decide what these measures should be. This distinction matters most where there are major landowners who want to be the ones who decide on landscape-wide changes, be it historically with sheep and the great Scottish Clearances, or the new ultra-rich who want to 'rewild'.[18]

For some time and in some cases, perhaps permanently, there will still be a number of activities for which the current incumbents will be the only practical option. This means that there will be a central

---

[16] When, for example, a wind farm and a power station simultaneously dropped off the UK network in August 2019, the system operator had to come up with emergency measures both to maintain the frequency on the system and bring on other power stations. Ofgem (2020), '9 August 2019 Power Outage Report', 3 January, www.ofgem.gov.uk/publications/investigation-9-august-2019-power-outage.

[17] See Helm, 'Cost of Energy Review'.

[18] See D. Helm (2022), 'Natural Capital, Carbon Offsetting and Land Use: A Discussion Paper', May, Scottish Land Commission, www.landcommission.gov.scot/downloads/628de8eb9c11a_Land%20Lines%20Natural%20capital-carbon%20offsetting%20and%20land%20use.pdf.

monopoly element for water companies, electricity and gas network companies, railway network companies and possibly for broadband at the centre of the communications sector. How to regulate these?

Price cap regulation for fixed periods is no longer appropriate under the system approach, for three reasons. First, the incumbents will no longer have many of the licence conditions, including the duty to supply. These are transferred to the system regulator. Second, the contracts are not best set as all-embracing five-year fixed-price ones. Third, the incumbents need not be restricted to narrowly defined activities, such as in electricity supply, networks and generation.

Taking each of these in turn, the transfer of the licence conditions to the system regulator in respect of resilience and security of supply (as well as other duties such as net zero, the protection of natural capital and the USOs) changes the role of incumbents from having responsibility for the system to having responsibility to fulfil a contract or contracts. These contracts are special only in their tailoring to the specific context. In wider markets where conditions dictate that there is only one credible bidder, it will be a negotiated contract, awarded on the basis of agreed rates of return. But even here, it is possible that other companies may bid for the incumbent contracts. For example, one water company may bid against another, and similarly for the energy networks.

The pluralisation of contracts is the result of having a system plan with a short, medium and longer term. The system regulator offers multiple contracts for different periods to ensure capital maintenance and planned enhancements, and can even invite initial bidders to specify the time period in their offers.

The third consequence of the system regulator having taken over the core licence conditions is that there can be a relaxation of the restrictions on companies' activities. The separation of network functions from other activities was necessary in order to home in on the specific licence requirements. This unbundling, which formed a big part of the creation of liberalised markets and the introduction of competition, was partly to avoid networks biasing investment to benefit their other activities, including the supply of services through the networks. This is no longer a problem in the system regulation model since the contracts are set by the regulator and the incumbents are at arm's length. The result is that these restrictions can be removed, and a single licence issued limited to ensuring that the contractors are fit and proper to be engaged in core systems. The network operators in electricity, for example, can deploy their skills in storage and batteries, into demand-side investments and even into generation. They can be more Austrian. The silo approach can be abandoned, less and less relevant in a period of rapid technical change. The system regulator gets more control, there is more competition to do the works and there is more scope for innovation, while reducing the growing regulatory intrusion into the detailed activities of the private businesses. Regulation can thereby be reduced.

The problem in applying the system regulation model to both health and education is that the outputs are hard to specify with precision, and where they are, they can distort behaviour towards the meeting of measurable targets. No one appears to have any clear idea of the detailed capital maintenance requirements, or indeed the enhancements. Incumbent managers and staff campaign for more money, and political parties compete over who can spend the most, and employ the most nurses, teachers, police and so on. Repeated attempts to reform the school syllabus and to set targets for health outcomes and waiting times neglect the incompleteness of imposed contracts. Children's education is not measured simply by the number of top grades (especially when a very large proportion of any cohort is given top grades), and health outcomes are not simply gauged by the waiting times or how many tests are carried out. In both cases there is a caring function, tailored for each individual.[19]

The incompleteness of contracts does not stop progress. On the contrary, incompleteness makes a coherent system plan all the more important, recognising uncertainty, the possibilities of shocks like coronavirus and explicit budgeting for resilience. Both education and health need system plans, rather than tick-box targets.

Generational Links

In most current models, regulation not only attempts to ensure the efficiency of the incumbent monopolies and to enforce the licence requirements on outputs, but also guarantees that the private companies can

---

[19] The fictitious 'Mr Chips' was not revered for the number of top grades his pupils achieved, but how he inspired them, their standards and the impact on the way they lived their lives – whether they were good citizens as well as exam-passing machines. J. Hilton (1934), *Goodbye, Mr Chips*, London: Hodder & Stoughton.

finance their functions. This is a critical element which helps to minimise the cost of capital, by ruling out the expropriation of investors by forcing prices down to the (relatively low or zero) marginal costs, rather than remunerating their (relatively high) average costs. Fixed and sunk capital costs are thereby guaranteed.[20]

When the companies were privatised in the UK, they took the core system assets with them.[21] These assets represented the past investments, which had been paid for in a pay-as-you-go fashion. Past consumers had paid for future assets, just as they had inherited the investments of their predecessors, right back to the Victorian sewers. At privatisation, this intergenerational chain was broken twice: once for the old assets; and again for new assets, which would be paid for through the repayment of debts by the next generation. In effect, the government sold the past (customer-paid) assets for a pile of cash, which it promptly spent on the current generation through lower taxes than would otherwise have been the case. It thereby violated core requirements of the sustainable economy and its first principle. Customers effectively paid twice.

The transferred assets went onto the private balance sheets and the regulators allowed these to earn a rate of return, reflecting the statutory duty to ensure that they could finance their functions. Since these investments had already been paid for by past customers and taxpayers, there is a good case to be made that these assets should have remained in the privatised accounts at an opening value of zero. The companies would then operate and maintain the assets, recovering their costs and making a return on new investments. It is the new investments that need to be protected from pure marginal cost pricing, and as the assets are enhanced, these are added to the RAB. The RAB should then be a core contract between the generations.

A problem the RAB assets cause to the system regulation model is in determining to whom they belong. There are several models. As new assets are created, they could stay with the incumbents, on their balance sheets, or they could transfer upon completion to the system regulators. The former limits the scope for auctions and competition

---

[20] It remains to sort out whether this is a guarantee that operating and capital maintenance costs will be covered from current revenues, whilst enhancements are covered by the duty to honour the resulting investment costs.

[21] The UK privatisation of the assets is different from the French example of letting franchises, keeping public ownership of the assets in a number of cases.

and entrenches the incumbents. The latter – as a build, transfer and operate model – creates assets on the public balance sheet, and in particular on the system regulators' accounts. This option is quite close to a nationalised industry with compulsory contracting-out of the works.

A third option is to create separate tradeable RABs.[22] These are placed into a holding company or similar vehicle, and debt-financed. Since the assets exist, they have an accounting value and the actions of managers can make no difference to these accounting numbers, so there should be no equity risk, which is transferred to consumers and taxpayers via the duty to finance functions. The debt is pretty close to government bonds since it has an implicit government guarantee and may be held mostly by pension funds.[23]

Now we have: the system regulators developing and implementing the system plans and auctions and letting contracts over the short, medium and long term; the creation of new assets by private companies; and the completed projects going into the RAB account and being refinanced with debt. The incumbent utility in effect 'sells' its completed new assets into the tradeable general RAB funds largely held by pension funds and other long-term infrastructure investment vehicles. The tradeable RAB fund represents the enhancement assets of the systems and is rather like a sovereign wealth fund. It in turn can be added to the national balance sheet, as a core element of the inter-generational bargain. From it, contributions are made to the citizens' dividend and hence to part of the basic income.

Closing Down the Economic Regulators

The system regulatory model allows for a much cleaner and more consistent regulatory architecture for the state to exercise the relevant controls and to meet the requirements of the sustainable economy. This is both top-down and bottom-up.

The top-down dimension comes from a wider national infrastructure plan and its consistency with the overall planning regime. The

---

[22] D. Helm (2008), 'Tradeable RABs and the Split Cost of Capital', January, www.dieterhelm .co.uk/regulation/regulation/tradeable-rabs/.
[23] Some existing utility debt has been bought by the Bank of England through QE. This is effectively what is going on in the UK in the RAB model being applied to new nuclear power stations.

sustainable economy requires an overarching long-term infrastructure plan for all the capitals – natural, physical, human and social. There have been a number of attempts to set out a national infrastructure plan, and often these have descended into a list of projects rather than an overarching coordination across the systems. In part, the failure to do this led to the setting-up in 2015 of the National Infrastructure Commission in the UK.

The bottom-up dimension allows for the clearing away of much of the regulatory bureaucracy that has emerged since privatisation in the late 1980s and into the 1990s. The numerous 'offices', one for each infrastructure system, have focused on the economic regulation of the specific monopolies, not the systems and not the environmental, social and other dimensions. In the system regulation model, they are not needed and can be closed down.[24] It adds to the bonfire of social security and taxation administration, which the basic income and flat-rate taxes facilitate, proposed in respect of social justice.

In the case of water, not only can Ofwat be closed down, but the production activities of the Environment Agency are separated out so they can compete for the catchment works (and probably best transferred out of the government sector), and the environmental regulatory function can be consolidated within a single regulatory body. This should be an Environmental Protection Agency.[25] In the case of energy and transport (and agriculture), the CCC provides an overarching set of carbon budgets, which the system regulators will need to meet. Both should be given the first principle as their overarching objective. The resulting clarity provides a blueprint for regulation in other countries.

Regulating the National Dividend and the Wealth Fund

When it comes to the USOs, basic income and the national dividend, the regulatory issues here are partly technical and partly constitutional. The technical issues arise in the context of the definition of inflows and outflows.

---

[24] See Helm, 'Cost of Energy Review', on closing Ofgem.
[25] In practice, this is going to be partly the Office for Environmental Protection under the Environment Act. The relationship between the Office for Environmental Protection and the Environment Agency is unfinished business.

The easiest institutional model is of a national fund with a cash inflow and with an immediate cash outflow. The fund in this model, like many charities, is a collection and distribution agency. The technical questions are about deciding how big the national dividend inflow is, and the nature of the distributions both in timing and the entitlements.

Recall this is a *national* dividend, based on the assets on the national balance sheet. These include the assets directly owned by the state, and possibly the RABs guaranteed by the state. The fund could, for example, assume that the sustainable economic growth rate is around 2 per cent per annum, and apply this to the ring-fenced assets in the government's control or ownership. As the growth rate goes up, so too it might be assumed does the national dividend. An Oxford college might take 3 per cent from its endowment per annum as a dividend to spend on its current activities. Many charities with endowments follow a similar path, although some are more aggressive.

It might be reasonable to apply the expected sustainable economic growth rate to the state-owned assets and state-guaranteed RABs. It should in theory be close to the risk-free rate, the return on government bonds. Where the state owns assets but chooses to provide these free of charge, for example the health and education assets, national parks and a host of other public goods, the citizen dividend is still relevant. It is just that it is paid in kind, not cash. There should be an explicit account of this, and the citizens' annual dividend statement should set these out as, in this example, a notional return (after the capital maintenance has been met). It applies only to the returns on enhancements and enhancement investment, not to the existing assets, which are in perpetuity.

That leaves the determination of sustainable economic growth. It cannot be GDP, which is a flows concept and takes little account of changes in the value of the underlying assets or of the capital maintenance required. The national balance sheet with debt liabilities set against assets, and with capital maintenance deducted from current revenues, produces very different numbers to GDP.

An example illustrates some of the measurement issues. As a result of the coronavirus lockdowns, many economies increased borrowing to pay for current spending, including for example the UK's public payment of 80 per cent of wages through furlough. This financing increases the debt on the balance sheet, and is typically unfunded. It is current expenditure paid for by borrowing. Either public expenditure will have to fall, or taxes will have to rise in the future, net of sustainable economic growth, by a sufficient amount to bring the current side into positive territory so it can pay off the balance sheet debt over time, or some form of default will be needed to write off the debt, whether outright or through inflation and currency depreciation. Selling off assets (as with privatisation) does not improve the position; neither does printing money.

In this example, it is obvious that we are all much worse off, echoing the point made by Robbins about the economic consequence of the First World War. The lockdowns have done *permanent* damage, and hence the *permanent* level of income and consumption consistent with asset value protection and proper capital maintenance is going to be lower. The national dividend should therefore be cut.

The problem is knowing by how much. One way of deciding the amount is to split the declared national dividend into two parts: a permanent income basic amount on a risk-averse basis (say 1 per cent), and an ex post payment adjustment in light of what actually happens. Given the scale of environmental problems that may happen this century, 1 per cent might actually turn out to be on the high side, so there would have to be some sort of clawback mechanism (as there would be for the Covid spending). If the outlook dims further, a mechanism might also be needed to cut the basic risk-averse amount. Conversely with, for example, rapid technical progress, it could be raised.

The above are all technical questions, and best dealt with by independent statistical bodies and a trust model of control over the fund itself, with legal protection under a constitution. These institutions will have to resist the inevitable political pressures. Politicians seeking re-election will want to pander to the immediate interests of their electorate. There will be inevitable pressures to paint a rosy picture of the economic prospects, talk up technical progress, talk down conflicts, pandemics and the possibilities of war, and try to raise the basic payment and increase the ex post payment too.

The distribution of the fund is straightforward provided it genuinely is on a per citizen basis, with no adjustments. It can be paid to the electoral roll on a fixed amount per annum (or quarterly or monthly to help low-income households with limited capacity to borrow and save to cope with fluctuations in their household budgets). There could be a cut-off above a certain income and wealth level (reflecting a modification to basic income). There are also decisions to be made about specific and special needs. These matters arise because of citizens' different health needs, locations and other personal constraints. To avoid the fund trustees making these decisions, there are two options: government can pay for any additional social security and health needs directly out of additional taxation, independent of the national dividend and basic income payments; or the government could give public guidance. In the latter case, it is imperative that if some payments to some citizens go up, others go down. This will particularly need constitutional oversight.

The cash-in, cash-out model of the fund sidesteps the question about whether the dividend component of the basic income is too expensive. No taxes are raised. It is the surplus (or deficit) after taxes have been collected and expenditure deducted. Redistribution is about current taxes and current spending: the dividend is the citizens' share in the returns on the assets, and the assets facilitate the citizens' capabilities and the associated USOs. The dividend is ultimately a return on equity.

The risk of political interference is not limited to the pay-outs. Governments might try to get the fund to leverage itself and start investing in assets directly, making it a form of national investment bank.[26] This is indeed what happens in some sovereign wealth funds. It is, however, only a problem if the fund owns the assets against which leverage can be built up. The cash-in, cash-out fund does not itself have any assets; these belong to the state and the core system infrastructure owners in the form of RABs. Once the fund gets assets, its functions are different. In the sustainable economy, the state focuses on ensuring that the assets are maintained intact (a current spending obligation, of no relevance to the national dividend, since the dividend is net of the capital maintenance) and ensuring investment in asset enhancements that add to the balance sheet, net of the extra debt on the balance sheet to fund the investments. In the investment case, assets and liabilities go up, dependent on whether the investment turns out to deliver a positive economic return net of the cost of capital.

A New Institutional Architecture

The institutional regulatory architecture of the sustainable economy is designed to separate out the overarching political choices from

---

[26] It might also seek to influence the choice of trustees, as US presidents do in proposing new appointments to the Supreme Court.

the effective delivery of the objectives and weights that the political process dictates. It is designed to have regard to the short, medium and longer terms. Of these periods, it is the longer term that is least likely to feature in political party rivalry and the immediate competition for votes. The institutions of the sustainable economy are designed to lean against the wind of short-term expediency, which promotes the consumption of current citizens without due regard to future citizens.

The system regulation model does just this. It starts with a set of accounting rules, separating out capital maintenance from capital enhancement, and all within the framework of a national balance sheet, independently constructed, updated and reported on. In this, it replicates the accountability and scrutiny of company accounts. The overarching national infrastructure plan fits into this accounting context. There follow the system plans, for catchments, regional and national energy systems, for road, rail and city transport infrastructures, and for broadband, fibre and mobile coverage.

These systems are all part of the national balance sheet because they are all underwritten by the state, whatever the formal property rights say. Ultimate control lies with the state, and indeed it is control that is one of the touchstones for accounting bodies in the allocation of assets between the private and public sectors. The question as to whether taxpayers or citizens as consumers pay is a subsidiary point, and less significant than it may seem.[27]

The health and education systems are part of the national assets and there is no reason why the same system regulatory approach should not be applied here, including a cost of capital requirement to represent the risks.

The overall returns on this portfolio of state-controlled assets, net of capital maintenance, are available as a dividend. This could go into a cash-in, cash-out fund, paid to all citizens as a basic dividend. The fund has to be independent of day-to-day interference, and to set an ex ante risk-averse dividend and an ex post correction. The amount paid may not be enough to take everyone out of poverty, but additional adjustments to income should come out of current revenues and hence taxation.

---

[27] During the coronavirus pandemic, it became clear that the state stood behind those systems and many of the companies in difficulty.

The citizen now has: USO provisions for natural capital, water, transport, energy and communications, and for health and education, plus an annual basic income dividend payment (topped up from taxation). These enable each to have the capabilities to participate in society, and provide the wider industry with the core inputs and routes to market, together with a labour force that is enabled to contribute to the national endeavour.

Putting in place institutional structures for the system regulators and the governance of the fund requires a new constitution, bringing the interests of citizens now and the next generation into the frame, all within the overall objective of maintaining and enhancing the assets over time.

11 A NEW CONSTITUTION

The sustainable economy's first principle requires that the interests of the next generation are taken into account. The next generation inherits as good if not better assets so that they can choose how to live their lives. What generations beyond this do is outside the scope of the sustainable economy.

These interests are flagrantly overlooked by the current generation. The systems are not properly maintained, let alone enhanced. When it comes to the environmental damage that continues to be caused by current unsustainable economies, the intergenerational rule is being systematically broken. Current spending is supported by borrowing, and the bias is the other way around, with the next generation subsidising the current one.

To prevent this disregard of the interests of future generations, and in recognition of their inability to vote, there needs to be some constitutional device to embed their interests, some form of a generational constitution. Without this constraint on majority rule by the current generation, and with constitutions ignoring the future constituency, we are doomed to more of the same. Drafting a precise constitution is a matter for legal experts. Here the focus is on the concept and the broad principles.

The Case for Constitutions

Most countries have constitutions and most of these are written down. Some are manipulated and ignored. Russia's constitution, for example, stated the maximum period a president could serve, until this is overturned. Even China had a constitution with a time limit on its presidency until it, too, is overturned. Putin and Xi Jinping show a callous disregard of the rules when it suits them. Neither of these examples is evidently better than the UK, which is one of the few democracies that does not have a proper written constitution. If one day the UK elects a Trump, then the absence of a constitution may be much regretted. It is the US constitution which prevented a Trump being a *ruler* rather than an elected president, and it is the checks and balances between the executive (the President), legislature (Congress and the Senate) and judiciary (the Supreme Court) branches of government, and the interactions between all of these, that provided some stability in the US during the Trump presidency.[1]

The sheer variety and experience of constitutions begs the question of what a good constitution might look like. Liberal political theory provides a conceptual way of thinking about a constitution, from John Locke onwards.[2] The liberal idea is to take the individuals, 'founding fathers', and ask them to come up with a set of rules which should frame and constrain the actions of governments (and hence limit a dictatorship of the majority of current voters over current minorities and the next generation's interests). From Locke to Rawls, the liberal constitution envisages an abstracted context in which, in ignorance of the subsequent positions in society (or simply ignoring them in John Stuart Mill's representative democracy[3]), each individual works out what would be a just society in which the rights of each are respected and the outcomes are fair and reasonable. It is a form of social contract.

---

[1] It would have been more difficult in the US to break international law, as the UK proposed to do over the Northern Ireland Protocol agreed as part of the BREXIT arrangements.

[2] J. Locke (1680), *Two Treatises of Government.*

[3] Volume XIX of *The Collected Works of John Stuart Mill* contains a number of Mill's essays on politics and his book *Considerations on Representative Government.* J.M. Robson (ed.) (1963–91), *Collected Works of John Stuart Mill*, 33 vols., Toronto: University of Toronto Press, London: Routledge & Kegan Paul, https://oll.libertyfund.org/title/robson-collected-works-of-john-stuart-mill-in-33-vols.

The most famous recent version of the liberal constitution is provided by John Rawls.[4] In order to derive the principles of his ideal state of justice, Rawls assumes that his delegates meet together in what he calls a veil of ignorance over their subsequent position in society. These are reasonable (and, in Rawls's case, rational) people, able to think beyond their immediate circumstances. They must be educated enough to understand the choices in front of them, and not be so poor themselves that they can focus only on immediate needs. It is a deliberately informationally restricted choice.[5]

In this veil of ignorance, Rawls claims his two principles of justice will be chosen. These are first that each person is to have an equal right to the most extensive basic liberty compatible with a similar liberty for all, and second that social and economic inequalities have to be attached to offices and positions open to all (Rawls's equality of opportunity principle).[6] These inequalities have to be to the greatest benefit of the least advantaged members of society (Rawls's difference principle), translated into economics as maximin – maximise the benefits to the least well-off – and raising the question of who exactly is the least well-off, and in what units. Thus we have: an overriding priority of liberty, equality of opportunity and the difference principle. Although Rawls does not require equality of outcomes, or the utilitarian greatest happiness to the greatest number, he is nevertheless both equality-leaning and quite close to utility maximisation, once the diminishing marginal utility of money is brought into consideration.

Abstraction is the crucial liberal element. It treats the autonomous individuals as coming together for purposes of mutual self-interest. This is in contrast with more communitarian traditions which see society as moulding the individuals as part of that society, following Jean-Jacques Rousseau.[7] It is also at variance with conservative traditions, which stress

---

[4] J. Rawls (1971), *A Theory of Justice*, Oxford: Oxford University Press.

[5] Ibid., pp. 136–42, section 24, 'The Veil of Ignorance'. On p. 137 he states: 'as far as possible...the only particular facts which the parties know is that their society is subject to the circumstances of justice and whatever this implies. It is taken for granted, however, that they know the general facts about human society.' Rawls goes on to list them, to include 'whatever general facts affect the choice of the principles of justice'.

[6] The two principles are listed in Rawls, *A Theory of Justice*, p. 60: 'First: each person is to have an equal right to the most extensive basic liberty compatible with a similar liberty for others. Second: social and economic inequalities are to be arranged so that they are both (a) reasonably expected to be to everyone's advantage, and (b) attached to positions and offices open to all.'

[7] J.-J. Rousseau (1762), *The Social Contract*; and *The Confessions of Jean-Jacques Rousseau*.

the slow evolution of social institutions and the special relationships built up through history, in the tradition of Hume and Edmund Burke.

One curious and decisive feature of the veil of ignorance is Rawls's assumption that the participants will all be risk-averse. If they are self-interested, each will want to make sure that if they turn out to be the worst-off in the society that follows, they will be looked after. This is a personalised version of the precautionary principle. Assuming this is why Rawls can assert that his individuals, in the veil of ignorance, choose the principle that any inequality is justified only if it is to the benefit of the worst-off in society, in case it is them. There is no room for *Dragon's Den*, *Love Island* and a host of popular media focused on success, winning and prizes.

Personal risk aversion is a very demanding and quasi-socialistic principle, and very different from the risk aversion in respect of systems in the sustainable economy. Modern capitalist and authoritarian societies are organised rather differently, with large incentives to make supernormal profits to motivate enterprise and investment. Rawls's approach is certainly not like the sort of society envisaged by Keynes with his animal spirits, and it is at odds with the Austrian tradition focused on incentives and entrepreneurs.

In theory, the Keynes and Austrian approaches could be reconciled by presenting a sort of trickle-down argument, where all the inequalities that result lift all boats, especially for the worst-off in the society. Capitalism in this trickle-down model has the unintended consequence of making the poor better off than they would be in a society that aimed directly for equality.[8] It is what Keynes might have supported as an unintended consequence of his multiplier, with demand-side stimuli creating the 'means to prosperity'.[9] The evidence for 'trickle-down' is scant, and equality does not motivate capitalists: they go after profits, and the competitive process erodes these so that innovation, technical progress and lower prices are all delivered, in the process also employing all those who want jobs at their marginal product or above. Capitalists do not go about trying to meet Rawls's difference principle.

---

[8] The claim against was presented as the Laffer curve.

[9] See J.M. Keynes (1933), 'Means to Prosperity', reprinted in J.M. Keynes (2010), *Essays in Persuasion*, London: Palgrave Macmillan. Writing in 1933, Keynes states that his scheme 'embodies an advance towards economic equality greater than any that we have made in recent times', p. 368.

Being at the Table

Who to include? The key feature of the sustainable economy is that it is concerned with the economy over time. The next generation matters. But future people are not here and cannot take part in the constitutional conventions writing the rules. How then to bring the next generation to the table? The critical principle is of fairness between the generations, and with it the idea that the current generation, like its predecessors, has a duty to act as good stewards.[10] This is what our first principle requires. The next generation should not be treated differently to the current one. Each generation comprises leaseholders, not freeholders, of the assets, natural or otherwise.

Amongst the reasons why we might want the next generation at the table is that they may have different preferences to ours. But this is hopeless: we cannot know how these might differ, and hence it is reasonable to assume that human nature is everywhere and always the same. It follows that we do not need them at the table because they may be different. Current people are in this sense representative of future people.

In any case, in the capabilities approach the detail of preferences does not matter because we are not trying to predetermine those choices. Crucially, we are not trying to make future people happy or to equalise utility across the generations in an effort to gain the greatest happiness over all time. The aim is more limited: to allow the next generation to exercise their choices in the ways that best suit them. We thereby escape the utilitarian's difficulties.

In the sustainable economy, the next generation must be empowered with the assets which provide for their capabilities to make their choices. The constitutional rule between the generations is a contract for the transfer of assets from the current to the next generation, and a contract which specifies the state of those assets and the duty of the current generation to be good stewards of those assets, which are temporarily in its care. The contract also transfers debts, incurred only in exchange for passing on enhanced assets. The balance sheet is the account that reflects both the stewardship (the capital maintenance) and the enhancements.

---

[10] Rawls has a 'just saving rule' to address this question, but it is not grounded on assets, capital maintenance and the sustainable economy set out here.

The stewardship approach to meeting the requirements of the sustainable economy has the advantage that there is no need to be precise about exactly who is and who is not in the next generation. It merely requires that the capital maintenance and other considerations are met. There may be specific cases where the time horizon makes a critical difference to adjudicating on compliance. There always will be, in any constitutional arrangement. This is for a supreme court to decide upon.

The rights embedded in this constitution are not simply the maximisation of freedom to exercise choices. The constitution includes the right to do what you want, subject to not harming the ability of others to do so, with 'others' including future citizens as well as current ones. But the contract between the generations also requires more than a negative refrain from harm to the next generation. It is more than Mill's *On Liberty*, Hayek's *Constitution of Liberty* or the first of Rawls's principles, and requires certain positive actions. Only Rawls spells this out in his second principle.

The negative freedom from interference from others that the liberal right advocates neglects the positive aspects of stewardship and the extent to which the assets have to be created and sustained by society. The negative liberty picture of atomistic individuals in the economists' perfect competition model assumes that the assets are all discrete, atomistic and small. It neglects the creation of the great system assets and the protection of the environment, the assets at the heart of the sustainable economy. These will not arise spontaneously from individual actions. They require positive intervention, and a significant role from the state.

Formalising Sticky Rights

Constitutional rules can never be absolute. There are no fundamental human rights to which any individual has an absolute trump card in respect of other citizens.[11] This is easily seen by looking at any of the individual rights in the American constitution. The right to bear arms is an example; another is religious freedom. In the first case, it is possible to construct cases where this would be a bad idea, and in the second,

---

[11] See R. Dworkin (1977), *Taking Rights Seriously*, Cambridge, MA: Harvard University Press, and his discussion of rights as trumps.

there can be bad religions. Even the right to life is not sacrosanct to each and every individual in every situation. The police do, from time to time, legitimately shoot and kill people. People die in pandemics even if, with enough resources, they could be saved. Soldiers die in defence of constitutions. Special forces kill Al-Qaeda leaders.

Rather, what a constitution does is make certain rights and rules *sticky*, hard but not impossible to overcome. Changing them requires going through a process which is typically subject to review, appeal and legal judgments. There are supermajority rules, extended periods to allow reconsideration, court hearings and adjudications, referenda and 'independent' regulators. Revisions must be feasible: the job is just to make them difficult when it can be argued that they might damage the interests of the next generation.

There is no perfect constitution: they are the products of their time of writing and specific historical circumstances, with very uncertain prospects and uncertain futures. Our age is one with new massive challenges. In our time, climate change and biodiversity loss are literally life-threatening.

Constitutions are designed to protect citizens from oppressive majorities. They are limits on democracy, and also protections against dictators. They allow for an orderly change of governments, rules for the election of governments and rules for their removal. Minorities are protected from abuse by powerful majorities. Protecting future generations from the possible tyranny of the current generation is an extension of this idea.

Constitutions are contracts between the members of a society at a point in time and over time. The contract sets out the principles that govern conduct. It lays down how these relationships will play out, how the law of the contract will be governed and how violations will be dealt with. The contract can be interpreted as a set of property rights, but, as we saw previously, there are no absolute property rights, and public goods pose special problems.

The First Principle

The first constitutional principle of the sustainable state is that each generation, as steward of the assets it inherits, must look after them and bequeath the next generation a set of assets at least as good as those it inherited. This should be written into the constitution.

This general principle of course requires interpretation, about which there will be public arguments and debates. As time passes, so technology, ideas and knowledge change. There is a difference between a rule that says that a specific set of physical assets must be maintained and one that says that the aggregate set of assets must be maintained, between a rule that gives priority to renewable natural capital over the man-made and human and social capital and a rule which protects all capitals. Some assets could be replaced by others.

Against this physical flexibility, it is possible to compare different operational outcomes. It might be that the capabilities can be held constant over time, but the physical values of the assets change as long as the operating values are as good.[12] To mainstream economists this is simply a recognition of substitutability within the bundle of assets. The next generation can get more iPhones, but there may be fewer swallows.

It is immediately apparent that full flexibility is unlikely to deliver the desired outcome because some assets, particularly renewable natural capital, are more important than others. But so too is full rigidity. This means that some assets should be physically maintained in almost all circumstances (subject to a judicial or other process) and others can be quite flexible. A great deal of physical capital has a limited life anyway, and buildings and equipment are constantly changing. On the other hand, biodiversity is largely given and extinctions are not just now but for all times. Even those bits of biodiversity that do not have any obvious use now may do to future generations. They are options, and once gone impossible to recreate unless we get really good at genetic recreation and environmental reconstruction to allow the resurrected species to flourish. The written constitution will need to prioritise some assets over others, and especially renewable natural capital, providing special protection. It needs targeted stickiness.

There are various ways some flexibility could be institutionalised. There could be a generational timescale for formal constitutional rules, with a presumption of no change unless clearly demonstrated to be relevant. There could be independent bodies to review which assets are maintained. Part of this reviewing function is statistical and related to the accounting rules and conventions; part is analogous to the

---

[12] On operating versus physical capital maintenance, see J. Edwards, J. Kay and C. Mayer (1987), *The Economic Analysis of Accounting Profitability*, Oxford: Clarendon Press; and G. Whittington (2017), *Value and Profit: An Introduction to Measurement in Financial Reporting*, Cambridge: Cambridge University Press.

Law Commission, in looking at past legislation and making recommendations for changes.[13] Part could be a once-in-twenty-five-years constitutional convention. Laws such as the Climate Change Act (amended) 2019 and the Environment Act 2021 set out statutory targets. These would have to be consistent with the constitutional rules, with the potential to appeal to a supreme court where there are allegations that they have fallen short of the requirements of the principles of the constitution.

The next step in a written constitution is to set out the rights, duties and obligations of *citizens* (not consumers) within this framework of assets. The central argument is that the entitlement of citizens is to the primary assets, and that these comprise the basic systems (the natural, physical, human and social capitals) which are the framework for the economy to function and for citizens to thrive. These USOs vary over time. They now include, for example, broadband. There cannot be a simple constitutional list, but there can be a process for deciding what they are and how they are changed over time. Where there is doubt, a supreme court could adjudicate.

Arguments about the boundary between what is and what is not in this category should not distract us from the core aspects all agree should be included. These might include the major utility networks, health and education. The constitution defines the general entitlements of citizens, and the process of deciding whether they are fulfilled. There will be borderline cases.

The USOs include the entitlement to the national dividend, reflecting the return on assets that all citizens have a stake in. In the sustainable economy, these include the RABs for all the main privatised utilities, as well as the return on assets directly owned by the government. Both are public assets. That return can come through the provision of the USO at below cost, and through a return to reflect the cost of capital.

Embedding the Polluter-Pays and Precautionary Principles

In meeting the overarching objective, there are two further principles essential to the sustainable economy. The first is the polluter-pays principle. Internalising the costs of pollution is a necessary condition of the sustainable economy.

---

[13] See for a description www.lawcom.gov.uk/.

There will be debates and disputes about who is the ultimate polluter and establishing responsibility. But then there are always debates about property rights, and the polluter-pays principle is in effect the right to protection from damage to property by other parties. The principle introduces stickiness by putting the question of responsibility for pollution into the constitutional context.

The second is the precautionary principle. The institutions that oversee compliance with this principle will have to make judgements about the gap between expectations and uncertainties. We do not know the full consequences of global warming; nor do we know how great the warming will be on the basis of the measures we are taking. Similarly, we have little idea how biodiversity will turn out as a result of a variety of policies that might or could be adopted.

The implication is that, for all the key systems, a margin for resilience should be introduced above the mean expected outcomes, to ensure that the next generation is *most likely* to end up a bit ahead. There are two reasons for this: it takes account of irreversibility and asymmetries; and of the damage already done. Some catch-up restitution is needed anyway. The first reason relies on the idea that the benefits to the next generation of avoiding risk are greater than the costs today of meeting them, because the bad outcomes are likely to be asymmetrically large and, in the case of renewable natural capital, irreversible. The second reason is an ethical one. Whatever the starting baseline for defining the current generation, there is little doubt that the natural capital and the climate have in fact been damaged by the current generation, and that the line is not being held, notwithstanding the technological advances that will benefit future generations (although not all technological advances are necessarily desirable).

In constitutional terms, it is impossible to specify the size of this precautionary margin. The constitution of the sustainable economy should require institutions and individuals, in discharging their functions, to have regard to the precautionary principle in respect of these primary assets. In practice, this will mean that any official challenged in the courts for failing to do so will need to show how assessments have been made and what steps have been taken to implement them. The precautionary and the polluter-pays principles are what goes in the constitution, while the process is the pragmatic means to meet it.

What Should Be Passed Down the Generations

Regarding the first overarching principle to leave at least as good a set of assets for the next generation, some consensus will be needed on which assets are deemed most important. The constitution should make provision for, and give priority to, primary assets, those considered of primary importance for capabilities.

This does not mean that other assets are unimportant, or that they might not become primary in due course. The constitution could simply state the importance of primary assets in general and leave it to governments and the courts to decide the particular cases that fall inside and outside this category.

The intermediary position is to set out the general headings and provide some steers within each. Taking them in turn, natural capital assets fall into the primary category, because to be deprived of them makes it very difficult for any individual or business to function. The sustainable economy needs sustained natural capital. It is a fair bet that it always will do.

Some types of natural capital are nevertheless more important than others. All the really important ones are renewable natural capital: stuff that nature gives us for free and keeps on giving us in perpetuity provided the stocks are not depleted to levels below which they can reproduce themselves. There are overlapping types of renewable natural capital at the species level, at the catchment and local ecosystems level, and at the global level, right up to the climate. The constitution would require that all these levels of natural capital be kept at least above the thresholds, to the extent that national boundaries allow. The constitutional protections might extend to protected areas, lands and marine areas set aside for current and future generations.

The other main type of natural capital is the non-renewables – stuff that can, unless recycled, be used only once (except over extremely long time periods). More mineral deposits may eventually be formed, but not enough for millions of years to add to the resource base. These sorts of natural capital cannot be maintained as stocks, even if there is some recycling. This is true also of the minerals needed for low-carbon technologies, notably for electric car batteries and wind and solar generators. Someone uses them and, in order to meet the sustainable economy requirements, there must be compensation for their use now by the current generation for the next generation who will not be able to consume them. Recycling has costs, even if it mitigates some of the depletion. The accounts should show the intergenerational spreading of the benefits.

Intergenerational accounts are key to demonstrating compliance with the first principle, and identifying violations. The non-renewables appear on the balance sheet, and as they are run down, there needs to be a corresponding and compensating adjustment. This can be to increase other assets, and in particular enhanced renewable natural capital, and could include contributions to future national dividend payments. The constitutional duty to maintain assets intact implies that conformity with these requirements does require that these accounts are kept and the balance sheet asset valuation cannot fall net of liabilities. It would otherwise be impossible to show how actions complied with the overarching first principle.

Human capital maintenance and enhancement are driven in the main through education and R&D. Education is a USO in the sustainable economy, a primary asset. Because people die, education needs to be continuously invested in to maintain the stock of human capital intact. The ideas, knowledge and technologies are assets-in-perpetuity, but only if people have access to them. The constitution can reflect this both by protecting basic and core R&D, as well as the research infrastructure that goes with it, and by enshrining a duty to provide universal education. The special additional requirement is to compel citizens to participate in education. It is a right and an obligation.

Physical capital comes in many different shapes, forms and sizes. For the bulk of the private sector there is no need to require constitutionally that it is protected. Frequently, depreciation applies, since physical assets decay and technology changes their economic values. However, there are some forms of physical capital which, though theoretically limited, in practice are best seen as assets-in-perpetuity. These provide citizens and businesses with water, energy, transport and communications. Since these are critical for capabilities, the general constitutional requirement to provide citizens with capabilities will be met through the provision of these basic system infrastructures. The principle is about the capabilities; the application is about the provision and capital maintenance of these systems. Citizens have a right to energy, water, transport and communications – and of course nature – reflected in USOs.

Finally, there is the complex and culturally dependent social capital. This is all about trust and resilience. It will be hard for a constitution to legislate for social capital, other than as a general principle, and hard for courts to decide whether this requirement is being met. A general reference is what is probably required here, recognising that it will be difficult to enforce. For example, commitments to religious freedoms may be included, but commitments to specific religions are to be avoided. Freedom of speech might require protection. Many constitutions make reference to these rights, without filling in the details. They flag them, leaving lots of leeway for interpretation. The flags have value even in such complex circumstances. Asking questions and shining a torch on what is going on is almost always a useful first step.

Limiting Government Discretion and the Importance of Rules

These rights and obligations need to be embedded in a constitution, otherwise they may be neglected as and when parliamentary majorities from time to time see it expedient to do so. A constitution is a limit to discretion by governments. The constitution is a set of rules, rules of the game that governments have to follow.

Historically, those keenest on limiting discretion have been conservatives, and conservative liberals in particular. The historical backdrop is the French Revolution: the fear that, in the absence of rules, revolutionary forces can tear up existing institutions. For those on the right, there is an assumption that revolutions lead to tyrannies. In the cases of the French Revolution in 1789, the Russian Revolution in 1917 and the Chinese Revolution in 1949, the evidence supports this hypothesis, eloquently set out by Burke and reinforced by Alexis de Tocqueville.[14]

Although many environmentalists find themselves on the left, and want to overturn 'capitalism', the central idea that there should be limits on discretion when it comes to nature is one that should appeal to them, as well as to conservatives. Discretion to cut down the rainforests, to destroy ancient woodlands and to build coal-fired power stations is in conflict with the idea that there should be rules to protect

---

[14] See E. Burke (1790), *Reflections on the French Revolution*, London: James Dodsley; A. de Tocquevillle (1835), *Democracy in America*, London: Saunders and Otley; and T. Paine (1792), *Rights of Man*, London: printed for J. Parsons as an alternative perspective.

natural capital. The absence of such constraints has not produced good outcomes. The sustainable economy principle of ensuring that the value of assets does not in aggregate go down, and the limitation on substitution between different asset classes, puts rules in the way of marginal calculations and discretion. Moreover, simple compensation rules and net gain policies tend not to be enough, not least because they get limited to individual assets, not ecosystems of natural capital.

Admittedly, the proposals for a new constitution are themselves revolutionary, in a sense similar to that in the context of the American Revolution. To develop the constitution outlined here would be a radical departure from the discretionary state that has built up piecemeal since the English Civil War and the Glorious Revolution of the seventeenth century. But then there is little chance of protecting natural capital, and having regard to the next generation, without entrenching these rights in a new constitution. Once in place, as with the American Constitution entrenching the American Revolution, the new constitution should be hard to change.

Ways of Amending Constitutions

Hard to change does not mean impossible. Constitutions are not straitjackets, but rather tight coats. Circumstances change, and there needs to be a way of amending constitutions. Around the world a number of devices have been tested and introduced. There are supermajorities requiring, say, two-thirds or more of a parliament to approve. Sometimes, the ability to change the constitution not only requires a supermajority but restricts this to an upper house or senate. Others use referenda, and some, like the Swiss, on a very regular basis.[15]

There is a particular dimension of this limit to discretion which comes up in the sustainable economy. Some decisions have medium- and longer-term horizons, in a context in which parliaments cannot typically bind their successors. An example is climate change and the adoption of targets for net zero by 2050. While new information may lead to ex post revision of the target, the very existence of long-term targets and plans can condition expectations and significantly reduce costs. If everyone knows that there is a legal requirement to meet net

---

[15] The Swiss example does not necessarily protect the environment. In June 2021, proposals to address climate change were rejected, for example.

zero by 2050, which is likely to be upheld by a supreme court under a constitution, and hence that the target will not be easily weakened, and if the energy sector knows there is a plan for fibre provision, and a target for the roll-out of electric vehicles, and the water sector knows that there is a requirement to increase tree cover in catchments, all their decisions can be implemented at lower cost. These commitments enable the system regulators to plan with less uncertainty and to do so consistently. Electric cars, for example, are likely to work better if the electricity networks are developed to cope in harmony.[16]

In all these examples, the constitution cannot mandate these planning activities in detail. Rather, they form part of the reasonable steps that governments should take to ensure that their conduct is consistent with the overarching first principle of leaving the next generation with a set of assets at least as good as those it inherited. Governments will need to show that they have acted in good faith, taken due notice of the polluter-pays and precautionary principles, and the system plans are one of the core ways of demonstrating this. Otherwise, the constitution should provide for legal challenge. It is an obvious step to align statutory duties of system regulators with the constitution's first principle and also the polluter-pays and precautionary principles. The constitution embeds these.

This constitutional approach feeds through into the stickiness of these longer-term plans. If, for example, the government makes proposals for transport which take out ancient woodlands, there could be a constitutional challenge since this violates the principles.[17] There may be circumstances where this damage to renewable capital is nevertheless justified. The power of constitutional stickiness is that compensatory offsetting benefits would need to be very considerable. The principles mandate this.

In practice, membership of the EU provides for some such stickiness. The EU Directives are underpinned by the European Court of Justice. The EU Air Quality Directive mandates that citizens should be protected from urban air pollution breaching certain thresholds, and governments can be challenged through the courts for failures. A government of an EU member state could try to change the Directive, but

---

[16] In regulation, this is sometimes called the 'fair bet principle'. See, for example, Ofcom (2020), 'Full Fibre Must Be Fair Bet', Dame Melanie Dawes speech to FTTH Council Europe, 3 December.

[17] See again HS2. Glaister, 'HS2: Levelling Up or the Pursuit of an Icon'.

it does not have sole power to do this, and in practice once a Directive is in place, it would need a majority coalition of member states and then the European Parliament to abolish it. Directives have a number of features that mirror constitutional constraints. They create stickiness.

'Taking back control', the slogan of the UK BREXIT campaign, could be interpreted as a desire to break free of rules and constraints in the name of whatever the current parliamentary majority in the House of Commons dictates in the interests of the current generation. It is already apparent that this control is and will be used on occasion to weaken environmental constraints.[18] Removing stickiness is likely to be to the overall detriment of the environment, even if there are specific counterexamples from time to time.

Outside the EU, there is no such protection in the UK, and the UK courts will struggle to hold the government to account for air quality violations, for example. An early example of the difficulties is the Climate Change Act. Under this Act, the CCC proposes five-year rolling carbon budgets, setting them for the next fifteen years. Parliament either accepts the proposals or the government has to come up with a new carbon budget which would have the same effect. The record of meeting the carbon budgets so far is poor,[19] but there is no constitutional court to appeal to since there is no constitution that this failure violates. The European Court of Justice, by contrast, could be (and was) appealed to for violation of the Air Quality Directive, and indeed it found against the UK government and required remediation. This is constitutionalism and the supporting courts in action, limiting discretion and developing and enforcing medium- and longer-term targets that are not easily changed.

Proving the Rules Are Being Followed

Central to the sustainable economy and its constitutional protection is that any government can be held to account and hence have its performance measured against the overarching principles, and especially the

---

[18] C. Burns and A. Jordan (2021), 'Environmental Regulation in the Post-BREXIT Era', 23 March, www.BREXITenvironment.co.uk/2021/03/23/environmental-regulation-post-BREXIT/.

[19] Climate Change Committee (2020), 'Reducing UK Emissions: 2020 Progress Report to Parliament', 25 June, www.theccc.org.uk/publication/reducing-uk-emissions-2020-progress-report-to-parliament/.

first principle. This requires government to maintain intergenerational accounts. The accounting framework for the sustainable economy is designed precisely to answer the stewardship question, and to shine a torch on how well the government is doing in meeting the overarching principle. Put another way, unless there is a way of measuring whether the net natural and other assets are going up in value or down, holding a government to account is going to be extremely difficult, whatever the constitution says.

The first principle requires that the assets are maintained. Meeting this condition would be radical, because it would force the capitals to be maintained and, in the process, require either less spending elsewhere or higher taxes. By not paying for capital maintenance out of current revenues, we are living beyond our means, and the manifestation of this is in the deterioration of the asset base. This is the climate change, the biodiversity loss, the deterioration of catchments, the potholes in the roads, and so on. It is why our infrastructures are often poor.

In the constitutional approach, a budget presented to parliament which did not provide for proper levels of capital maintenance could be struck down by the courts. Governments proposing to reduce taxes and pay for current-account spending by borrowing would face legal challenge. This possibility would encourage finance ministers to set out how they are in fact meeting their capital maintenance obligations. In particular, ministers could not pretend that they are controlling public expenditure by putting off maintenance. Cutting capital maintenance, allowing the potholes in the road to get bigger, would fall foul of the courts. All budgets would be under the scrutiny of the offices protecting the constitution.

This may sound very intrusive and it could encourage vexatious legal challenges, but this need not be the case. All governments have to do is comply with the constitution, and there could be independent bodies, for example an enhanced office for budget responsibility, with the duty to check and opine on whether the constitutional requirements have been met. It could be built into the budgeting process. It need not delay action: the challenges would be ex post, and need not hold up implementation.

More generally, the balance sheet and the accounts presented by government could be audited by an independent body. This is something that happens in some countries automatically. In France, there is an accounts court (*Le Chambre des Comptes*). The difference between the current situation and the constitutional one is that reporting on accounts and accounting practice would have teeth: if the accounts are found to be inconsistent with the constitution then legal action could follow. Put simply, it would be constitutionally illegal to cook the books, rather than as at present just embarrassing to have this pointed out.

Embedding the Intergenerational Constitution

The gap between the overarching constitutional principles and the way the constitution is interpreted and implemented is mediated by a range of institutions, all ultimately within the oversight of a supreme court. These are bodies that can be created to ensure that the first principle is properly embedded in practical outcomes. This is a key role for the regulatory institutions. The core headings are: the systems, the citizens' entitlements and the macroeconomic frameworks.

Each of these has a substantive role in the sustainable economy. Plans must be consistent with the first principle. In the sustainable economy, the system regulators for each of the main infrastructures have this planning function, guided by central government and consistent with the constitution. The system regulators have the duty to ensure resilience, security of supply and other long-range objectives like net zero. They can use markets to auction the system requirements, but not the systems themselves. Private companies or other organisations deliver them.

To meet the citizens' entitlements to fully participate in society, the USO requirements link to the national dividend. There will need to be a cash-in, cash-out fund with trustees, and the national accounts will need to show the surplus year-by-year net of capital maintenance. Much of this is technical and about the arithmetic and payments procedures, but there will also be some discretion over the projected economic growth. For this reason, the precautionary principle could entail a two-part payment, ex ante and ex post, as already outlined. It is the job of the fund's trustees to ensure that the rules are followed. The trustees' articles (its internal constitution) will need to be consistent with the overall constitution, and open to legal challenge.

The macroeconomic implications of the overarching constitutional first principle are considerable and radical. The sustainable economy rules should include: balancing the current account of the national accounts, net of capital maintenance, with limited discretion to allow for exceptional surpluses and deficits; providing a mechanism for a fund to build up so that deficits resulting from or in response to crises are temporary; and ensuring that the balance sheet is non-declining. This means that any and all investments that enhance assets' values can be matched by debt and the state can borrow to invest. Increases in debt are matched by the assets the borrowing creates. Projects that do not add value – trophy projects – would most likely fall foul of this rule and would need some funding contribution deducted from the current accounts. This is not a cap on debt per se, as for example in the German debt rules,[20] but rather a rule that assets must be created to match or exceed debt liabilities except in exceptional, limited and temporary circumstances. It leaves government and its primary macroeconomic policy institutions, like the Bank of England, open to legal challenge.

The rules for monetary policy include an interest rate to be set in real terms in line with expected sustainable economic growth, linking the present to the future and setting the returns and hence incentives for saving. This can be enshrined in the mandate set by governments to the central bank. The government must make sure that the mandate itself is consistent with the first principle.

In terms of institutions, it is surprisingly simple to follow the above rules. Much of the institutional architecture is in place, even in the UK, and without a constitution. The current-account balance is an accounting exercise with limited discretion over the short-term deficits. This could be a task added onto the existing UK Office for Budget Responsibility, backed up by the existing National Audit Office, all under constitutional oversight.

Setting interest rates following the rules above could remain with the Bank of England and its Monetary Policy Committee. There are already rules (like the 2 per cent inflation target), and the sustainable economy macroeconomic rules could supplant them. In the US, the Federal Reserve already carries out these functions, and in the EU, the ECB has the relevant powers. The sustainable economy rules require a forecast of sustainable growth and a feedback correction rule;

[20] The debt limit, enshrined in the German constitution, limits new public debt to a maximum of 0.35 per cent of GDP.

and the process for setting the interest rate is again under the eye of the courts and the supreme court. The Bank of England would have to set out clear reasons for the decisions it takes. This procedure is an extension of what it already does. The difference in the sustainable economy is that it could be challenged.

As regards QE, this would be treated as an extreme and emergency measure, and there would be an automatic adjustment to the national balance sheet. In order for the balance sheet to continue to add up, there would need to be a provision for repairing the damage done by QE, and the Bank of England, the US Federal Reserve and the ECB would be required to set an exit strategy *before* they embarked on QE.[21]

The Stability Benefits

The advantages of the sets of rules above, and the institutions to deliver each of them, are measured by not only fulfilling the overarching objective, the first principle, but by doing so in a predictable and inherently stable way. It turns the macroeconomic financial instability and short-term planning cycles for the infrastructure systems into a predictable and stable macroeconomic framework and medium- and longer-term system planning. The extra dimension added in the sustainable economy is that all of the above must be carried out consistent with the first principle, and also with the polluter-pays and precautionary principles.

The sustainable economy rests on sustainable consumption, that is consumption that can be sustained by the current generation without prejudicing the opportunities and capabilities of the next generation. With the rules for systems and system planning, for the national dividend and for the setting of interest rates and the budgets for governments, the level of sustainable consumption is predictable and need not change significantly from year to year.

It is also likely that the sustainable economy constitution will help to maximise the sustainable consumption path because it will

---

[21] There is a similar example relating to the exercise of QE by the ECB – the German courts have examined its consistency with the overarching constitution of Germany and found it initially worrying. See also House of Lords Economic Affairs Committee (2021), 'Quantitative Easing: A Dangerous Addiction?', 1st Report of Session 2021–2 HL Paper, 16 July.

enhance productivity. Instead of the last two decades of extreme financial instability, repeated economic and financial crises and very low productivity growth, the proper maintenance and enhancement of the infrastructures will feed through to lower costs for every business, the employment opportunities will help enhance human capital and the national dividend will contribute to flexible labour markets.

Long-term credible and stable investment plans will lower the costs of capital. Households will be able to save and invest in the context of greater financial stability, and the state will be able to ensure a smoother flow of savings into investments, and enhance those investments where they improve the balance sheet by targeting savings for investments into the four capitals, financed primarily by debt. Borrowing will be for investment, not consumption, for the future people and not for the present. Social capital, and especially trust between the generations, will be enhanced.

Constitutions are never perfect, and there are costs as well as benefits from going down the constitutional route. But without constitutional protection of the interests of the next generation, the chances of getting to the sustainable economy are slim. Constitutions are imperfect ways of creating stickiness in the face of actions that benefit the current generation at the expense of the next. They are not once-and-for-all, as the social contract theorists like Rawls would have us choose in a veil of ignorance. They are live frameworks of rules, sticky but nevertheless capable of evolution. It remains for the detail to be filled in to translate the principles of the sustainable economy into a practical and workable constitution.

12 CONCLUSIONS: IT COULD GO EITHER WAY

There is only one credible position to take. We can expand our horizons and grow and prosper. We can make this a green and prosperous land. But that prosperity is not likely to materialise on the current economic model, because it is seriously flawed both in its objectives and in its inner workings. We will not 'save the planet' by more of the same. What is required is a very radical recalibration. It is not markets and capitalism themselves that are the problem; it is the ways they are being channelled in the twenty-first century by largely ignoring the environmental consequences. We have a choice, a pathway we could take. The challenge is urgent. To get onto a sustainable consumption path, and thence onto a sustainable economic growth path, requires some brave and more radical surgery. We don't have time to wait and see.

The sustainable economy is very different from the existing economic model. Its ambitions are limited to leaving the next generation with a set of assets at least as good as we inherited. This first principle of the sustainable economy requires very limited foresight. No economic forecasts, no focus on ever-rising GDP. Just the basics: making sure that future citizens have the basics to choose how to live their lives. And not the future generally, but limited to the next generation specifically.

As we stare into the unknown world of the next generation, trying to make them happy gives way to something more solid: making sure the assets are in place. It turns the spotlight back onto us and what we are doing to the planet, and especially its natural capital. What we have to do is in fact very simple: we have to do the capital maintenance, and follow the polluter-pays and precautionary principles. It is us who are taking risks with the planet, and us who are the polluters and who are not paying for the pollution we cause and us who are putting the next generation at risk. It is us as citizens who are not fulfilling our obligations.

The rules of the sustainable economy are simple too: to follow these principles, we should not behave with the kind of blatant selfishness currently on display. We should not saddle the next generation with piles of debt raised to pay for our current consumption. The next generation can be burdened with debt only where they are blessed with new assets worth at least as much as the liabilities that are incurred to make the investment, to enhance their future. Building better assets, better ideas and knowledge and enhancing natural capital are good things to borrow for.

Right now, the next generation is being screwed by us. As populations age, as the majority becomes skewed to the pensioners, the demands for more public services grow, but not the corresponding willingness to vote for higher taxes. The young are inheriting lots of debt, lots of climate change and a lot less biodiversity. They are also getting increasingly inadequate infrastructures. Instead of making sure the energy, water and transport systems are in good shape for the challenges of this century, the old systems of the twentieth century are often patched up with sticking plasters. Water leaks out of the pipes, sewers cannot cope, energy networks struggle to accommodate the new demands from electric cars and the roll-out of fibre looks to the consumers in densely populated cities, and less the citizens in the more peripheral and rural areas.

This is not some accident that has befallen the young. It is very much by design of the economic orthodoxies of our time, which match the interests of the majority – a majority that is increasingly focused on the old. The prevalence of Keynesian economic policies panders to this narrow electoral base, to the inevitable tyranny of this majority. A focus on aggregate demand, on keeping up consumption, has not produced higher productivity and higher GDP growth, its measures of success. It has at times brought very negative real interest rates, fiscal deficits and, consistent with this paradigm about how to manage an economy, it has ended up with QE, as many rulers in the past also did. In ordinary language, this is printing money.

Perhaps it is not too extreme to claim that the first principle has been turned on its head: the next generation will inherit a set of debts and degraded assets to maximise the benefits to the current generation. Worse, the polluted should pay, and we should sail as close to the wind as possible when it comes to taking risks with climate change and biodiversity loss. If these are the principles, we are doing pretty well at meeting them.

It is at the heart a consumerist ideology, spending now and to hell with the consequences. Old-fashioned values, like thrift and saving for a rainy day, about paying one's way, are thrown out of the window. The Victorian approach that Keynes and Bloomsbury so disparaged is dead and buried. Conspicuous consumption, which was once a criticism hurled at the rich and famous, has been democratised through the new forms of communication, and 'influencers' are the high bar of disposable fashions and 'image'. If this is what Keynes wanted, he should rest easy in his grave.

What should make him less easy are the consequences of his success. Whereas, for Keynes, the economic prospects of the grandchildren were an ever-enlarging set of consumption possibilities, it has turned out for them to be a less happy place, and a potential disaster for the environment.

It is at this late hour that choices have to be made. They 'have' to be made because the consequence of an unstainable economy is that it will not be sustained and the point of no return is approaching fast. In making this choice, the missing bit is being able to envisage what that sustainable economy would actually look like. Its architecture is, like the problem itself, at heart remarkably simple.

Its starting point is its most fundamental one. It is to throw off the central idea that humans are best regarded as consumers only, and the sole path to happiness, the maximisation of utility, is to achieve the highest level of consumption. There is more to life than spending, and turning economics away from pure consumerism towards citizens, recognising that citizens have common and equal rights and responsibilities, shifts the focus dramatically. The central concern is making sure that these citizens have the capabilities to thrive. Citizens are of course also consumers, but they are also more than just consumers.

Putting citizens centre stage and recognising that we have very fuzzy glasses to peer into the future leads to the second radical point of departure: the centrality of assets, and in particular primary assets. This is why the first principle is defined as leaving the next generation with a set of assets at least as good as the current one inherited. It is all about systems and assets rather than utility and flows, creating the platform for the young to launch themselves into adulthood, to build careers and families and do all this to the maximum of their capacity.

Choices are made now in the radical uncertainty which is the human lot, and what makes life so interesting. There is little that is more boring than certainty as to what the future may hold. Imagine if you know how your life was going to unfold, and when you are going to die. It is all predetermined and there is nothing you can do about it. That is what certainty entails. Living such a life would probably not be a life worth living. Instead, we should embrace the uncertainty that is at the heart of the human condition, and be risk-averse about it. We should be precautionary, as good Victorians would have been.

In living our lives as good citizens, and accounting for our behaviour, the idea of a day of reckoning is quite helpful. It contains the idea that we should account for our conduct. To do this, the sustainable economy asks for accounts. The sustainable economy has proper accounts with balance sheets that reflect the assets, and their management in perpetuity. They tell us what assets we have and how well we are protecting and enhancing them, whether we are being good stewards on behalf of the young in the next generation.

The sustainable economy has a simple measure of this. It is the test of whether the assets are being properly maintained, so they don't depreciate, and hence we avoid consuming the capital. Capital maintenance is the central organising concept to achieve the first principle. It is what needs to be done, before we can spend. What we can safely and responsibly spend is after deducting capital maintenance before determining the amount of spending consistent with sustainable consumption and growth.

Only when the natural ecosystems are protected and properly managed, the energy system delivers low-carbon electricity securely, the water system delivers drinking water and cleans up the sewage, the trains, buses and electric cars have networks to travel on, and everyone has access to fibre communications can enhancements be brought into the picture and borrowing be contemplated.

Borrowing to spend does not wash in the sustainable economy, except in the event of a big and sudden economic shock, and even then there has to be a recognition and a plan to repay it. Three recent shocks have shown how easy the borrowing bit is, and how hard the repayment catch-up is to deal with: the financial shock in 2007/8, the Covid pandemic and the energy price crisis. There are no signs that the borrowing associated with each of these shocks will be repaid, and no clear plans to do so. Default is the likely exit, and inflation is the traditional means. It is now and it was in the 1970s. The debt is not sustainable and hence will not be sustained.

Many governments have tried to commit to credible financial rules, and 'borrowing for investment only' is the one that repeatedly gets invoked, for good reason. It is the right fiscal rule. The problem is that it is investment not capital maintenance that counts, and creative governmental accounting often gets health and education and a host of other things conveniently renamed as investment. It is the right rule, and in the sustainable economy it has a clear and hard meaning. The hard bit is that in the sustainable economy, it is actually followed in practice. The watchwords of the sustainable economy are: 'shine the torch'. Look closely, peer through the fabric of lies and wishful think-ing that underlie many national accounts, and ask what is really going on. Don't believe the political hype about 'things can only get better', that 'growth will pay for itself', and that tax cuts and more spend-ing are what make for a stairway to heaven. Shining the torch on the ambulance queues, what is actually going on in the classroom, at the state of the infrastructures, at the rising debts and rising inequalities, reveals a story that few politicians – and us who vote for them – wish to acknowledge, let alone do something about.

The polluter-pays principle makes markets the servants of the overall objectives, not the carriers of destructive subsidies to pollut-ers. It is hard to overestimate how radical this would be. Take the 2022 energy price crisis. If and when oil and gas prices fall back to a better reflection of their (non-carbon) costs of production, and if then a proper carbon tax is added back to reflect the scale of the damage from carbon emissions and at a level necessary to meet the net zero targets on a sustainable basis, the high energy prices experi-enced in late 2022 would become the norm. The fact that consumers clamoured for bail-outs, and had insufficient funds to pay the bills, is a measure of just how big the switch to polluter pays would actually be. Add in taxes on methane, and the environmental damage from mining all those minerals needed for electric car batteries and for the magnets in wind turbines, and energy in a useable form would be treated as a scarce resource (energy itself is anything but scarce). This is not a message that governments want to give in extolling the virtues of net zero. They would have us believe that decarbonisation is the route to cheaper energy and hence more disposable income to spend. It probably won't be, and serious decarbonisation is going to hurt – probably a lot.

The sustainable economy is radically challenging. Making us the polluters pay, making us pay for the capital maintenance of the core primary assets and especially renewable natural capital, and making us save to invest in enhancing these assets is going to require a big adjustment to our spending and the ways we live our lives. There is quite a lot of pain in getting onto the sustainable path. In the macro-economic mess that most countries are in, and after two decades of monetary and fiscal stimuli, and QE, there is little scope for tax cuts, more and more unsecured borrowing and dithering over paying for carbon and other pollution. These will only make matters much worse.

The shock would be profound. It upends the consumerist world all are so addicted to. There would be immediate and more long-term casualties. They would not just be the oil and gas and coal companies, the fertiliser and plastics manufacturers, and the conventional steel and cement makers. They would be citizens' bottom lines. The sustainable economy has to deliver social justice, not just in steady state, but to manage the transition from here to there, and to do so without creating a global slump and mass unemployment, and dire poverty too. It has to do it from a starting line that the last two decades have made much more unequal.

The good news is that there are plenty of sources of funding available once we are prepared to think radically enough, and admit that tax and welfare sticking-plaster changes are wholly inadequate for the challenges ahead. And, in focusing on citizens, there are plenty of resources to tackle their capabilities to participate in society now and for the young in the next generation. Again, simplicity is both the right call, and perfectly plausible to achieve. Complexity is the enemy of effective relief of poverty and ensuring efficiency in both spending and taxation. In the sustainable economy, there are two bits to all this: the provision of broadly universal services and a modified universal income paid to a significant number of citizens from a combination of taxation and a national dividend, so that wages are flexible, and that the Keynesian encouragement of ever-greater unfunded fiscal deficits is abandoned.

The obvious question which haunts this book is whether or not there is any chance that the framework set out here will be adopted, whether the voters will elect leaders on a policy platform like this, and whether the autocrats in countries like China and Russia will see it in their interests to follow. Or even whether any political leader is actually prepared to confront us with the consequences of our selfish ways.

It has to be admitted that the prospects are slim. The immediate politics has focused on 'the cost of living crisis', yet more borrowing to cover current spending, and even tax cuts. If anything, there is an acceleration in the pursuit of the sorts of economic policies that got us into this mess. In a world of Xi Jinping, what chance is there that the world's largest polluter will change tack? Faced with drought and serious environmental shocks already, China's response is to double down on buying more coal. Putin's Russia, underpinned by the great Russian fossil-fuel industries, does not take kindly to carbon taxes and decarbonisation. Putin's priorities are territorial expansion and military aggression, not addressing the environmental crises. Helping to wreck the planet should be treated as just as serious as Putin's horrors in Ukraine. For both, he should be an international pariah. In the US, the ghost of Trump lurks.

Rather than despair, there are two ways of advancing against this gloomy outlook. The first is to tell people about the upsides of taking the path in this book, stressing the benefits to the current as well as future generations, and explaining why an enlightened self-interest might actually be better met through the benefits of a more environmentally benign consumption and growth path. The second is to spell out what might happen if we ignore the environmental destruction all around us, and what the consequences might be when the unsustainable hits the brick wall and is no longer sustained.

The upsides are impressive. In *Green and Prosperous Land*, I set out the opportunities within just the UK, for the urban areas, the rivers, agriculture, the uplands and the coasts. Better air quality in cities, trees and green spaces improving mental and physical health and for children to play, improving river quality and thereby lowering the costs of cleaning it up for water supplies, and diverting the subsidies to farmers to pay for greener public goods. Once properly accounted for and brought into the evaluation of both current spending and future investment, these are all projects that have positive economic values. Add in the carbon sequestration opportunities from better land and coastal management, many of which are both cheaper than some current emissions reductions opportunities, and offer up the many other returns to the natural capitals over and above the carbon offsets.

These are all no regrets, even before the biodiversity gains are added on top, and make economic sense as soon as sensible pricing is introduced. Just doing all these sensible things now would make a big difference, and show people the great upside potential of the sustainable economy. Recall that not to price pollution is to court inefficiency, since an efficient economy includes all the costs. Proper pricing changes the patterns of world trade, benefits the local over the global and stops carbon leakage. What's not to like about all this?

And there is another different and optimistic reason for radical change. Part of what makes us human is our inherent sociability. We care about others and especially about our relatives and very specifically our children. If we build the sustainable economy, we can look them in the eye with the integrity that comes from behaving in an ethically acceptable way. Our lives are better if we can realise a better future for them. A life worth living is one that has principles and a sense of doing the right thing.

The final upside cuts against many of the more gloomy environmentalists. These are the no-growthers. Many green activists tell us that not only should we mend our ways, but we should also forsake all future aspirations for economic growth. This is profoundly wrong. The sustainable economy can and will grow, and potentially strongly, as a result of the growth of ideas, knowledge and technology. This is investment that can be financed legitimately through debt, creating new and better assets and hence passing on the liabilities associated with them to the next generation. This is in one sense a pretty obvious point: all economic growth is now driven by this form of capital, Karl Popper's 'World 3', the bundle of theories and hypotheses that have stood the test of repeated attempts to bring them down, and all the new additions to this body of knowledge. The bit of growth that we benefit from now comes from the huge advances in technology in the late nineteenth century, what the Victorians gave us in evolution, and modern organic chemistry, all built on great theoretical leaps forward. The reasons why the citizens of the sustainable economy can regard the step away from current unsustainable consumption to the sustainable consumption path as a temporary set-back is because ideas, knowledge and technology are marching on at an incredible pace.

The choice is whether to make sure there is a world within which this great advance in this form of capital can be realised and enjoyed, or whether we blow this great opportunity by destroying the climate and the biodiversity, the natural capital upon which the whole edifice of economic life is constructed. In all but the very short term, it is a great bargain to switch to the sustainable economy, and a disaster in the making not to do so.

That brings us back to the downsides of not acting now. These are already upon us and the consequences are going to get much worse. If our leaders are not persuaded to act in ways that grasp the opportunities in front of them, they (and therefore we) will have to confront the consequences, and there have been a number of attempts to spell out why the costs of action now to head off the worst impacts are lower than those we will have to pay when the unsustainable is not sustained.

The risk is that climate change continues unabated. Indeed, that is what is most likely going to happen. People will move, some people will starve and ecosystems will cross tipping points. The era of mass migration would make what is now going on in the Mediterranean look like a picnic. The Arctic warming is already pointing that way, and rises in sea level will accelerate. The tundra might melt and the consequent methane leakage might have planetary impacts. The question is whether the consequences are revealed too late in the day to turn the situation around.

What tips the balance is whether the interests of the next generation get a fair hearing. If the young and the next generation were properly at the table, it might all be rather different. That's why the sustainable economy needs a constitution. To turn the situation around, we need to embed the future in our deliberations. That constitution would entrench the rights of the next generation and ensure the stewarding of the natural and other assets so that their life chances are as good as ours. This is because they would have the capabilities to choose how to live their lives. We do not owe them equal happiness, whatever happiness means. But we do owe them our duty to be good leaseholders and to hand over a better world, both environmentally and with more and better ideas and technologies. We do not need to worry about the distant future. If we leave a decent inheritance to the next generation, it will be their duty to look after the one after that. It would in any case be an enormous step forward.

When the American rebels got rid of the British in the eighteenth century, they sat down to start again, from first principles, and to write these down in their new constitution. Two hundred and fifty years later, it is still standing, having seen off a number of less-than-perfect presidents and broadly protected individual rights against the tyranny of the majority. Now is the time for another such radical departure, to see off the tyranny of the current selfish generation over the next. Again, it is about principles and citizens.

We come back to the choice. The sustainable economy is within our reach. We can do this. There have been previous examples in history when consumption has had to give way to investment in order to meet a higher-order objective. Sadly, these have generally been during and immediately after wars. The challenge for our age and our generation is whether the global environmental threats are big enough yet to motivate radical change. There are lots of upsides in moving to the sustainable economy, which a war economy does not yield. But it does require us, the current generation, to mend our economic ways and put the planet on a sustainable path. It requires quite radical change, not just a tilt of the tiller. It can and should be done. Whether now turns out to be what the great naturalist Edward Wilson called 'nature's last stand' will be shown in time. It is for history to reveal how it will end.

The legacy we leave is for us to choose.[1]

---

[1] See chapter 3, 'Nature's Last Stand', in E.O. Wilson (2002), *The Future of Life*, London: Little, Brown.

WEBSITES

https://annualreporting.info/intfinrepstan/8-concepts-of-capital-and-capital-maintenance/

https://data.worldbank.org/indicator/NY.GDP.MKTP.CD?locations=RU

https://datacommons.org/place/country/RUS?utm_medium=explore&mprop=amount&popt=EconomicActivity&cpv=activitySource per cent2CGrossDomesticProduction&hl=en

https://docs.cdn.yougov.com/hdemoi825d/Internal_ClimateChangeTracker_220720_GB_W.pdf

https://ec.europa.eu/clima/eu-action/eu-emissions-trading-system-eu-ets_en

https://ember-climate.org/insights/research/subsidies-for-drax-biomass/

https://ourworldindata.org/co2-and-other-greenhouse-gas-emissions

https://tfl.gov.uk/info-for/investors/borrowing-programme

https://tradingeconomics.com/commodity/carbon

https://ukcop26.org/glasgow-leaders-declaration-on-forests-and-land-use/

www.gov.uk/government/news/sale-of-horticultural-peat-to-be-banned-in-move-to-protect-englands-precious-peatlands

www.harper-adams.ac.uk/news/203518/the-hands-free-hectare-project

www.imf.org/en/Publications/fandd/issues/2021/09/quantum-computings-possibilitiesand-perils-deodoro

www.lawcom.gov.uk/

www.ofgem.gov.uk/publications/ofgem-publishes-report-its-regulation-energy-market

www.ons.gov.uk/economy/environmentalaccounts/methodologies/naturalcapital.

www.reuters.com/business/environment/brazil-demand-us-pay-upfront-stalls-deal-save-amazon-forest-2021-04-15/

www.seai.ie/data-and-insights/seai-statistics/key-statistics/electricity/

www.wildlifetrusts.org/news/governments-set-low-bar-phase-out-gardeners-use-peat

BIBLIOGRAPHY

Abraham, K.G. and Mallatt, J. (2022), 'Measuring Human Capital', *Journal of Economic Perspectives*, 36(3), 103–30.

Arrow, K., Dasgupta, P., Goulder, L. et al. (2004), 'Are We Consuming Too Much?', *Journal of Economic Perspectives*, 18(3), 147–72.

Barber, L. (2008), 'No More Mr Nice Guy', interview with Boris Johnson in *The Guardian*, 19 October, www.theguardian.com/culture/2008/oct/19/boris-london.

Barro, R.J. (1974), 'Are Government Bonds Net Wealth?', *Journal of Political Economy*, 82(6), 1095–117.

Becker G. (1964), *Human Capital*, 2nd edn, New York: Columbia University Press.

Becker, G. (1965), 'A Theory of the Allocation of Time', *Economic Journal*, 75(299), 493–517.

Becker, G. (1981), *A Treatise on the Family*, Cambridge, MA: Harvard University Press.

Beckerman, W. (1968), *An Introduction to National Income Analysis*, London: Weidenfeld and Nicholson.

Beesley, M. and Littlechild, S. (1989), 'The Regulation of Privatized Monopolies in the United Kingdom', *RAND Journal of Economics*, 20(3), 454–72.

Bergholt, D., Furlanetto, F. and Maffei-Faccioli, N. (2022), 'The Decline of the Labor Share: New Empirical Evidence', *American Economic Journal: Macroeconomics*, 14(3), 163–98.

Berlin, I. (1958), *Two Concepts of Liberty*, Oxford: Clarendon Press, reprinted in I. Berlin (1969), *Four Essays on Liberty*, Oxford: Oxford University Press.

Bernanke, B.S. (2022), *21st Century Monetary Policy: The Federal Reserve from the Great Inflation to COVID-19*, New York: W.W. Norton & Co.

Beveridge, W. (1942), 'Social Insurance and Allied Services', Cmd. 6404.

Burke, E. (1790), *Reflections on the French Revolution*, London: James Dodsley.

Burns, C. and Jordan, A. (2021), 'Environmental Regulation in the Post-BREXIT Era', 23 March, www.BREXITenvironment.co.uk/2021/03/23/environmental-regulation-post-BREXIT/.

Byatt, I.C. (1986), 'Accounting for Economic Costs and Prices: A Report to HM Treasury by an Advisory Group' (the Byatt Report), 2 vols., HMSO.

Callaghan, J. (1976), Prime Minister, speech to Labour Party Conference.

Campbell, G. (2014), 'Government Policy during the British Railway Mania and the 1847 Commercial Crisis', in N. Dimsdale and A. Hotson (eds.), *British Financial Crises since 1825*, Oxford: Oxford University Press.

Chancellor, E. (2022), *The Price of Time: The Real Story of Interest*, London: Penguin Books.

Chandler, A. (1977), *The Visible Hand: The Managerial Revolution in American Business*, Cambridge, MA: Belknap Press.

Clark, C. (2012), *The Sleepwalkers: How Europe Went to War in 1914*, London: Allen Lane.

Climate Change Committee (2019), 'Net Zero: The UK's Contribution to Stopping Climate Change', May, www.theccc.org.uk/publication/net-zero-the-uks-contribution-to-stopping-global-warming/.

Climate Change Committee (2020), 'Building Back Better – Raising the UK's Climate Ambitions for 2035 Will Put Net Zero Within Reach and Change the UK for the Better', 9 December, www.theccc.org.uk/2020/12/09/building-back-better-raising-the-uks-climate-ambitions-for-2035-will-put-net-zero-within-reach-and-change-the-uk-for-the-better/.

Climate Change Committee (2020), 'Reducing UK Emissions: 2020 Progress Report to Parliament', 25 June, www.theccc.org.uk/publication/reducing-uk-emissions-2020-progress-report-to-parliament/.

Climate Change Committee (2020), 'The Sixth Carbon Budget', December, www.theccc.org.uk/wp-content/uploads/2020/12/The-Sixth-Carbon-Budget-The-UKs-path-to-Net-Zero.pdf.

Coase, R. (1960), 'The Problem of Social Cost', *Journal of Law and Economics*, 3, 1–44.

Crafts, N. (2021), 'Artificial Intelligence as a General-Purpose Technology: An Historical Perspective', *Oxford Review of Economic Policy*, 37(3), 521–36.

Dasgupta, P. (2019), *Time and the Generations*, New York: Columbia University Press.

Dasgupta, P. (2021), 'Final Report – The Economics of Biodiversity: The Dasgupta Review', 2 February.

de Tocquevillle, A. (1835), *Democracy in America*, London: Saunders and Otley.

Dearden, L., Fitzsimons, E. and Wyness, G. (2011), 'The Impact of Tuition Fees and Support on University Participation in the UK', IFS Working Paper W11/17, 5 September, Institute for Fiscal Studies.

DeCanio, S.J. (2003), *Economic Models of Climate Change: A Critique*, London: Palgrave Macmillan.

Defra and The Rt Hon Michael Gove MP (2018), 'A Green Future: Our 25 Year Plan to Improve the Environment', https://assets.publishing.service.gov.uk/government/uploads/system/uploads/attachment_data/file/693158/25-year-environment-plan.pdf.

Deming, D.J. (2022), 'Four Facts about Human Capital', *Journal of Economic Perspectives*, 36(3), 75–102.

Dimbleby, H. (2021), 'The National Food Strategy: The Plan – An Independent Review for Government', 15 July, www.nationalfoodstrategy.org/.

Dworkin, R. (1977), *Taking Rights Seriously*, Cambridge, MA: Harvard University Press.

Economy, E.C. (2010), *The River Runs Black: The Environmental Challenge to China's Future*, Ithaca: Cornell University Press.

Edel, L. (1979), *Bloomsbury: A House of Lions*, London: The Hogarth Press.

Edwards, J., Kay, J. and Mayer, C. (1987), *The Economic Analysis of Accounting Profitability*, Oxford: Clarendon Press.

Ellerman, A.D., Valero, V. and Zaklan, A. (2015), 'An Analysis of Allowance Banking in the EU ETS', Working Paper, EUI RSCAS, 2015/29, Florence School of Regulation, Climate, https://cadmus.eui.eu/handle/1814/35517.

Environment Agency (2022), 'Working with Nature', Chief Scientist's Group report, July, https://assets.publishing.service.gov.uk/government/uploads/system/uploads/attachment_data/file/1094162/Working_with_nature_-_report.pdf.

European Commission (2021), 'Proposal for a Regulation of the European Parliament and of the Council Establishing a Carbon Border Adjustment Mechanism', COM(2021) 564 final, 14 July.

Fearnside, P.M. (2022), 'Amazon Environmental Services: Why Brazil's Highway BR-319 Is So Damaging', *Ambio*, 51, 1367–70.

Financial Reporting Council (2021), 'Key Facts and Trends in the UK Accounting Profession', www.frc.org.uk/getattachment/e976ff38-3597-4779-b192-1be7da79d175/FRC-Key-Facts-Trends-2021.pdf.

Financial Times (2008), 'Good Question, Ma'am', 14 November, www.ft.com/content/5b306600-b26d-11dd-bbc9-0000779fd18c.

Friedman, B.M. (2021), *Religion and the Rise of Capitalism*, New York: Alfred A. Knopf.

Frost, R.L. (1915), 'The Road Not Taken', first published in *The Atlantic Monthly*, August.

Gatti, L.V., Basso, L.S., Miller, J.B. et al. (2021), 'Amazonia as a Carbon Source Linked to Deforestation and Climate Change', *Nature*, 595, 388–93.

Glaister, S. (2021), 'HS2: Levelling Up or the Pursuit of an Icon', Institute of Government, July, www.instituteforgovernment.org.uk/sites/default/files/hs2-levelling-up-stephen-glaister.pdf.

Glover, J. (1984), *What Sort of People Should There Be?*, Harmondsworth: Penguin Books.

Godfrey-Smith, P. (2016), 'Popper's Philosophy of Science: Looking Ahead', chapter 4 in J. Shearmur and G. Stokes (eds.), *The Cambridge Companion to Popper*, Cambridge: Cambridge University Press, pp. 104–24.

Gordon, R.J. (2016), *The Rise and Fall of American Growth: The U.S. Standard of Living since the Civil War*, Princeton: Princeton University Press.

Graves, A.R. and Morris, J. (2013), 'Restoration of Fenland Peatland under Climate Change', Report to the Adaptation Sub-Committee of the Committee on Climate Change, Cranfield University, Bedford, www.theccc.org.uk/wp-content/uploads/2013/07/Report-for-ASC-project_FINAL-9-July.pdf.

Greaves, H. and Ord, T. (2017), 'Moral Uncertainty about Population Ethics', *Journal of Ethics and Social Philosophy*, 12(2), 135–67.

Hallmann,C.A., Sorg, M., Jongejans, E. et al. (2017), 'More than 75 Percent Decline over 27 Years in Total Flying Insect Biomass in Protected Areas', *Plos One*, 18 October, https://journals.plos.org/plosone/article/file?id=10.1371/journal.pone.0185809&type=printable.

Harris, A.L. (1959), 'J.S. Mill on Monopoly and Socialism: A Note', *Journal of Political Economy*, 67, 604–11.

Harris, J. (1997), *William Beveridge: A Biography*, revised edn, Oxford: Clarendon Press.

Harris, J.A. (2015), *Hume: An Intellectual Biography*, Cambridge: Cambridge University Press.

Hartwick, J.M. (1977), 'Intergenerational Equity and the Investing of Rents from Exhaustible Resources', *American Economic Review*, 67(5), 972–4.

Hassan, J.A. (1983), 'The Impact and Development of the Water Supply in Manchester, 1568–1882', *Historic Society of Lancashire and Cheshire*, 133, 25–45.

Hayek, F.A. von (1944), *The Road to Serfdom*, Chicago: University of Chicago Press.

Hayek, F.A. von (1948), *Individualism and Economic Order*, Chicago: Chicago University Press.

Hayek, F.A. von (1948), 'The Meaning of Competition', in *Individualism and Social Order*, Cambridge: Cambridge University Press.

Hayek, F.A. von (1960), *The Constitution of Liberty*, Chicago: University of Chicago Press.

Heald, D. (1989), 'The Valuation of Power Stations by the Modern Equivalent Asset Method', *Fiscal Studies*, 10(2), 86–108.

Helm, D. (2003), *Energy, the State and the Market: British Energy Policy since 1979*, Oxford: Oxford University Press.

Helm, D. (2006), 'Regulatory Reform, Capture, and the Regulatory Burden', *Oxford Review of Economic Policy*, 22(2), 169–85.

Helm, D. (2008), 'Tradeable RABs and the Split Cost of Capital', January, www.dieterhelm.co.uk/regulation/regulation/tradeable-rabs/.

Helm, D. (2015), *Natural Capital: Valuing the Planet*, New Haven: Yale University Press.

Helm, D. (2017), 'Cost of Energy Review', Independent Review for the Department of Business, Energy and Industrial Strategy, October.

Helm, D. (2018), *Burn Out: The Endgame for Fossil Fuels*, updated edn, New Haven: Yale University Press.

Helm, D. (2019), 'The Systems Regulation Model', 12 February, www.dieterhelm .co.uk/regulation/regulation/the-systems-regulation-model/.

Helm, D. (2020), *Green and Prosperous Land: A Blueprint for Rescuing the British Countryside*, revised edn, London: William Collins.

Helm, D. (2020), 'Thirty Years after Water Privatization – Is the English Model the Envy of the World', *Oxford Review of Economic Policy*, 36(1), 69–85.

Helm, D. (2021), *Net Zero: How We Stop Causing Climate Change*, revised edn, London: William Collins.

Helm, D. (2022), 'Natural Capital, Carbon Offsetting and Land Use: A Discussion Paper', May, Scottish Land Commission, www.landcommission .gov.scot/downloads/628de8eb9c11a_Land%20Lines%20Natural%20 capital-carbon%20offsetting%20and%20land%20use.pdf.

Helm, D. (2022), 'The Retreat from Net Zero', 4 July, www.dieterhelm.co.uk/ energy/climate-change/the-retreat-from-net-zero/.

Helm, D., Hepburn, C. and Ruta, G. (2012), 'Trade, Climate Change, and the Political Game Theory of Border Carbon Adjustments', *Oxford Review of Economic Policy*, 28(2), 368–94.

Helm, D., Kay, J. and Thompson, D. (1989), *The Market for Energy*, Oxford: Clarendon Press.

Hicks, J.R. (1935), 'Annual Survey of Economic Theory: The Theory of Monopoly', *Econometrica*, 3, 1–20.

Hicks, J.R. (1939), *Value and Capital: An Inquiry into Some Fundamental Principles of Economic Theory*, Oxford: Clarendon Press.

Hicks, J.R. (1955), 'Economic Foundations of Wage Policy', *Economic Journal*, 65(259), 389–404.

Hicks, J.R. (1982), *Money, Interest and Wages: Collective Essays on Economic Theory*, vol. III, Oxford: Blackwell.

Hilton, J. (1934), *Goodbye, Mr Chips*, London: Hodder & Stoughton.

HM Government (2020), 'The Ten Point Plan for a Green Industrial Revolution', November.

HM Government (2021), 'Net Zero Strategy: Build Back Greener', October, p. 9.

HM Treasury (1978), 'The Nationalised Industries', Cmnd. 7131, HMSO.

HM Treasury (2020), 'National Infrastructure Strategy: Fairer, Faster, Greener', November, https://assets.publishing.service.gov.uk/government/uploads/system/uploads/attachment_data/file/938539/NIS_Report_Web_Accessible.pdf.

HM Treasury (2020), 'Net Zero Review 2020: Interim Report', December, https://assets.publishing.service.gov.uk/government/uploads/system/uploads/attachment_data/file/1004025/210615_NZR_interim_report_Master_v4.pdf.

House of Lords Economic Affairs Committee (2021), 'Quantitative Easing: A Dangerous Addiction?', 1st Report of Session 2021–2 HL Paper, 16 July.

Howson, S. and Winch, D. (1977), *The Economic Advisory Council, 1930–39: A Study in Economic Advice during Depression and Recovery*, Cambridge: Cambridge University Press.

Johansen, L. (1985), 'Richard Stone's Contributions to Economics', *Scandinavian Journal of Economics*, 87(1), 4–32.

Jones, C. (2005), 'The Optimal Provision of Goods', chapter 10 in C. Jones (ed.), *Applied Welfare Economics*, Oxford: Oxford University Press.

Jones, C.I. (2019), 'Paul Romer: Ideas, Nonrivalry, and Endogenous Growth', *Scandinavian Journal of Economics*, 121(3), 859–83.

Kahn, R. (1931), 'The Relation of Home Investment to Unemployment', *Economic Journal*, 41(162), 173–98.

Kahn, R (1984), *The Making of the Keynes' General Theory*, Cambridge: Cambridge University Press.

Kay, J. (2010), *Obliquity: Why Our Goals Are Best Achieved Indirectly*, London: Profile Books.

Kelton, S. (2021), *The Deficit Myth: How to Build a Better Economy*, London: John Murray.

Keynes, J.M. (1930), *A Treatise on Money*, London: Macmillan.

Keynes, J.M. (1931), 'Economic Possibilities for Our Grandchildren', reprinted in J.M. Keynes (2010), *Essays in Persuasion*, London: Palgrave Macmillan.

Keynes, J.M. (1933), 'Means to Prosperity', reprinted in J.M. Keynes (2010), *Essays in Persuasion*, London: Palgrave Macmillan.

Keynes, J.M. (1940), *How to Pay for the War: A Radical Plan for the Chancellor of the Exchequer*, London: Macmillan.

Knight, F.H. (1921), *Risk, Uncertainty and Profit*, Boston: Houghton Mifflin.

Kuhn, T. (1962), *The Structure of Scientific Revolutions*, Chicago: University of Chicago Press.

Labour Party (2019), 'It's Time for Real Change, Labour Party Manifesto 2019', www.labour.org.

Lai, O. (2021), 'Billionaires' Single Space Flight Produces a Lifetime's Worth of Carbon Footprint: Report', 15 December, https://earth.org/billionaires-single-space-flight-produces-a-lifetimes-worth-of-carbon-footprint-report/.

Landshoff, P. (2020), 'The State of the Fenland Peat: Why Peatland Loss Is a Serious Challenge and What We Can Do About It', 21 May, www.zero.cam.ac.uk/who-we-are/blog/state-fenland-peat-why-peatland-loss-serious-challenge-and-what-we-can-do-about-it.

Lange, O. (1938), *On the Economic Theory of Socialism*, Minneapolis: University of Minnesota Press.

Lawson N. (1982), 'The Market for Energy', speech to the British Institute of Energy Economics, Cambridge, June, reproduced in D. Helm, J. Kay and D. Thompson (eds.) (1989), *The Market for Energy*, Oxford: Clarendon Press.

Lenton, T.M., Rockström, J., Gaffney, O., Rahmstorf, S., Richardson, K., Steffen, W. and Schellnhuber, H.J. (2019), 'Climate Tipping Points – Too Risky to Bet Against', *Nature*, 27 November, www.nature.com/articles/d41586-019-03595-0.

Levy, P. (1975), 'The Bloomsbury Group', chapter 8 in M. Keynes (ed.) (1975), *Essays on John Maynard Keynes*, Cambridge: Cambridge University Press.

Liberal Industrial Inquiry (1928), *Britain's Industrial Future, Being the Report of the Liberal Industrial Inquiry of 1928* (the 'Yellow Book'), London: Ernest Benn; second impression, with a foreword by David Steel, 1977.

Lipsey, R.G. and Lancaster, K. (1956), 'The General Theory of Second Best', *Review of Economic Studies*, 24(1), 11–32.

Local Government Board (1873), '1873 Return of Owners of Land', presented to both Houses of Parliament by Command of Her Majesty, Volume 1, HMSO 1875.

Locke, J. (1680), *Two Treatises of Government*.

McKenna, G. (2007), *The Puritan Origins of American Patriotism*, New Haven: Yale University Press.

Malthus, T.R. (1798), *An Essay on the Principle of Population as It Affects the Future Improvement of Society, With Remarks on the Speculations of Mr. Godwin, M. Condorcet and Other Writers*, London: J. Johnson.

Maniw, N.G. (2020), 'A Skeptic's Guide to Modern Monetary Theory', *AEA Papers and Proceedings*, 110, 141–4.

Marx, K. (1951), *Theories of Surplus Value: A Selection from the Volumes Published between 1905 and 1910 as 'Theorien über den Mehrwert'*, ed. K. Kautsky, taken from Karl Marx's preliminary manuscript for the projected fourth volume of *Das Kapital*, translated from the German by G.A. Bonner and E. Burns, London: Lawrence & Wishart.

Marx, K. and Engels, F. (1848), 'The Communist Manifesto', in K. Marx (1969), *Karl Marx and Frederick Engels: Selected Works*, vol. i, Moscow: Progress Publishers, pp. 98–137.

Matthew, H. (1979), 'Disraeli, Gladstone, and the Politics of Mid-Victorian Budgets', *Historical Journal*, 22(3), 615–43.

Mayer, C. (2013), 'Unnatural Capital Accounting', Natural Capital Committee, https://assets.publishing.service.gov.uk/government/uploads/system/uploads/attachment_data/file/516947/ncc-discussion-paper-unnatural-capital-accounting.pdf.

Mayer, C. (2019), *Prosperity: Better Business Makes the Greater Good*, Oxford: Oxford University Press.

Miles, D.K., Stedman, M. and Heald, A.H. (2021), 'Stay at Home, Protect the National Health Service, Save Lives: A Cost Benefit Analysis of the Lockdown in the United Kingdom', *International Journal of Clinical Practice*, 75(3).

Mises, L. von (1949), *Human Action: A Treatise on Economics*, London: William Hodge.

More, T. (1516), *Utopia*.

National Audit Office (2017), 'HM Revenue & Customs 2016–17 Accounts', NAO, London.

National Audit Office (2017), 'A Short Guide to Department for Work and Pensions', NAO, London.

Nelson, R.R. and Winters, S.G. (1982), *An Evolutionary Theory of Economic Change*, Cambridge, MA: Belknap Press.

Newbery, D.M. (1997), 'Rate-of-Return Regulation Versus Price Regulation for Public Utilities', Department of Applied Economics, Cambridge University, www.econ.cam.ac.uk/people-files/emeritus/dmgn/files/palgrave.pdf.

Nordhaus, W. (2007), 'A Review of the Stern Review on the Economics of Climate Change', *Journal of Economic Literature*, 45(3), 686–702.

Nordhaus, W. (2018), 'Projections and Uncertainties about Climate Change in an Era of Minimal Climate Policies', *American Economic Journal: Economic Policy*, 10(3), 333–60.

Nordhaus, W. (2019), 'Climate Change: The Ultimate Challenge for Economics', *American Economic Review*, 109(6), 1991–2014.

Nozick, R. (1974), *Anarchy, State, and Utopia*, Oxford: Basil Blackwell.

O'Brien, D.P. (1975), *The Classical Economists*, Oxford: Clarendon Press.

O'Hear, A. (1980), *Karl Popper*, London: Kegan & Paul.

Ofcom (2020), 'Full Fibre Must Be Fair Bet', Dame Melanie Dawes speech to FTTH Council Europe, 3 December.

Ofgem (2020), '9 August 2019 Power Outage Report', 3 January, www.ofgem.gov.uk/publications/investigation-9-august-2019-power-outage.

Ofwat (2017), 'Ofwat's Price Review: Delivering More of What Matters. Our Final Methodology for the 2019 Price Review – Executive Summary', 13 December.

Ofwat (2017), 'UK Government Priorities and Our 2019 Price Review Final Methodology', 13 December.

Ofwat (2017), 'Welsh Government Priorities and Our 2019 Price Review Final Methodology', 13 December.

Olson, M. (1982), *The Rise and Decline of Nations*, New Haven: Yale University Press.

Orwell, G. (1933), *Down and Out in Paris and London*, London: Victor Gollancz Ltd.

Orwell, G. (1937), *The Road to Wigan Pier*, London: Victor Gollancz Ltd.

Orwell, G. (1944), 'George Orwell's Review of Hayek's The Road to Serfdom', in G. Orwell (1988), *The Complete Works of George Orwell*, vol. xvi: *I Have Tried to Tell the Truth 1943–44*, London: Secker and Warburg.

Orwell, G. (1968), *The Collected Essays, Journalism and Letters of George Orwell*, vol. i, London: Secker and Warburg.

Paine, T. (1792), *Rights of Man*, London: printed for J. Parsons.

Parfit, D. (1984), *Reasons and Persons*, Oxford: Oxford University Press.

Parijs, P. van and Vanderborght, Y. (2017), *Basic Income: A Radical Proposal for a Free Society and a Sane Economy*, Cambridge, MA: Harvard University Press.

Patinkin, D. (1965), *Money, Interest, and Prices: An Integration of Monetary and Value Theory*, New York: Harper & Row.

Peart, S. (1991), 'Sunspots and Expectations: W. S. Jevons's Theory of Economic Fluctuations', *Journal of the History of Economic Thought*, 13(2), 243–65.

Phillipon, T. (2019), *The Great Reversal: How America Gave Up on Free Markets*, Cambridge, MA: Harvard University Press.

Pigou, A.C. (1920), *The Economics of Welfare*, Basingstoke: Palgrave Macmillan.

Popper, K. (1945), *The Open Society and Its Enemies*, 4th revised edn, 1962, London: Routledge & Kegan Paul.

Popper, K. (1963), *Conjectures and Refutations: The Growth of Scientific Knowledge*, London: Routledge & Kegan Paul.

Popper, K. (1979), *Objective Knowledge: An Evolutionary Approach*, revised edn, Oxford: Clarendon Press.

Quinn, W. and Turner, J.D. (2021), *Boom and Bust: A Global History of Financial Bubbles*, Cambridge: Cambridge University Press.

Ramsey, F.P. (1928), 'A Mathematical Theory of Saving', *Journal of Economics*, 38(152), 543–59.

Rawls, J. (1971), *A Theory of Justice*, Oxford: Oxford University Press.

Rebanks, J. (2020), *English Pastoral: An Inheritance*, London: Penguin Books.

Rennert, K., Prest, B.C., Pizer, W.A. et al. (2021), 'The Social Cost of Carbon: Advances in Long-Term Probabilistic Projections of Population, GDP,

Emissions, and Discount Rates', *Brookings Papers on Economic Activity*, BPEA Conference Drafts, 9 September.

Robbins, L. (1934), *The Great Depression*, London: Macmillan,

Robson, J.M. (ed.) (1963–91), *Collected Works of John Stuart Mill*, 33 vols., Toronto: University of Toronto Press; London: Routledge & Kegan Paul, https://oll.libertyfund.org/title/robson-collected-works-of-john-stuart-mill-in-33-vols.

Romer, P.M. (1987), 'Growth Based on Increasing Returns to Specialization', *American Economic Review*, 77(2), 56–62.

Rousseau, J.-J. (1762), *The Social Contract*.

Rousseau, J.-J. (1782), *The Confessions of Jean-Jacques Rousseau*.

Rowthorn, R. and Maciejowski, J. (2020), 'A Cost–Benefit Analysis of the Covid-19 Disease', *Oxford Review of Economic Policy*, 36(S1), S38–S55.

Rumsfeld, D. (2002), US Department of Defence news briefing, 12 February.

Samuelson, P.A. (1947), *Foundations of Economic Analysis*, Cambridge, MA: Harvard University Press.

Sargent, T.J. and Wallace, N. (1975), '"Rational" Expectations, the Optimal Monetary Instrument, and the Optimal Money Supply Rule', *Journal of Political Economy*, 83(2), 241–54.

Savage, L.J. (1951), 'The Theory of Statistical Decision', *Journal of the American Statistical Association*, 46(253), 55–67.

Say, J.B. (1803), *A Treatise on Political Economy*.

Schelling, T.C. (2005), 'An Astonishing Sixty Years: The Legacy of Hiroshima', Prize Lecture, Department of Economics and School of Public Policy, University of Maryland, 8 December.

Schoemaker, P.J. (1982), 'The Expected Utility Model: Its Variants, Purposes, Evidence and Limitations', *Journal of Economic Literature*, 20(2), 529–63.

Schumpeter, J. (1942), *Capitalism, Socialism, and Democracy*, New York: Harper & Bros.

Scott, M. (1991), *A New View of Economic Growth*, Oxford: Oxford University Press.

Sen, A.K. (1970), 'The Impossibility of a Paretian Liberal', *Journal of Political Economy*, 78, 152–7.

Sen, A.K. (1980), 'Equality of What?', reprinted in A.K. Sen (1982), *Choice, Welfare and Measurement*, Oxford: Basil Blackwell.

Sen, A.K. (1983), 'Poor, Relatively Speaking', *Oxford Economic Papers*, 35(2) 153–69.

Sen, A.K. (2009), *The Idea of Justice*, London: Allen Lane.

Shackle, G.L.S. (1969), *Decision Order and Time in Human Affairs*, 2nd edn, Cambridge: Cambridge University Press.

Shackle, G.L.S. (1972), *Epistemics and Economics*, Cambridge: Cambridge University Press.

Sidgwick, H. (1874), *The Methods of Ethics*, London: Macmillan and Co.

Skidelsky, R. (1983), *John Maynard Keynes: Hopes Betrayed, 1883–1920*, London: Macmillan.

Skidelsky, R. (1992), *John Maynard Keynes: The Economist as Saviour, 1920–1937*, vol. II, London: Macmillan.

Skidelsky, R. (2000), *John Maynard Keynes: Fighting for Freedom, 1937–1946*, London: Macmillan.

Skidelsky, R. (2010), *Keynes: The Return of the Master*, vol. i, London: Penguin Books.

Slater, M. (2018), *The National Debt: A Short History*, London: C. Hurst & Co. Publishers Ltd.

Smith, A. (1759), *The Theory of Moral Sentiments*.

Smith, A. (1776), *An Inquiry into the Nature and Causes of the Wealth of Nations*.

Solow, R.M. (1987), 'We'd Better Watch Out', book review, *New York Times*, 12 July, p. 36.

Solow, R.M. (1993), 'An Almost Practical Step towards Sustainability', *Resources Policy*, 16(3), 162–72.

Son, J. and Feng, Q. (2019), 'In Social Capital We Trust?', *Social Indicators Research*, 144, 167–89.

Sowell, T. (1972), *Say's Law: An Historical Analysis*, Princeton: Princeton University Press.

Stern, N. (2007), *The Economics of Climate Change: The Stern Review*, HM Treasury, Cambridge: Cambridge University Press.

Strachey, L. (1918), *Eminent Victorians*, London: Chatto & Windus.

Taleb, N.N. (2007), *The Black Swan: The Impact of the Highly Improbable*, London: Allen Lane.

Tawney, R.H. (1926), *Religion and the Rise of Capitalism: A Historical Study*, London: J. Murray.

Tietenberg, T.H. and Lewis, L. (2018), *Environmental and Natural Resource Economics*, London: Routledge.

Tynan, N. (2007), 'Mill and Senior on London's Water Supply: Agency, Increasing Returns, and Natural Monopoly', *Journal of the History of Economic Thought*, 29(1), 49–65.

Ulph, D. (2014), 'UK Tax System Complexity: Causes and Consequences', *Tax Journal*, 17 December.

United Nations (1987), 'Report of the World Commission on Environment and Development: Our Common Future' (the Brundtland Report), https://sustainabledevelopment.un.org/content/documents/5987our-common-future.pdf.

United Nations General Assembly (1992), 'Report of the United Nations Conference on Environment and Development', Annex I Rio Declaration on Environment and Development, Principle 15.

Veblen, T. (1899), *The Theory of the Leisure Class: An Economic Study of Institutions*, New York: Macmillan.

Voltaire, F.-M.A. (1759), *Candide, ou L'Optimisme*.

Wapshott, N. (2011), *Keynes Hayek: The Clash that Defined Modern Economics*, New York: W.W. Norton.

Weber, M. (1905), *The Protestant Spirit and the Rise of Capitalism*, reprinted 2002, London: Penguin Books.

Weitzman, M.L. (2007), 'A Review of the Stern Review on the Economics of Climate Change', *Journal of Economic Literature*, 45(3), 703–24.

Westad, O.A. (2017), *The Cold War*, Allen Lane.

Whittington, G. (1988), 'The Byatt Report: A Review Essay', *British Accounting Review*, 20, 77–87.

Whittington, G. (2017), *Value and Profit: An Introduction to Measurement in Financial Reporting*, Cambridge: Cambridge University Press.

Wicksell, K. (1907), 'The Influence of the Rate of Interest on Prices', *Economic Journal*, 17(66), 213–20.

Wiener M.J. (1981), *English Culture and the Decline of the Industrial Spirit, 1850–1980*, Cambridge: Cambridge University Press.

Wilk, R. and Barros, B. (2021), 'Private Planes, Mansions and Superyachts: What Gives Billionaires like Musk and Abramovich such a Massive Carbon Footprint', *The Conversation*, 16 February, https://theconversation.com/private-planes-mansions-and-superyachts-what-gives-billionaires-like-musk-and-abramovich-such-a-massive-carbon-footprint-152514.

Wilson, E.O. (2002), *The Future of Life*, London: Little, Brown.

INDEX

natural capital (cont.)
  natural vs. other capitals, 55–6
  for the next generation, 31–2, 207–8
  non-renewable and renewable,
    5–7, 57–9
  other capital dependent upon, 32–3
  as primary asset, 56–9
  as public good, 118–19
  a sustainable economy, 7–14
  system regulation model, 179–81
negative interest rates, 149
neo-Ricardian effect, 146–7
neo-Ricardian equivalent theory, 146–7
net zero
  constitutional principles, 210–11
  cost estimates, 98–9
  and fossil fuels, 18–19
networks, infrastructure systems, 59–63
non-renewable natural capital, 5–7, 57–9
nuclear power, 18–20

open societies, 48–9
operational capital maintenance, 77–8
Orwell, George, 164
outflows, institutional model, 191–4
outsourcing net zero, 101
overpopulation, 24

pay-as-you-go principle, 88–9
peat, ban on, 112
pesticides, polluter-pays principle,
  104–5
physical capital, 59–63, 208–9
Pigou, Arthur, 95, 100
Pigouvian taxes, 95–8
  Austrian approach, 105–6
  global agreements, 110–11
planning
  Austrian economics and
    entrepreneurs, 46–8
  system regulation model, 190–1
politics, see also constitutions
  EU membership, 211–12
  forecasting and uncertainty, 37–9
  Keynesian approach, 138–40

from the Labour Standard to the
  Consumption Standard, 140–1
limiting government discretion and
  the importance of rules, 209–10
open societies, 48–9
our legacy, 218–27
polluter-pays principle, 102–5
the problem with planning, 49–51
polluter-pays principle
  in the absence of global enforcement,
    109–11
  Coase bargaining as alternative,
    99–101
  in constitutional terms, 205–6
  impact on consumption, 9–11, 93–4
  justifications for, 102–5
  market failure, 94–9
  our legacy, 222–3
  pollution taxes (Austrian school
    approach), 105–6
pollution
  capital maintenance, 77–8
  living beyond our means, 107–9
  market failure, 94–9
  prices, 113
  regulating and prohibiting, 111–13
  remedial investments, 81–2
  taxes (Austrian economics approach),
    105–6
Popper, Karl, 65–7
population, see world population
poverty
  distributional argument, 25–6
  inequality and the problem of the
    ultra-rich, 166–9
  pure impartiality, 21–4
  social insurance, 163–4
  social justice, 12
precautionary principle
  asymmetric risks, 44–6
  Austrian economics and
    entrepreneurs, 46–8
  in constitutional terms, 205–6
price, incorporating pollution costs,
  113, see also Pigouvian taxes

Printed in the USA
CPSIA information can be obtained
at www.ICGtesting.com
LVHW080733241123
764522LV00007B/263

9 781009 449182